D0607595

Effective
Succession
Planning

SECOND EDITION

Effective
Succession
Planning

SECOND EDITION

Ensuring
Leadership Continuity
and Building Talent from Within

WILLIAM J. ROTHWELL

AMACOM
American Management Association
New York • Atlanta • Boston • Chicago • Kansas City • San Francisco • Washington, D. C.
Brussels • Mexico City • Tokyo • Toronto

This publication is designed to provide accurate and authoritative information in regard to the subject matter covered. It is sold with the understanding that the publisher is not engaged in rendering legal, accounting, or other professional service. If legal advice or other expert assistance is required, the services of a competent professional person should be sought.

Library of Congress Cataloging-in-Publication Data

Rothwell, William J., 1951–
Effective succession planning : ensuring leadership continuity and building talent from within / William J. Rothwell.—2nd ed.
p. cm.
Includes bibliographical references and index.
ISBN 0-8144-7080-7
1. Leadership. 2. Executive succession—United States. 3. Executive ability. 4. Organizational effectiveness. I. Title.

HD57.7.R689 2001
658.4'092—dc21

00-055831

Printing number

10 9 8 7 6 5 4 3

This book is dedicated to my wife,
Marcelina Rothwell,
and to my daughter,
Candice Rothwell.
Without their patience,
this book would never have been written.

Contents

List of Exhibits   xiii

Preface   xvii

Acknowledgments   xxvii

Part I:
Background Information about Succession Planning and
Management   1

Chapter 1:   What Is Succession Planning and
Management?   3

Five Ministudies: Can You Solve These Succession
Problems?   3
Defining Succession Planning and Management   5
Distinguishing Succession Planning and Management from
Replacement Planning   7
The Importance of Succession Planning and
Management   7
Reasons for a Succession Planning and Management
Program   9
Approaches to Succession Planning and
Management   21
Ensuring Leadership Continuity in Organizations   24
Summary   29

Chapter 2:   Trends Influencing Succession Planning
and Management   31

Introductory Activity: Drivers of Change and the
Trends   32

What Trends Are Influencing Succession Planning and
    Management?   32
What Does All This Mean for Succession Planning and
    Management?   38
Summary   38

Chapter 3:   The Need for a Newer Approach   40

Case Study 1   40
Case Study 2   44
Case Study 3   48
Characteristics of Effective Succession Planning and
    Management Programs   53
The Life Cycle of Succession Planning and Management
    Programs: Five Generations   57
Identifying and Solving Problems with Various Approaches
    to Succession Planning and Management   68
Requirements for a Fifth-Generation Approach   73
Key Steps in a Fifth-Generation Approach to Succession
    Planning and Management   73
Summary   76

Chapter 4:   Competency Identification and Values
              Clarification: Keys to Succession Planning
              and Management   77

What Are Competencies?   77
How Are Competencies Used in Succession Planning and
    Management?   78
Conducting Competency Identification Studies for
    Succession Planning and Management   79
Using Competency Models in Succession Planning and
    Management   80
What Are Values, and What Is Values Clarification?   80
How Are Values Used in Succession Planning and
    Management?   83
Conducting Values Clarification Studies for Succession
    Planning and Management   84
Using Values Clarification in Succession Planning and
    Management   85
Bringing It All Together: Competencies and
    Values   85
Summary   86

Part II:
Laying the Foundation for a Succession Planning and Management Program 87

Chapter 5: Making the Case for Change 89

Assessing Current Problems and Practices 89
Demonstrating the Need 96
Determining Organizational Requirements 102
Linking Succession Planning and Management Activities to
    Organizational and Human Resource Strategy 103
Benchmarking Succession Planning and Management
    Practices in Other Organizations 108
Obtaining and Building Management Commitment to
    Systematic Succession Planning and
    Management 113
Summary 116

Chapter 6: Starting Up a Systematic Succession
Planning and Management Program 118

Clarifying Program Roles 118
Formulating a Mission Statement 122
Writing Policy and Procedures 128
Identifying Target Groups 129
Setting Program Priorities 134
Addressing the Legal Framework in Succession Planning
    and Management 136
Establishing Strategies for Rolling Out a Succession
    Planning and Management Program 138
Summary 147

Chapter 7: Refining the Program 148

Preparing a Program Action Plan 148
Communicating the Action Plan 149
Conducting Succession Planning and Management
    Meetings 152
Training on Succession Planning and
    Management 156
Counseling Managers about Succession Planning Problems
    in Their Areas 164
Summary 167

Part III:
Assessing the Present and the Future   169

Chapter 8:   Assessing Present Work Requirements and
              Individual Job Performance   171

  Identifying Key Positions   172
  Three Approaches to Determining Work Requirements in
    Key Positions   176
  Using Full-Circle, Multi-Rater Assessments   182
  Appraising Performance   184
  Creating Talent Pools: Techniques and
    Approaches   187
  Summary   192

Chapter 9:   Assessing Future Work Requirements and
              Individual Potential   193

  Identifying Key Positions for the Future   193
  Three Approaches to Determining Future Work
    Requirements in Key Positions   197
  Assessing Individual Potential   202
  Summary   212

Part IV:
Closing the "Developmental Gap": Operating and
Evaluating a Succession Planning and Management
Program   213

Chapter 10:   Developing Internal Successors   215

  Testing Bench Strength   215
  Formulating Internal Promotion Policy   219
  Preparing Individual Development Plans   221
  Developing Successors Internally   229
  Summary   237

Chapter 11:   Assessing Alternatives to Internal
              Development   239

  Assessing Alternatives   239
  Deciding What to Do   249
  Summary   249

Chapter 12:   Applying Online and High-Tech Approaches
              to Succession Planning and Management
              Programs   253

     How Are Online and High-Tech Methods
        Defined?   253
     In What Areas of Succession Planning and Management
        Can Online and High-Tech Methods Be
        Applied?   254
     How Are Online and High-Tech Applications
        Used?   255
     What Specialized Competencies Are Required by
        Succession Planning and Management Coordinators to
        Use These Applications?   269
     Summary   270

Chapter 13:   Evaluating Succession Planning and
              Management Programs   271

     What Is Evaluation?   271
     What Should Be Evaluated?   272
     How Should Evaluation Be Conducted?   275
     Summary   281

Chapter 14:   Predictions for the Future of Succession
              Planning and Management   287

     Prediction 1: Decision-Makers Will Seek Flexible Strategies
        to Address Future Organizational Talent
        Needs   290
     Prediction 2: Decision-Makers Will Seek Integrated
        Retention Policies and Procedures   293
     Prediction 3: Succession Planning and Management Issues
        Will Have a Global Impact   297
     Prediction 4: Succession Issues Will Be Influenced by Real-
        Time Technological Innovations   300
     Prediction 5: Succession Planning and Management Will
        Emerge as an Issue in Government Agencies, Academic
        Institutions, and Nonprofit Enterprises   300
     Prediction 6: Succession Planning and Management Will
        Lead to an Increasing Policy of Organizational
        Openness   302

Prediction 7: Succession Planning and Management Will
   Increasingly Be Integrated with Career
   Development   302
Prediction 8: Succession Planning and Management Will
   Be Heavily Influenced by Concerns about Work/Family
   Balance and Spirituality   303
Summary   303

Notes   309

Index   325

About the Author   337

List of Exhibits

P-1: Age Distribution of the U.S. Population, Selected Years, 1965–2025

P-2: U.S. Population by Age, 1965–2025

1-1: Demographic Information about Respondents to a 1999 Survey on Succession Planning and Management: Industries

1-2: Demographic Information about Respondents to a 1999 Survey on Succession Planning and Management: Size

1-3: Demographic Information about Respondents to a 1999 Survey on Succession Planning and Management: Job Functions of Respondents

1-4: Reasons for Succession Planning and Management Programs

1-5: Strategies for Reducing Turnover and Increasing Retention

1-6: Workforce Reductions among Survey Respondents

2-1: An Assessment Questionnaire: How Well Is Your Organization Managing the Consequences of Trends Influencing Succession Planning and Management?

3-1: Characteristics of Effective Succession Planning and Management Programs

3-2: Assessment Questionnaire for Effective Succession Planning and Management

3-3: A Simple Exercise to Dramatize the Need for Succession Planning and Management

3-4: Chief Difficulties with Succession Planning and Management Programs

3-5: The Seven-Pointed Star Model for Systematic Succession Planning and Management

4-1: Approaches to Competency Identification

5-1: Strategies for Handling Resistance to Implementing Succession Planning and Management

5-2: The Importance of Succession Planning and Management

5-3: Making Decisions about Successors (in Organizations without Systematic Succession Planning and Management)

5-4: A Questionnaire for Assessing the Status of Succession Planning and Management in an Organization

5-5: A Worksheet for Demonstrating the Need for Succession Planning and Management

5-6: An Interview Guide for Determining the Requirements for a Succession Planning and Management Program

5-7: An Interview Guide for Benchmarking Succession Planning and Management Practices

5-8: Opinions of Top Managers about Succession Planning and Management

5-9: Opinions of Human Resource Professionals about Succession Planning and Management

5-10: Actions to Build Management Commitment to Succession Planning and Management

6-1: A Model for Conceptualizing Role Theory

6-2: Management Roles in Succession Planning and Management: A Grid

6-3: A Worksheet to Formulate a Mission Statement for Succession Planning and Management

6-4: A Sample Succession Planning and Management Policy

6-5: Targeted Groups for Succession Planning and Management

6-6: An Activity for Identifying Initial Targets for Succession Planning and Management Activities

6-7: An Activity for Establishing Program Priorities in Succession Planning and Management

6-8: U.S. Labor Laws

7-1: A Worksheet for Preparing an Action Plan to Establish the Succession Planning and Management Program

7-2: Sample Outlines for In-House Training on Succession Planning and Management

8-1: A Worksheet for Writing a Key Position Description

8-2: A Worksheet for Considering Key Issues in Full-Circle, Multi-Rater Assessments

8-3: The Relationship between Performance Management and Performance Appraisal

8-4: Approaches to Conducting Employee Performance Appraisal

8-5: A Worksheet for Developing an Employee Performance Appraisal Linked to a Position Description

9-1: A Worksheet for Environmental Scanning
9-2: An Activity on Organizational Analysis
9-3: An Activity for Preparing Realistic Scenarios to Identify Future Key Positions
9-4: An Activity for Preparing Future-Oriented Key Position Descriptions
9-5: Steps in Conducting Future-Oriented ''Rapid Results Assessment''
9-6: How to Classify Individuals by Performance and Potential
9-7: A Worksheet for Making Global Assessments
9-8: A Worksheet to Identify Success Factors
9-9: An Individual Potential Assessment Form
10-1: A Sample Replacement Chart Format: Typical Succession Planning and Management Inventory for the Organization
10-2: Succession Planning and Management Inventory by Position
10-3: A Simplified Model of Steps in Preparing Individual Development Plans (IDPs)
10-4: A Worksheet for Preparing Learning Objectives Based on Individual Development Needs
10-5: A Worksheet for Identifying the Resources Necessary to Support Developmental Experiences
10-6: A Sample Individual Development Plan
10-7: Methods of Grooming Individuals for Advancement
10-8: Key Strategies for Internal Development
11-1: Deciding When Replacing a Key Job Incumbent Is Unnecessary: A Flowchart
11-2: A Worksheet for Identifying Alternatives to the Traditional Approach to Succession Planning and Management
12-1: Continua of Online and High-Tech Approaches
12-2: A Hierarchy of Online and High-Tech Applications for Succession Planning and Management
12-3: A Worksheet for Brainstorming When and How to Use Online and High-Tech Methods
13-1: The Hierarchy of Succession Planning and Management Evaluation
13-2: Guidelines for Evaluating the Succession Planning and Management Program
13-3: A Worksheet for Identifying Appropriate Ways to Evaluate Succession Planning and Management in an Organization

13-4:   A Sample "Incident Report" for Succession Planning and Management

13-5:   Steps for Completing a Program Evaluation of a Succession Planning and Management Program

13-6:   A Checksheet for Conducting a Program Evaluation for the Succession Planning and Management Program

14-1:   A Worksheet to Structure Your Thinking about Predictions for Succession Planning and Management in the Future

14-2:   A Worksheet to Structure Your Thinking about Alternative Approaches to Meeting Succession Needs

14-3:   Age Distribution of the U.S. Population in 2025

14-4:   Age Distribution of the Chinese Population in 2025

14-5:   Age Distribution of the Population in the United Kingdom in 2025

14-6:   Age Distribution of the French Population in 2025

14-7:   Important Characteristics of Career Planning and Management Programs

14-8:   An Assessment Sheet for Integrating Career Planning and Management Programs with Succession Planning and Management Programs

Preface

The world continues to face the crisis of leadership that was described in the preface to the first edition of this book. Indeed, "a chronic crisis of governance—that is, the pervasive incapacity of organizations to cope with the expectations of their constituents—is now an overwhelming factor worldwide."[1] That statement is as true today as it was when that book was published in 1994. Evidence can still be found in many settings: Citizens continue to lose faith in their elected officials to address problems at the national, regional, and local levels; the religious continue to lose faith in high-profile church leaders who have been stricken with sensationalized scandals; and consumers continue to lose faith in business leaders to act responsibly and ethically.[2]

A crisis of governance is also widespread inside organizations. Employees wonder what kind of employment they can maintain when a new employment contract has changed the relationship between workers and their organizations. Employee loyalty is a relic of the past,[3] victim of the downsizing craze so popular in the 1990s and that persists in some organizations to the present day, at precisely the time when a continuing economic expansion in the United States has made retention of high-potential intellectual capital an important key to competitive success and turnover a constraint on business growth. Changing demographics makes the identification of successors key to the future of many organizations when the legacy of the 1990s cutbacks in the middle management ranks, traditional training ground for senior executive positions, has come home to roost. If that is hard to believe, consider that 20 percent of the best-known companies in the United States may lose 40 percent of their senior executives to retirement within the next five years.[4] Demographics tell the story: The U.S. population is aging, and that could mean many retirements soon. (See Exhibits F-1 and F-2.)

Amid the twofold pressures of pending retirements in senior executive ranks and the increasing value of intellectual capital and knowledge management, it is more necessary than ever before for organizations to plan for leadership continuity and employee advancement at all levels. But that is easier said than done. It is not consistent with long-standing tradi-

Exhibit P-1: Age Distribution of the U.S. Population, Selected Years, 1965–2025

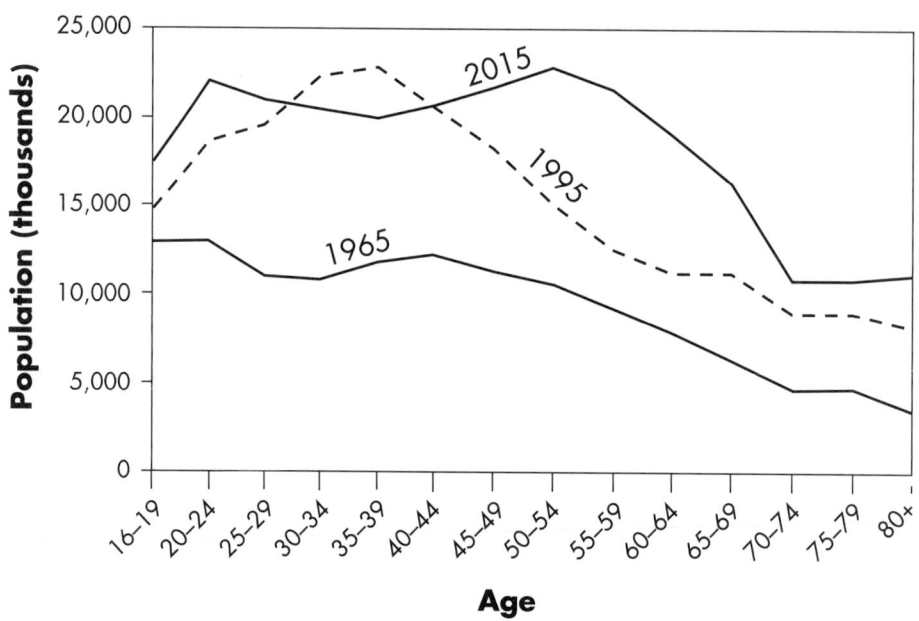

SOURCE: Stacy Poulos and Demetra S. Nightengale, "The Aging Baby Boom: Implications for Employment and Training Programs." Presented at http://www.urban.org/aging/abb/agingbaby.html. This report was prepared by the U.S. Department of Labor under Contract No. F-5532-5-00-80-30.

tion, which favors short-term thinking on succession planning and management (SP&M) issues. Nor is it consistent with the continuing current trends favoring slimmed-down staffing and the use of contingent workers, which often create a shallow talent pool from which to choose future leaders.

In previous decades, labor in the United States was plentiful and easily taken for granted. Managers had the leisure to groom employees for advancement over long time spans and to overstaff as insurance against turnover in key positions. That was as true for management as for nonmanagement employees. Most jobs did not require extensive prequalification. Seniority, as measured by time with an organization or in an industry, was sufficient to ensure advancement. Succession planning and management activities properly focused on leaders astride the peak of tall organizational hierarchies because organizations were controlled from the top down and were thus heavily dependent on the knowledge, skills, and attitudes of top management leaders. But times have changed. Few organizations have the luxury to overstaff in the face of fierce competition from abroad and economic restructuring efforts. That is particularly true in high-technology

Exhibit P-2: U.S. Population by Age, 1965–2025

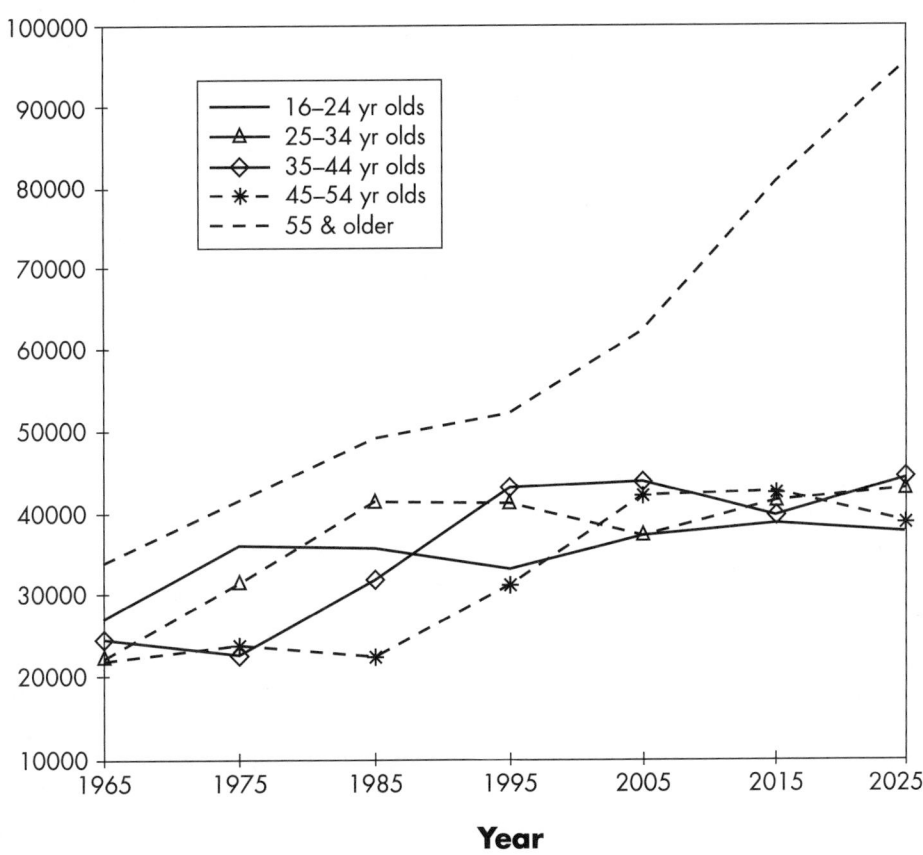

SOURCE: Stacy Poulos and Demetra S. Nightengale, "The Aging Baby Boom: Implications for Employment and Training Programs." Presented at http://www.urban.org/aging/abb/agingbaby.html. This report was prepared by the U.S. Department of Labor under Contract No. F-5532-5-00-80-30.

companies where several months' experience may be the equivalent of one year in a traditional organization.

At the same time, products, markets, and management activities have grown more complex. Many jobs now require extensive prequalification, both inside and outside organizations. A track record of demonstrated and successful job performance, more than mere time in position, and leadership competency have become key considerations as fewer employees compete for diminishing advancement opportunities. As employee empowerment has broadened the ranks of decision-makers, leadership influence can be exerted at all hierarchical levels rather than limited to those few granted authority by virtue of their management positions.

For these reasons, organizations must take proactive steps to plan for future talent needs at all levels and implement programs designed to ensure that the right people are available for the right jobs in the right places and at the right times to meet organizational requirements. Much is at stake in this process: "the continuity of the organization over time requires a succession of persons to fill key positions."[5] There are important social implications as well. As management guru Peter Drucker explains:[6]

> The question of tomorrow's management is, above all, a concern of our society. Let me put it bluntly—we have reached a point where we simply will not be able to tolerate as a country, as a society, as a government, the danger that any *one of our major companies will decline or collapse because it has not made adequate provisions for management succession.* [emphasis added]

Research adds weight to the argument favoring SP&M. First, it has been shown that firms in which the CEO has a specific successor in mind are more profitable than those in which no specific successor has been identified. A possible reason is that selecting a successor "could be viewed as a favorable general signal about the presence and development of high-quality top management."[7] In other words, superior-performing CEOs make SP&M and leadership continuity top priorities. Succession planning and management has even been credited with driving a plant turnaround by linking the organization's continuous improvement philosophy to individual development.[8]

But ensuring leadership continuity can be a daunting undertaking. The rules, procedures, and techniques used in the past appear to be growing increasingly outmoded and inappropriate. It is time to revisit, rethink, and even reengineer SP&M. That is especially true because, in the words of one observer of the contemporary management scene, "below many a corporation's top two or three positions, succession planning [for leadership talent] is often an informal, haphazard exercise where longevity, luck, and being in the proverbial right place at the right time determines lines of succession."[9] A haphazard approach to SP&M bodes ill for organizations in which leadership talent is diffused—and correspondingly important—at all hierarchical levels.

The Purpose of This Book

Succession planning and management and leadership development figure prominently on the agenda of many top managers. Yet, despite senior management interest, the task often falls to Human Resource Management (HRM) and Human Resource Development (HRD) professionals to spearhead and coordinate efforts to establish and operate planned succession programs and avert succession crises. In that way, they fill an important, proactive role demanded of them by top managers, and they ensure that SP&M issues are not lost in the shuffle of fighting daily fires.

But SP&M is rarely, if ever, treated in most undergraduate or graduate college degree programs—even in those specifically tailored to preparing HRM and HRD professionals. For this reason, HRM and HRD professionals often need assistance when they coordinate, establish, operate, or evaluate SP&M programs. This book is intended to provide that help. It offers practical, how-to-do-it advice on SP&M. The book's scope is deliberately broad. It encompasses more than *management* succession planning, which is the most frequently discussed topic by writers and consultants in the field. Stated succinctly, the purpose of this book is to reassess SP&M and offer a fresh but practical approach to ensuring leadership continuity in key positions and building leadership talent from within.

Succession planning and management should support strategic planning and strategic thinking and should provide an essential starting point for management and employee development programs. Without it, organizations will have difficulty maintaining leadership continuity—or identifying appropriate leaders when a change in business strategy is necessary. While most large blue-chip corporations operate SP&M programs, small and medium-sized businesses also need them. In fact, inadequate succession plans are a common cause of small business failure as founding entrepreneurs fade from the scene, leaving no one to continue their legacy,[10] and as tax laws exert an impact on the legacy of those founders as they pass away.

Whatever an organization's size or your job responsibilities, then, this book should provide useful information on establishing, managing, operating, and evaluating SP&M programs.

Sources of Information

As I began writing this book I decided to explore state-of-the-art succession planning and management practices. I consulted several major sources of information:

1. *A tailor-made survey.* In late 1999 I surveyed over 700 HRM professionals about SP&M practices in their organizations. Selected survey results, which were compiled in April 2000, are published in this book for the first time. This survey was an update of an earlier survey conducted for the first edition of this book. While the response rate to this survey was disappointing, the results do provide interesting information.

2. *Phone surveys and informal benchmarking.* I spoke by phone with vendors of specialized succession planning software and discussed SP&M with HRD professionals in major corporations.

3. *Other surveys.* I researched other surveys that have been conducted on SP&M in recent years and, giving proper credit when due, I summarize key findings of those surveys at appropriate points in the book.

4. *Web searches.* I examined what resources could be found on the World Wide Web relating to important topics in this book. Many are summarized in Chapter 12.

5. *A literature search.* I conducted an exhaustive literature review on SP&M—with special emphasis on what has been written on the subject since the last edition of this book. I also looked for case-study descriptions of what real organizations have been doing.

6. *Firsthand experience.* Before entering the academic world, I was responsible for a comprehensive Management Development (MD) program in a major corporation. As part of that role I coordinated management SP&M. My experiences are reflected in this book. Since entering academe, I have also done consulting on the topic of SP&M.

The aim of these sources is to ensure that this book will provide a comprehensive and up-to-date treatment of typical *and* best-in-class SP&M practices in organizations of various sizes and types operating in different industries.

The Scheme of This Book

Effective Succession Planning: Ensuring Leadership Continuity and Building Talent from Within is written for those wishing to establish, revitalize, or review an SP&M program within their organizations. It is geared to meet the needs of HRM and HRD executives, managers, and professionals. It also contains useful information for chief executive officers, chief operating officers, general managers, university faculty members who do consulting, management development specialists who are looking for a detailed treatment of the subject as a foundation for their own efforts, SP&M program coordinators, and others bearing major responsibilities for developing management, professional, technical, sales, or other employees.

The book is organized in four parts. Part I sets the stage. Chapter 1 opens with dramatic vignettes illustrating typical—and a few rivetingly atypical—problems in SP&M. The chapter also defines succession planning and management, distinguishes it from replacement planning, emphasizes its importance, explains why organizations sponsor such programs, and describes different approaches to succession planning and management.

Chapter 2 describes five key trends influencing succession planning and management. Those trends are: (1) the need for speed; (2) a seller's market for skills; (3) reduced loyalty among employers and workers; (4) the importance of intellectual capital and knowledge management; and (5) the key importance of values and competencies. The chapter clarifies what these trends mean for SP&M efforts.

Chapter 3 opens with several case-study descriptions of SP&M programs. The chapter draws conclusions from the cases about the characteristics of effective SP&M programs, describes the life cycle of SP&M programs, identifies and solves common problems with various approaches to SP&M, and describes the requirements and key steps in a fifth-generation approach to SP&M.

Chapter 4 defines competencies, explains how they are used in SP&M, summarizes how to conduct competency identification studies for SP&M and use the results, defines values, and explains how values and values clarification can guide SP&M efforts.

Part II consists of Chapters 5 through 7. It lays the foundation for an effective SP&M program.

Chapter 5 describes how to make the case for change, often a necessary first step before any change effort can be successful. The chapter reviews such important steps in this process as assessing current SP&M practices, demonstrating business need, determining program requirements, linking SP&M to strategic planning and human resource planning, benchmarking SP&M practices in other organizations, and securing management commitment.

Building on the previous chapter, Chapter 6 explains how to clarify roles in an SP&M program; formulate the program's mission, policy, and procedure statements; identify target groups; and set program priorities. It also addresses the legal framework in SP&M and provides advice about strategies for rolling out an SP&M program.

Chapter 7 rounds out Part II. It offers advice on preparing a program action plan, communicating the action plan, conducting SP&M meetings, designing and delivering training to support SP&M, and counseling managers about SP&M problems uniquely affecting them and their areas of responsibility.

Part III is comprised of Chapters 8 and 9. It focuses on assessing present work requirements in key positions, present individual performance, future work requirements, and future individual potential. Crucial to an effective SP&M program, these activities are the basis for subsequent individual development planning.

Chapter 8 examines the present situation. It addresses the following questions:

△ How are key positions identified?

△ What three approaches can be used to determining work requirements in key positions?

△ How can full-circle, multi-rater assessment be used in SP&M?

△ How is performance appraised?

△ What techniques and approaches can be used in creating talent pools?

Chapter 9 examines the future. Related to Chapter 8, it focuses on these questions:

△ What key positions are likely to emerge in the future?

△ What will be the work requirements in those positions?

△ What is individual potential assessment, and how can it be carried out?

Part IV consists of Chapters 10 through 14. Chapters in this part focus on closing the developmental gap by operating and evaluating an SP&M program.

Chapter 10 offers advice for testing the organization's overall bench strength, explains why an internal promotion policy is important, defines the term *Individual Development Plan* (IDP), describes how to prepare and use an IDP to guide individual development, and reviews important methods to support internal development.

Chapter 11 moves beyond the traditional approach to SP&M. It offers alternatives to internal development as the means by which to meet replacement needs. The basic idea of the chapter is that underlying a replacement need is a work need that must be satisfied. There are, of course, other ways to meet work needs than by replacing a key position incumbent. The chapter provides a decision model to distinguish between situations when replacing a key position incumbent is—and is not—warranted.

Chapter 12 examines how to apply online and high-tech approaches to SP&M programs. The chapter addresses four major questions: (1) How are online and high-tech methods defined? (2) In what areas of SP&M can online and high-tech methods be applied? (3) How are online and high-tech applications used? and (4) What specialized competencies are required by succession planning coordinators to use these applications?

Chapter 13 is about evaluation, and it examines possible answers to three simple questions: (1) What is evaluation? (2) What should be evaluated in SP&M? and (3) How should an SP&M program be evaluated?

Chapter 14 concludes the book. It offers eight predictions about SP&M. More specifically, I end the book by predicting that SP&M will: (1) prompt efforts by decision-makers to find flexible strategies to address future organizational talent needs; (2) lead to integrated retention policies and procedures that are intended to identify high-potential talent earlier, retain that talent, and preserve older high-potential workers; (3) have a global impact; (4) be influenced increasingly by real-time technological innovations; (5) become an issue in government agencies, academic institutions, and nonprofit enterprises in a way never before seen; (6) lead to increasing organizational openness about possible successors; (7) increasingly be integrated with career development issues; and (8) be heavily influenced in the future by concerns about work/family balance and spirituality.

William J. Rothwell
University Park, Pennsylvania

Acknowledgments

Writing a book resembles taking a long journey. Researching, drafting, and repeatedly revising a book requires more time, effort, patience, and self-discipline than most authors care to admit or many have the dedication to pursue.

Yet no book is written in isolation. Completing such a journey requires any author to seek help from many people, who provide advice—and directions—along the way.

This is my opportunity to thank those who have helped me. I would therefore like to extend my sincere appreciation to my graduate research assistant, Mr. Chen Wei (Wayne Chen), for helping me send out and analyze the results of the survey, updated from the first edition of this book, on succession planning and management. I would also like to thank the following individuals, listed in alphabetical order, for their help in reviewing drafts of this manuscript at various stages of completion and offering their valuable insights on ways to improve it:

Dr. Joseph Benkowski
Dr. David Dubois
Dr. Marsha King
Dr. Stephen B. King
Dr. Robert K. Prescott

These individuals provided me with valuable advice, information, and encouragement, though I bear ultimate responsibility for the quality of the final product. Now that I am at the end of the journey, I owe them a debt of gratitude for their help along the way.

Finally, I would also like to thank Adrienne Hickey and other staff members at AMACOM, who offered numerous useful ideas on the project while also demonstrating enormous patience with me.

Part I
Background Information about Succession Planning and Management

Part I provides background information about succession planning and management (SP&M). It introduces SP&M with a series of dramatic vignettes that allow you to assess how well-positioned your organization is to handle common succession problems. This part also:

- △ Defines SP&M
- △ Distinguishes SP&M from replacement planning
- △ Describes the importance of SP&M
- △ Lists reasons for an SP&M program
- △ Reviews approaches to SP&M
- △ Reviews key trends influencing SP&M and explains their implications
- △ Provides case-study descriptions of SP&M programs
- △ Lists key characteristics of effective SP&M programs
- △ Describes the life cycle of SP&M programs
- △ Explains how to identify and solve problems with various approaches to SP&M
- △ Lists the requirements and key steps for a fifth-generation approach to SP&M
- △ Defines competencies and explains how they are used in SP&M
- △ Describes how to conduct and use competency identification studies for SP&M
- △ Defines values and values clarification and explains how they are used in SP&M
- △ Describes how to conduct and use values clarification studies for SP&M

Chapter 1

What Is Succession Planning and Management?

Five Ministudies: Can You Solve These Succession Problems?

How is your organization handling succession planning and management (SP&M)? Read the following vignettes and, on a separate sheet, describe how *your* organization would solve the problem presented in each. If you can offer an effective solution to all the vignettes, then your organization may already have an effective SP&M program in place; if not, your organization may have an urgent need to devote more attention to it.

Vignette 1

An airplane crashes in the desert, killing all on board. Among the passengers: top managers of Acme Engineering, a successful consulting firm. When the vice president of human resources at Acme is summoned to the phone to receive the news, she gasps, turns pale, looks blankly at her secretary, and breathlessly voices the first question that enters her mind: "Now who's in charge?"

Vignette 2

Georgina Myers, supervisor of a key assembly line, has just called in sick after two years of perfect attendance. She personally handles all purchasing and production scheduling in the small plant as well as overseeing the assembly line. The production manager, Mary Rawlings, does not know how the plant will function in the absence of this key employee. But she is sure that production will be lost today because Georgina has no trained backup.

Vignette 3

Marietta Diaz was not promoted to supervisor. She is convinced that she is a victim of racial and sexual discrimination. Her manager, Wilson Smith, assures her that is not the case. As he explains to her, "You just don't have the skills and experience to do the work. Gordon Hague, who was promoted, already possesses those skills. The decision was based strictly on individual merit and supervisory job requirements." But Marietta remains troubled. How, she wonders, could Gordon have acquired those skills in his previous nonsupervisory job?

Vignette 4

Morton Wile is about to retire as CEO of Multiplex Systems. For several years he has been grooming L. Carson Adams as his successor. Adams has held the posts of executive vice president and chief operating officer, and his performance has been exemplary in those positions. Wile has long been convinced that Adams will make an excellent CEO.

But, as his retirement date approaches, Wile has recently been hearing questions about his choice. Several division vice presidents and members of the board of directors have asked him privately how wise it is to allow Adams to take over, since (it is whispered) he has long had a high-profile extramarital affair with his secretary and is rumored to be an alcoholic. How, they wonder, can he be chosen to assume the top leadership position when he carries such personal baggage?

Wile is reluctant to talk to Adams about these matters. But he is sufficiently troubled to think about initiating an executive search for a CEO candidate from outside the company.

Vignette 5

Linda Childress is general manager of a large consumer products plant in the Midwest. She has helped her plant weather many storms. The first was a corporate-sponsored voluntary early retirement program, which began eight years ago. In that program Linda lost her most experienced workers. Among its effects in the plant: costly work redistribution, retraining, retooling, and automation.

The second storm was a forced layoff which occurred five years ago. It was driven by fierce foreign competition in consumer products manufacture. The layoff cost Linda fully one-fourth of her most recently hired workers and many middle managers, professionals, and technical employees. It also led to a net loss of protected labor groups in the plant's workforce to a level well below what had taken the company ten years of ambitious efforts to achieve. Other consequences: increasingly aggressive union action in the plant; isolated incidents of violence against management personnel by disgruntled workers; growing evidence of theft, pilferage, and employee sabotage; and skyrocketing absenteeism and turnover rates.

The third storm swept the plant on the heels of the layoff. Just three years ago corporate headquarters announced a company-wide Total Quality Management program. Its aims: to improve product quality and customer service, build worker involvement and empowerment, reduce scrap rates, and meet competition from abroad. While the goals were laudable, the program was greeted with skepticism because it was introduced so soon after the layoff. Many employees—and supervisors—voiced the opinion that "corporate headquarters is using Total Quality to clean up the mess they created by chopping heads first and asking questions about work reallocation later." However, since job security is an issue of paramount importance to everyone at the plant, the external consultant sent by corporate headquarters to introduce Total Quality received grudging cooperation. But the Total Quality initiative has created side effects of its own. One is that executives, middle managers, and supervisors are uncertain about their roles and the results expected of them. Another is that employees, pressured to do better work with fewer resources, are complaining bitterly about compensation practices that they feel do not reflect their increased responsibilities, efforts, or productivity.

Against this backdrop, Linda has noticed that it is becoming more difficult to find backups for hourly workers and ensure leadership continuity in the plant's middle and top management ranks. Although the company has long conducted an annual "succession planning and management" ritual in which standardized forms, supplied by corporate headquarters, are sent out to managers by the plant's human resources department, Linda cannot remember when the forms were actually used during a talent search. The major reason, Linda believes, is that managers and employees have rarely followed through on the Individual Development Plans (IDPs) established to prepare people for advancement opportunities.

Defining Succession Planning and Management

As the vignettes above illustrate, organizations need to plan for talent to assume key leadership positions or backup positions on a temporary or permanent basis.

Among the first writers to recognize that universal organizational need was Henri Fayol (1841–1925). Fayol's classic fourteen points of management, first enunciated early in the twentieth century and still widely regarded today, indicate that management has a responsibility to ensure the "stability of tenure of personnel."[1] If that need is ignored, Fayol believed, key positions would end up being filled by ill-prepared people.

Succession planning and management (SP&M) is the process that helps ensure the stability of tenure of personnel. It is perhaps best understood as *any effort designed to ensure the continued effective perform-ance of an organization, division, department, or work group by making provision for the development, replacement, and strategic application of key people over time.*

Succession planning has been defined as

> a means of identifying critical management positions, starting at the levels of project manager and supervisor and extending up to the highest position in the organization. Succession planning also describes management positions to provide maximum flex-ibility in lateral management moves and to ensure that as individ-uals achieve greater seniority, their management skills will broaden and become more generalized in relation to total orga-nizational objectives rather than to purely departmental objec-tives.[2]

Succession planning should not stand alone. It should be paired with *suc-cession management*, which

> assumes a more dynamic business environment. It recognizes the ramifications of the new employment contract, where corpo-rations no longer (implicitly) assure anyone continued employ-ment, even if he or she is doing a good job.[3]

An SP&M program is thus a *deliberate and systematic effort by an organi-zation to ensure leadership continuity in key positions, retain and de-velop intellectual and knowledge capital for the future, and encourage individual advancement.* Systematic "succession planning occurs when an organization adapts specific procedures to insure the identification, de-velopment, and long-term retention of talented individuals."[4]

Succession planning and management need not be limited solely to *management* positions or *management* employees. Indeed, an effective succession planning and management effort should also address the needs for critical backups and individual development in any job category—including key people in the professional, technical, sales, clerical, and pro-duction ranks. The need to extend the definition of SP&M beyond the management ranks is becoming more important as organizations take ac-tive steps to build high-performance and high-involvement work environ-ments in which decision-making is decentralized and leadership is diffused throughout an empowered workforce.

One aim of SP&M is to match the organization's available (present) talent to its needed (future) talent. Another is to help the organization meet the strategic and operational challenges facing it by having the right people at the right places at the right times to do the right things. In these senses, SP&M should be regarded as a fundamental tool for *organizational learning* because SP&M should ensure that the lessons of organizational experience—what is sometimes called *institutional memory*—will be preserved and combined with reflection on that experience to achieve continuous improvement in work results (what is sometimes called *double loop learning*).[5] Stated in another way, SP&M is a way to ensure the continued cultivation of leadership and intellectual talent and manage the critically important knowledge assets of organizations.

Distinguishing Succession Planning and Management from Replacement Planning

Succession planning and management should not be confused with *replacement planning*, though they are compatible and often overlap. The obvious need for some form of replacement planning is frequently a driving force behind efforts that eventually turn into SP&M programs—as Vignette 1 at the opening of this chapter dramatically illustrates. That need was only dramatized by the 1996 plane crash of U.S. Secretary of Commerce Ron Brown, which claimed the lives of over thirty other top executives.

In its simplest form, replacement planning is a form of risk management. In that respect it resembles other organizational efforts to manage risk, such as ensuring that fire sprinkling systems in computer rooms are not positioned so as to destroy valuable computer equipment in case of fire, or segregating accounting duties to reduce the chance of embezzlement. The chief aim of replacement planning is to reduce the chance of catastrophe stemming from the immediate and unplanned loss of key job incumbents.

However, SP&M goes beyond simple replacement planning. It is proactive and attempts to ensure the continuity of leadership by cultivating talent from within the organization through planned development activities. It should be regarded as an important tool for implementing strategic plans.

The Importance of Succession Planning and Management

Many requirements must be satisfied if organizations are to survive in a fiercely competitive environment. One key requirement is that replacements must be available to assume critically important positions as they become vacant. Indeed, "succession planning, like a relay race, has to do with passing on responsibility. . . . Drop the baton and you lose the race."[6]

Numerous surveys over the years have emphasized the importance of SP&M. Chief executives consistently cite the issue as one of their major concerns. Leadership succession has also surfaced as an issue of concern to corporate boards:[7]

> A survey by Korn/Ferry International of corporate board member policies and practices asked chairpersons to assess the importance of issues facing their companies in the next five years. Those typically seen as trendsetters—the billion-dollar companies—rated *management succession as the third most important issue* [*emphasis added*], on the heels of financial results and strategic planning. According to Lester Korn, CEO of the search firm, boards are beginning to realize that they have "the same obligations to protect the human resource asset base for the shareholders as they do to protect the balance sheet of the corporation."

There are several reasons why both CEOs and corporate boards are so interested in SP&M.

First, top managers are aware that the continued survival of the organization depends on having the right people in the right places at the right times. Strategic success is, in large measure, a function of having the right leadership. Leaving the development of those leaders to chance, and hoping for the best, may have worked at one time. Ignoring the development of leaders and depending on headhunters to find replacements for key people may also have worked at one time. But these approaches are not working now. Some effort must be made to ensure that the organization is *systematically* identifying and preparing high-potential candidates for key positions.

Second, as continuing downsizing and other cost containment efforts have led to reductions in the middle management ranks—a traditional training ground and source of top management talent—there are simply fewer people available to advance to the top ranks from within. That means that great care must be taken to identify promising candidates early and actively cultivate their development. Individuals who are *both* high performers on their present jobs and high potentials for future leadership positions should not be taken for granted, especially in a seller's labor market where talented workers can barter their abilities with other companies. The reason: Slimmed-down organizations have reduced their absolute numbers. Worse yet, members of this group are differentially affected by downsizing, because as work is redistributed after a downsizing, high performers end up shouldering more of the burden to get the work out while (in most cases) the rewards they receive are held constant. They are thus more likely to become dissatisfied and leave the organization than their less productive peers. To avoid that problem—which can be disastrous for the future leadership continuity of the organization—top managers must take active steps to reward them and advance them through vertical and horizontal career moves in a manner commensurate with their increased contributions.

Third, when SP&M is left informal and thus unplanned, job incumbents tend to identify and groom successors who are remarkably like themselves in appearance, background, and values. They establish a "bureaucratic kinship system" that is based on "homosocial reproduction."[8] As Rosabeth Moss Kanter explained:[9]

> Because of the *situation* in which managers function, because of the position of managers in the corporate structure, social similarity tends to become extremely important to them. The structure sets in motion forces leading to the replication of managers as the same kind of social individuals. And the men who manage reproduce themselves in kind.

As a consequence, white males tend to pick as successors other white males. That practice, of course, perpetuates such problems as the so-called *glass ceiling*, and other subtle forms of employment discrimination. To avoid these problems and promote diversity and multiculturalism in the workplace, systematic efforts must be made to identify and groom the best successors for key positions—not just those who superficially resemble the present key job incumbents.

Succession planning and management is important for other reasons as well. Indeed, it "forms the basis for (1) communicating career paths to each individual; (2) establishing development and training plans; (3) establishing career paths and individual job moves; (4) communicating upward and laterally concerning the management organization; and, (5) creating a more comprehensive human resources planning system."[10]

Reasons for a Succession Planning and Management Program

Why should an organization support a systematic SP&M program? To answer that question, I updated a survey that I sent out in 1993 for the first edition of this book. (The first survey was mailed to 350 randomly selected members of the American Society for Training and Development [ASTD] in October 1993.) The survey for the second edition of this book was mailed in December 1999 to 742 members of the Society for Human Resources Management (SHRM). A follow-up mailing was sent in January 2000, and a second follow-up mailing went out in February 2000. Thirty-one (31) surveys were returned. Only 30 surveys provided useful information. While that response rate is most disappointing, it does provide useful—if not representative—information. Of the respondents, 12 (40 percent) indicated that their organizations are presently operating a systematic SP&M program; the remaining respondents (60 percent) reported that their organizations are *not* operating a systematic SP&M program. Exhibit 1-1 presents demographic information about the respondents' industries; Exhibit 1-2 charts the sizes of the respondents' organizations; Exhibit 1-3 presents information about the respondents' job functions; and Exhibit 1-4 summarizes the respondents' perceptions about the chief reasons why their organizations operate systematic SP&M programs.

Reason 1: Provide Increased Opportunities for "High Potential" Workers

My survey respondents indicated that the most important reason to sponsor systematic SP&M is to "provide increased opportunities for 'high potential' workers." Although definitions of "High Potentials" (HiPos) may differ, they are usually regarded as those employees who have the potential

Exhibit 1-1: Demographic Information about Respondents to a 1999 Survey on Succession Planning and Management: Industries*

In what industry is your organization classified?

Industry	Frequency**	Percentage
Manufacturing	7	23.33%
Transportation/Communication/Electric/Gas	2	6.67%
Retail Trade	1	3.33%
Finance/Insurance/Real Estate	9	30.00%
Healthcare	3	10.00%
Government/Armed Forces	1	3.33%
Other Services	7	23.33%
Other Services include		
Market Research		
Education		
Hospitality		

*SOURCE: William J. Rothwell, *Results of a Survey on Succession Planning and Management Practices*, unpublished survey results (University Park, Pa.: The Pennsylvania State University, 2000).
**Not all respondents chose to answer this question.

Exhibit 1-2: Demographic Information about Respondents to a 1999 Survey on Succession Planning and Management: Size*

How many people does your organization employ?

Number of employees	Frequency**	Percentage
0–99	0	0.00%
100–249	2	6.67%
250–499	5	16.67%
500–1999	12	40.00%
2000–4999	3	10.00%
5000 or more	8	26.67%

*Source: William J. Rothwell, *Results of a Survey on Succession Planning and Management Practices*, unpublished survey results (University Park, Pa.: The Pennsylvania State University, 2000).
**Not all respondents chose to answer this question.

for future advancement. Hence, a very important reason for SP&M is to identify appropriate ways to accelerate HiPo development and improve the retention of talented people with potential.[11] A few important retention strategies are summarized in Exhibit 1-5.

Reason 2: Identify "Replacement Needs" as a Means of Targeting Necessary Training, Employee Education, and Employee Development

The second reason cited by survey respondents for organizations to sponsor systematic SP&M is to "identify 'replacement needs' as a means of

Exhibit 1-3: Demographic Information about Respondents to a 1999 Survey on Succession Planning and Management: Job Functions of Respondents*

What is your job function?

Job Function	Frequency**	Percentage
Trainer	0	0.00%
Personnel Manager	9	30.00%
Other	21	70.00%
VP HR		
HR Director		
Corporate Employment Director		
Assistant VP Compensation & Benefits		
Executive Development Consultant		
HRD Specialist		

*Source: William J. Rothwell, *Results of a Survey on Succession Planning Practices*, unpublished survey results (University Park, Pa.: The Pennsylvania State University, 2000).
**Not all respondents chose to answer this question.

Exhibit 1-4: Reasons for Succession Planning and Management Programs*

There are many reasons why decision-makers may wish to establish an SP&M program in an organization. For each reason listed in the left column below, please *circle a response code in the right column* indicating *how important you believe that reason to be for your organization*. Use the following scale: 1 = Not at all important; 2 = Not important; 3 = Somewhat important; 4 = Important; 5 = Very important.

Reasons for Sponsoring Succession Planning and Management Programs	How Important Do You Believe This Reason to Be?				
	Mean	SD	Mode	Median	Response
A Contribute to implementing the organization's Strategic Business Plans	4.17	0.84	5	4	40.00%
B Cope with effects of downsizing	1.50	0.67	1	1	40.00%
C Cope with the effects of voluntary separation programs—such as early retirement offers and employee buyouts	1.75	0.75	1,2	2	40.00%
D Help individuals realize their career plans within the organization	3.92	1.24	5	4	40.00%
E Improve employee morale	3.17	1.27	2,3,4	3	40.00%
F Improve employees' ability to respond to changing environmental demands	3.67	1.16	3,4	4	40.00%
G Reduce headcount to essential workers only	1.33	0.49	1	1	40.00%
H Increase the talent pool of promotable employees	4.33	0.89	5	4.5	40.00%
I Identify "replacement needs" as a means of targeting necessary training, employee education, and employee development	4.33	1.07	5	5	40.00%

J	Decide which workers can be terminated without damage to the organization	1.75	1.14	1	1.5	40.00%
K	Encourage the advancement of diverse groups—such as minorities or women—in future jobs within the organization	3.67	1.23	4	4	40.00%
L	Provide increased opportunities for "high potential" workers	4.58	0.67	5	5	40.00%
M	Tap the potential for intellectual capital in the organization	3.83	0.94	3	3.5	40.00%
O	Others					
	Preparation for "immediate loss" of key manager for whatever reason;					
	Retention;					
	Provide for transitional management in event of precipitous cessation of duties by a senior manager due to death, disability, or removal					

*SOURCE: William J. Rothwell, *Results of a Survey on Succession Planning and Management Practices*, unpublished survey results (University Park, Pa.: The Pennsylvania State University, 2000).

targeting necessary training, employee education, and employee development." In other words, SP&M becomes a driving force to identify justifiable employee training, education, and development needs. Training helps employees meet their current job responsibilities; employee education prepares them to advance to future responsibilities; and employee development can be a tool for individual enlightenment or organizational learning.

Reason 3: Increase the Talent Pool of Promotable Employees

Respondents in organizations sponsoring systematic SP&M cited the third most important reason as to "increase the talent pool of promotable em-

Exhibit 1-5: Strategies for Reducing Turnover and Increasing Retention

Possible Causes of Turnover *People leave the organization because they:*	Possible Strategies for Increasing Retention
Are dissatisfied with their future prospects in the organization or believe they have better prospects for the future in another organization	△ Assess the extent of this problem by using attitude surveys (paper-based or online), by using exit interviews with departing workers, and by running selected focus groups to gather information △ Give people hope by establishing and communicating about a succession planning and management program △ Establish or improve job posting programs, job rotations, and other efforts to give people more exposure and visibility within the organization △ Improve communication about the future of the organization and what that might mean for individuals in it
Dislike their supervisors and/ or their supervisors' approach to supervision	△ Assess the extent of this problem by using attitude surveys (paper-based or online) and by using exit interviews with departing workers △ Improve supervisory training, with special emphasis on sources of dissatisfaction that influence turnover △ Establish or improve job posting programs, job rotations, and other efforts to give people more exposure and visibility within the organization
Dislike the kind of work that they do or the kind of assignments that they have been given	△ Assess the extent of this problem by using attitude surveys (paper-based or online), by using exit interviews with departing workers, and by running selected focus groups to gather information △ Establish or improve job posting programs, job rotations, and other efforts to give people more exposure and visibility within the organization

Dislike their wage or salary level, believe it is not competitive, or believe they are not compensated in a way commensurate with their contributions	△ Assess the extent of this problem by using attitude surveys (paper-based or online), by using exit interviews with departing workers, and by running selected focus groups to gather information △ Conduct regular wage and salary surveys outside the organization △ Clarify the organization's philosophy of rewards ("do we want to pay only at competitive levels? If so, why?") △ Make use of innovative reward and compensation practices that go beyond mere considerations of wages to include alternative reward and alternative recognition programs and "cafeteria rewards" tailored to individual needs
Are stressed out or burned out from too much work or too little personal rest and recreational time	△ Assess the extent of this problem by using attitude surveys (paper-based or online), by using exit interviews with departing workers, and by running selected focus groups to gather information △ Take steps to add a component on work-life balance in descriptions of high-potentials and high performance and communicate that change to the organization △ Add to the social life of the organization by stepping up social activities and re-examining to whom and how work is allocated

ployees." Succession planning and management formalizes the process of preparing people to fill key positions in the future. Of course, the term *talent pool* may mean a group of individuals—rather than one identifiable successor—from which possible successors for key positions may be selected.

Reason 4: Contribute to Implementing the Organization's Strategic Business Plans

Succession planning and management should not be conducted in a vacuum; rather, it should be linked to, and supportive of, organizational strategic plans, human resource plans, human resource development plans, and other organizational planning activities. Perhaps for this reason, my survey respondents indicated that the fourth most important reason to sponsor systematic SP&M is to "contribute to implementing the organization's strategic plan."

Strategic planning is the process by which organizations choose to survive and compete. It involves formulating and implementing a long-term plan by which the organization can take maximum advantage of its internal organizational strengths and external environmental opportunities while minimizing the effects of internal organizational weaknesses and external environmental threats.

To implement a strategic plan, organizations require the right people in the right places at the right times. Without them, strategic plans cannot be realized. Hence, leadership identification and succession is critical to the successful implementation of organizational strategy. Particularly at top management levels, as Thomas Gilmore explains, "performance criteria are rarely cut and dried. They often flow from a strategic plan which the chief executive is responsible for developing and carrying out."[12] At least five different approaches may be used to integrate strategic plans and succession plans:[13]

1. *The top-down approach*. Corporate strategy drives SP&M. Leaders identified through a systematic SP&M process support the successful implementation of strategy.

2. *The market-driven approach*. Succession planning and management is governed by marketplace needs and requirements. As necessary talent is required to deal with competitive pressures, it is sought out.

3. *The career planning approach*. Succession planning and management is tied to strategic plans through individual career planning processes. In consultation with their organizational superiors and others, individuals examine their own career goals in light of the organization's strategy and make decisions about how they can take best contribute to emerging organizational needs while also improving their own chances for eventual advancement.

4. *The futuring approach*. Succession planning and management becomes a vehicle for anticipating talent needs stemming from corporate strategy. It is viewed as a way to scan external environmental conditions and match the organization's internal talent to the demands created by those conditions.

5. *The rifle approach*. Succession planning and management is focused on solving specific, identifiable problems confronting the organiza-

tion—such as higher-than-expected turnover in some organizational levels or job categories.

Consider what role SP&M should play in supporting the strategic plans of *your* organization. In doing that, realize that "there is no one universal approach that works well across all companies; rather, effective companies match their succession strategies to their business strategies."[14]

Related to strategic planning is human resource planning (HRP), which is "the process of analyzing an organization's human resource needs under changing conditions and developing the activities necessary to satisfy these needs."[15] HRP is comprehensive in scope, examining an organization's workforce and work requirements. One result of HRP should be a long-term plan to guide an organization's personnel policies, programs, and procedures.[16]

Few authorities dispute the growing importance of HRP. As Manzini and Gridley note:[17]

> The need for people with increasingly specialized skills, higher managerial competencies, and commitment to new levels of excellence, with professional qualifications in disciplines that did not exist a few decades ago—at costs commensurate with their contribution to organizational objectives—is and will continue to be the overriding 'business' concern of the organization.

Succession planning and management is integrally related to HRP, though SP&M is usually more focused on *leadership* needs and *leadership* skills. Many techniques and approaches that have evolved for use in HRP may also be applied to SP&M.

Succession planning and management may also be integrated with human resource development (HRD), which is perhaps best understood as "the integrated use of training and development, Organization Development, and career development to improve individual, group, and organizational effectiveness."[18] HRD is thus linked to *planned* learning activities sponsored by organizations. HRD planning (HRDP) is "the process of changing an organization, stakeholders outside it, groups inside it, and people employed by it through planned learning so they possess the knowledge and skills needed in the future."[19]

Succession planning and management should focus on identifying and developing *critically important leadership talent*. Moreover, SP&M may rely on means other than planned learning or promotion from within to meet talent requirements. For instance, critical succession needs may be met by external recruitment or internal transfer, or other means. However, SP&M should be a consideration in HRDP, though the results of one survey revealed that (at least with management personnel) SP&M is a driving force behind developmental activities in fewer than 39 percent of responding firms.[20]

Reason 5: Help Individuals Realize Their Career Plans within the Organization

Organizations make a substantial investment in the training of their employees. Employee performance may improve with experience as individuals advance along a learning curve in which they master organization-specific and job-specific knowledge. When individuals leave an organization, their loss can be measured.[21] If they remain with one employer to realize their career plans, then the employer benefits from their experiences. In this sense, then, SP&M can serve as a tool by which individuals can be prepared for realizing their career plans within the organization. That reason was cited by my survey respondents as the fifth most important for organizations to sponsor systematic SP&M.

Reason 6: Tap the Potential for Intellectual Capital in the Organization

Intellectual capital refers to the value of the human talents of an organization. Tapping the potential for intellectual capital was cited as the sixth most important reason for an SP&M program in an organization. It is thus an important strategy in making and realizing investments in intellectual capital in the organization.

Reason 7: Encourage the Advancement of Diverse Groups

The workforce in the United States is only becoming more diverse, reflecting the nation's population. Unfortunately, not all workers have historically been treated equally or equitably. Discrimination, while prohibited by federal and state laws, still occurs. Indeed, the realization of that prompted Supreme Court Justice Thurgood Marshall to explain that, as a black in America in 1991, he did not feel free.[22] While reactions to that view may vary, there is increasing recognition of a need to promote *multiculturalism*, which

> involves increasing the consciousness and appreciation of differences associated with the heritage, characteristics, and values of many different groups, as well as respecting the uniqueness of each individual. In this approach, diversity has a broad meaning that encompasses sex and ethnic groups along with groups

based on such attributes as nationality, professional discipline, or cognitive style.[23]

Perhaps as an indication of increasing recognition that organizations have a responsibility to pursue diversity at all levels, respondents to my survey indicated that "encouraging the advancement of diverse groups" was the seventh most important reason for organizations to sponsor systematic SP&M.

Many organizations build in to their SP&M programs special ways to accelerate the development of protected labor classes and diverse groups.

Reason 8: Improve Employees' Ability to Respond to Changing Environmental Demands

An eighth reason to sponsor systematic SP&M is to "improve employees' ability to respond to changing environmental demands," according to the respondents to my survey. "One role of the leader," writes Gilmore, "is to shield the organization from ambiguity and uncertainty so that people can do their work."[24] Organizations sponsor SP&M as one means by which to prepare people to respond to—or even anticipate—changing environmental demands. People groomed for key positions transform the ambiguity and uncertainty of changing external environmental demands into vision and direction.

Reason 9: Improve Employee Morale

Succession planning and management can be a means by which to improve employee morale by encouraging promotion from within. Indeed, promotions from within "permit an organization to utilize the skills and abilities of individuals more effectively, and the opportunity to gain a promotion can serve as an incentive."[25] Once that goal is achieved, the promoted employee's example heartens others. Moreover, particularly during times of forced layoffs, promotions from within and "inplacement" (movements from within of individuals otherwise slated for layoff) can boost morale and can help offset the negative effects of "survivor's syndrome."[26]

Reason 10: Cope with the Effects of Voluntary Separation Programs

My respondents identified "coping with the effects of voluntary separation programs" as the tenth most important reason that organizations sponsor systematic SP&M. Voluntary separation is closely related to forced layoffs and is often a preliminary step to it. In a voluntary separation, employees are offered incentives to leave the organization—such as prorated pay by years of service or years added to retirement. Like a forced layoff, a voluntary separation requires work to be reallocated as productive employees leave the organization. That requires some effort to identify "successors." Hence, SP&M can be valuable in identifying how—and to whom—work should be reallocated after workforce restructuring.

Reason 11: Decide Which Workers Can Be Terminated without Damage to the Organization

When making hiring decisions, employers have long considered an individual's potential for long-term advancement as well as his or her suitability for filling an immediate job vacancy. Perhaps for this reason, then, survey respondents cited "deciding which workers can be terminated without damage to the organization" as the eleventh most important reason for organizations to sponsor SP&M.

Reason 12: Cope with the Effects of Downsizing

A twelfth reason cited by survey respondents for organizations to sponsor systematic SP&M is to "cope with effects of downsizing." Downsizing has been—and continues to be—a fact of life in corporate America. While not as widely publicized as it once was, downsizing, the evidence suggests, has continued unabated since before the first edition of this book was published in 1994. Middle managers and professionals have been particularly affected. While jobs may be eliminated, work does not go away. As a consequence, there is often a need to identify those who can perform activities even when nobody is assigned special responsibility for them. Succession planning and management can be a tool for that purpose.

The respondents to my survey confirm that organizations have continued to undergo radical workforce restructuring in recent years, a trend first pinpointed in the 1994 edition of this book. (See Exhibit 1-6.)

Reason 13: Reduce Headcount to Essential Workers Only

The thirteenth reason for organizations to sponsor succession planning and management, as cited by my survey respondents, is to "reduce headcount to essential workers only." In an age of fierce competition, processes must be reengineered to decrease cost, reduce cycle time, and increase quality and output. Processes must be reexamined in light of results required, not activities that have traditionally been performed. In such environments, "companies don't need people to fill a slot, because the slot will only be roughly defined. Companies need people who can figure out what the job takes and do it, people who can create the slot that fits them.

Exhibit 1-6: Workforce Reductions among Survey Respondents

In the last 5 years, has your organization experienced (circle all responses in the right column below that apply)?

Events	Frequency	Percentage
A layoff	12	40.00%
An early retirement offer	5	16.67%
A reduction in force	17	56.67%
A hiring freeze	8	26.67%
Reduction by attrition	12	40.00%
Other	9	30.00%
Selected early retirement/separation packages		
None of the above		
Increase in growth and staffing needs		

*SOURCE: William J. Rothwell, *Results of a Survey on Succession Planning and Management Practices*, unpublished survey results (University Park, Pa.: The Pennsylvania State University, 2000).

Moreover, the slot will keep changing."[27] Headcount will also shift to keep pace with shifting requirements.

Approaches to Succession Planning and Management

There are numerous approaches to SP&M. They may be distinguished by *direction, timing, planning, scope, degree of dissemination,* and *amount of individual discretion.*

Direction

Who should make the final decisions in SP&M? The answer to that question has to do with *direction.*

A *top-down approach* to succession planning and management is directed from the highest levels. The corporate board of directors, CEO, and other top managers oversee program operations—with or without the assistance of a part-time or full-time SP&M coordinator, a leadership development specialist, or a human resource generalist assigned to help with the program. The highest-level leaders make decisions about how competence and performance will be assessed for present positions, how future competence and potential will be identified, and what developmental activities—if any—will be conducted with a view toward preparing individuals for advancement and building the organization's bench strength of leadership talent.

In contrast, a *bottom-up approach* to SP&M is directed from the lowest levels. Employees and their immediate supervisors actively participate in all activities pertaining to SP&M. They are also on the lookout for promising people to assume leadership positions. Decisions about SP&M are closely tied to *individual career planning programs*, which help individuals assess their present strengths and weaknesses and future potential. Top managers receive and act on decisions made at lower levels.

A *combination approach* attempts to integrate top-down and bottom-up approaches. Top managers are actively involved in establishing SP&M procedures, and remain involved in the SP&M program. Employees and their immediate supervisors are also actively involved in every step of the process. Some effort is made to integrate SP&M and individual career planning.

Often, a succession plan without a career plan is a wish list because designated HiPos may not aspire to the career goals to which others think they should aspire. A career plan without a succession plan is a road map without a destination.

Timing

How much time is devoted to SP&M issues—and when is that time devoted to it? The answer to that question has to do with *timing*.

Succession planning and management may be conducted *fitfully, periodically,* or *continuously*. When handled fitfully, systematic SP&M does not exist because no effort is made to plan for succession—with the result that every vacancy can become a crisis. When handled periodically, SP&M is carried out on a fixed schedule—usually quarterly or annually. Often it distinctly resembles an employee performance appraisal program, which is typically part of the SP&M effort. Managers complete a series of forms that may include a performance appraisal, an individual potential assessment (or full-circle, multi-rater assessment), an individual development plan (IDP), and a replacement chart for their areas of responsibility. This information is then turned over to the human resources department and/or to an individual assigned responsibility for SP&M.

When handled continuously, SP&M requires ongoing decision-making, information-gathering, and action-taking. Less attention is devoted to forms than to results and developmental activities. Employees at all levels are expected to contribute to the continuous improvement of themselves and others in the organization through mentoring, networking, sponsorship, training, education, development, and other means.

Planning

How much planning is conducted for succession? The answer to that question has to do with the *planning* component of an SP&M program.

Succession planning and management may be a *systematic* effort that is deliberately planned and is driven by a written, organization-wide statement of purpose and a policy. On the other hand, it may be an *unsystematic* effort that is left unplanned and informal. An unsystematic effort is driven by the idiosyncrasies of individual managers rather than by a deliberate plan and strategy for preparing individuals for advancement and for ensuring leadership continuity.

Scope

How many—and what kinds—of people in the organization are covered by succession plans? The answer to that question has to do with program *scope*.

Succession planning and management may range from the *specialized* to the *generalized*. A specialized program targets leadership continuity in selected job categories, job levels, functions, or locations. Often, such programs grow out of crises—such as excessive turnover in selected areas of the organization. On the other hand, a generalized program aims to prepare individuals for advancement in all job categories, job levels, functions, and locations. It is often a starting point for identifying individualized training, education, and development needs and for meeting individual career goals.

Degree of Dissemination

How many people participate in SP&M processes? The answer to that question has to do with the program's *degree of dissemination*. It is a philosophical issue that stems from—and influences—the organization's culture.

The degree of dissemination may range from *closed* to *open*. A closed SP&M program is treated as top secret. Managers assess the individual potential of their employees without the input of those affected by the assessment process. Decisions about whom to develop—and how to develop them—are limited to a "need-to-know" basis. Individual career goals may—or may not—influence these decisions. Top managers are the sole owners of the SP&M program and permit little or no communication about it. Secrecy is justified on two counts: (1) succession issues are proprietary to the organization and may reveal important information about strategic plans that should be kept out of the hands of competitors; and (2) decision-makers worry that employees who are aware of their status in succession plans may develop unrealistic expectations or may "hold themselves hostage." To avoid these problems, decision-makers keep the SP&M process and its outcomes confidential.

On the other hand, an open SP&M program is treated with candor. Work requirements, competencies, and success factors at all levels are identified and communicated. The SP&M process—and its possible outcomes—are described to all who ask. Individuals are told how they are regarded. However, decision-makers do not promise high performers with high potential that they are guaranteed advancement; rather, they send the message that "you must continue to perform in an exemplary way in your current job *and* take active steps to prepare yourself for the future to benefit from it. While no promises will be made, preparing yourself for the future will usually help you qualify for advancement better than not preparing yourself."

Amount of Individual Discretion

How much say do individuals have in assessing their current job performance and their future advancement potential? The answer to that question has to do with the *amount of individual discretion* in a succession planning and management program.

There was a time in U.S. business when it was assumed that everyone wanted to advance to higher levels of responsibility and that everyone was willing to relocate geographically whenever asked to do so. Such assumptions are no longer safe to make: Not everyone is willing to make the sacrifices that go with increased responsibility, and not everyone is willing to sacrifice work-life balance; not everyone is willing to relocate due to the complexities of dual-career families, situations where elderly parents require care, and the like.

Mandated succession planning and management ignores individual career goals. Decision-makers identify the best candidates for jobs, regardless of individual preferences. Whenever a vacancy occurs, internal candidates are approached first. While given right of refusal, they may also be pressured to accept a job change for the good of the organization.

Verified succession planning and management appreciates the importance of the individual in SP&M. Decision-makers identify desirable candidates for each job and then verify their interest in it by conducting career planning interviews or discussions. When a vacancy occurs, internal candidates are approached—but decision-makers are already aware of individual preferences, career goals, and interests. No pressure is exerted on the individual; rather, decision-makers seek a balance in meeting organizational succession needs and individual career goals.

Ensuring Leadership Continuity in Organizations

There are two main ways to ensure leadership continuity and thereby fill critically important positions. These may be generally classified as *tradi-*

tional and *alternative*. Each can have important implications for SP&M. Hence, each warrants brief review.

Traditional Approaches

In 1968, Haire noted that people can make only six types of job movements in any organization: in (*entry*), out (*termination*), up (*promotion*), down (*demotion*), across (*lateral transfer*), or progress in place (*development in the current position*).[28] Any one—or all—of these traditional approaches can, of course, be used as a means to meet succession needs for key positions.

Moving people into an organization (*entry*) is associated with recruitment and selection. In short, "hiring off the street" is one way to find successors for key positions. However, people hired from outside represent a gamble: They have little stake in the organization's status quo, though they may have valuable knowledge in which the organization is otherwise deficient. They may generate conflict trying to put new ideas into action. That conflict may be destructive or constructive.

Top managers may be reluctant to hire more than a certain percentage of outsiders for key positions because they do represent a gamble. Their track records are difficult to verify, and their ability to work harmoniously in a new corporate culture may be difficult to assess. If they fail, outsiders may be difficult to terminate both because managers can be reluctant to "fire" people and because wrongful discharge litigation is an issue of growing concern.

Moving people out of an organization (*termination*) is associated with layoffs, downsizings, reductions in force, firings, and employee buyouts. It is generally viewed negatively, continuing to carry a social stigma for those "let go" and to be a public relations concern for organizations that regularly terminate individuals with or without cause. Yet, if properly used, termination can be an effective tool for removing less-than-effective performers from their positions, thereby opening up opportunities for promising high-potential employees with proven track records.

Moving people up in an organization (*promotion*) is associated with upward mobility, advancement, and increased responsibility. Succession planning and management has long been linked with this approach more than any other. Indeed, replacement charts—while increasingly outdated—remain tools of SP&M in many organizations. They usually imply an upward progression from within the organization—and often within the same division, department, or work unit. Career maps show the competency requirements necessary for advancement and are often substituted now for replacement charts. Job posting programs can also be paired with replacement charting or career maps so as to communicate vacancies and provide a means of allowing movement across functions, departments, and locations.

Promotion from within does have distinct advantages: It sustains (or improves) employee morale, and it smooths transitions by ensuring that key positions are filled by those whose personalities, philosophies, and skills are already known to others in the organization.

However, experts advise limiting the percentage of positions filled through internal promotion. One reason is that it tends to reinforce the existing culture. Another reason is that it can end up perpetuating the racial, sexual, and ethnic composition already present in the leadership ranks.

There are other problems with strict promotion-from-within approaches to succession planning and management. First, exemplary job performance in one position is no guarantee of success in a higher-level position. Requirements at different organizational levels are not identical—and that is particularly true in management. Effective promotion from within requires planning and rarely occurs by luck.

Moving people down in an organization (*demotion*), like terminating them, is commonly viewed negatively. Yet it, too, can be an effective source of leadership talent on some occasions. For instance, when an organizational unit is being disbanded, effective performers from that unit may fill vacancies in other parts of the organization. Individuals may even accept demotions voluntarily if they believe that such moves will increase their job security or improve their long-term career prospects.

Moving people across an organization (*lateral transfer*) is becoming more common in the wake of downsizing. (It is sometimes linked to what has come to be called *inplacement*.[29]) That, too, can be a valuable means by which to cross-fertilize the organization, giving new perspectives to old functions or activities. Job rotations, either temporary or permanent moves from one position to others as a means of relieving ennui or building individual skills, are a unique form of transfer that can also be used in succession planning and management.[30]

Finally, progress in place (*development in the current position*) represents a middle ground between lateral transfer and upward mobility. It has become more common as opportunities for advancement have diminished in the wake of fierce global competition. Progress in place is based on the central premise that no job—no matter how broad or complex—fully taps individual potential. As a result, individuals can be developed for the future while remaining where they are, doing what they have always done, and gradually shouldering new duties or assignments. Stagnation is thus avoided by "loading" the job horizontally or vertically. (*Horizontal loading* means adding job responsibilities similar to what the individual has already done; *vertical loading* means offering new job responsibilities that challenge the individual to learn more.)

Related to progress in place is the notion of *dual career ladders* in which individuals may advance along two different career tracks: a *management track* (in which advancement is linked to increasing responsibility for people) and a *technical track* (in which advancement is linked to increasingly sophisticated responsibility within a given function or area of expertise). The organization may establish special rewards, incentives, and compensation programs to encourage advancement along dual career tracks.

Alternative Approaches

Experienced managers know that there is more than one way to fill a critical position. Job movements, described in the previous section, represent a traditional approach, commonly associated with SP&M. Alternative approaches are probably being increasingly used as managers in cost-sensitive organizations struggle to meet SP&M challenges while finding themselves restricted in the external hiring and internal promoting that they may do.

One alternative approach might be called *organizational redesign*. When a vacancy occurs in a key position, decision-makers do not automatically "move someone into that place"; rather, they break up the work duties and reallocate them across the remaining key positions or people. The desired effect is to reduce headcount while holding results constant. It also develops the remaining key people by giving them exposure to a new function, activity, or responsibility. However, if rewards do not match the growing workload, exemplary performers who have been asked to do more may grow disenchanted. There is also a limit to how much can be loaded on people before they are incapable of performing effectively.

A second alternative approach is *process redesign*. Decision-makers do not automatically assume that a key position needs to be replaced when it becomes vacant; rather, they review that function from top to bottom, determining whether it is necessary at all—and if it can be done in new ways that require fewer people.

A third alternative approach is *outsourcing*. Rather than assume that all key positions need to be performed internally, decision-makers periodically reassess whether activities can be more cost-effectively handled externally. If headcount can be reduced through outsourcing, the organization can decrease succession demands.

A fourth alternative approach involves *trading personnel temporarily with other organizations*. This approach builds on the idea that organizations can temporarily trade resources for their mutual benefit. Excess capacity in one organization is thus tapped temporarily by others. An advantage of this approach is that high performers or high potentials who are not immediately needed by one organization can be pooled for use by others, who usually offset their salaries and benefits. A disadvantage is that lending organizations risk losing these talented workers completely if they are spirited away by those having greater need of their services and greater ability to reward and advance them.

A fifth alternative approach involves establishing *talent pools*. Instead of identifying *one* likely successor for each critical position, the organization sets out to develop *many* people for *many* positions. That is accomplished by mandated job rotations so that high potentials gain exposure to many organizational areas and are capable of making multifaceted contributions. While that sounds fine in theory, there are practical difficulties with using this approach. One is that productivity can decline as new leaders play musical chairs and learn the ropes in new organizational settings.

A sixth alternative approach is to establish *two-in-the-box* arrangements. Motorola has been known to use this approach. "Since most Motorola businesses are run by a general manager and an assistant general manager, the assistant slot is used to move executives from one business to another for a few years so they can gain a variety of experiences."[31] A form of overstaffing that would not be appealing to some organizations, this approach permits individual development through job rotations while preserving leadership continuity. It is akin to forming an executive team in which traditional functional senior executives are replaced by a cohesive team that collectively makes operating decisions, effectively functioning in the place of a chief operating officer.[32]

A seventh alternative approach is to establish *competitive skill inventories* of high-potential workers *outside the organization*. Rather than develop organizational talent over time, an organization identifies predictable sources of high-potential workers and recruits them on short notice as needed. A disadvantage of this approach is that it can engender counterattacks by organizations that have been "robbed" of talent.

Of course, there are other alternative ways by which to meet successor needs in key positions. Here is a quick review of a few of them:

△ *Temping*. The organization makes it a practice to hire individuals from outside on a short-term basis to fill in during a search for a successor. The "temps" become candidates for consideration. If they do not work out, however, the arrangement can be severed on short notice.

△ *Job sharing*. An experienced employee in a key position temporarily shares the job with another as a means of on-the-job training—or assessing how well the candidate can perform.

△ *Part-time employment*. Prospective candidates for key positions are brought in on a part-time basis. They are carefully assessed before employment offers are made.

△ *Consulting*. Prospective candidates for key positions are brought in as consultants on projects related to the position duties. Their performance is carefully assessed before employment offers are made.

△ *Overtime*. Prospective candidates from within the organization are asked to work in other capacities in addition to their current jobs. This represents overtime work. The employer then assesses how well the individuals can perform in the key positions, making allowances for the unusual pressure under which they are functioning.

△ *Job rotation*. Prospective candidates for key positions are developed from within by rotating, for an extended time span, into another job or series of jobs in preparation for the future.

△ *Retirees*. The organization looks to individuals with proven track records to return to critical positions temporarily—or permanently.

The important point about SP&M is that numerous approaches may be used to satisfy immediate requirements. However, a continuing and systematic program is necessary to ensure that talent is being prepared inside the organization.

Summary

This chapter opened with five dramatic vignettes to illustrate the importance of succession planning and management (SP&M), which was defined as *any effort designed to ensure the continued effective performance of an organization, division, department, or work group by making provision for the development, replacement, and strategic application of key people over time*. A succession planning and management program was defined as *a deliberate and systematic effort by an organization to ensure leadership continuity in key positions, retain and develop intellectual and knowledge capital for the future, and encourage individual advancement*. Succession planning and management is proactive and should not be confused with more limited-scope and reactive replacement planning, which is a form of risk management.

Succession planning and management is important for several reasons: (1) the continued survival of the organization depends on having the right people in the right places at the right times; (2) as a result of recent economic restructuring efforts in organizations, there are simply fewer people available to advance to the top ranks from within; (3) succession planning and management is needed to encourage diversity and multiculturalism in organizations and to avoid "homosocial reproduction" by managers; and (4) succession forms the basis for communicating career paths, establishing development and training plans, establishing career paths and individual job moves, communicating upward and laterally, and creating a more comprehensive human resources planning system.

Organizations sponsor systematic succession planning and management programs for various reasons. The three most important, based on my 1999 survey, are:

△ *Reason 1*: To provide increased opportunities for "high potential" workers

△ *Reason 2*: To identify "replacement needs" as a means of targeting necessary training, employee education, and employee development

△ *Reason 3*: To increase the talent pool of promotable employees

Approaches to succession planning and management may be distinguished by *direction, timing, planning, scope, degree of dissemination,* and *amount of individual discretion*. Succession needs may be met through *traditional* and *alternative* approaches. Succession planning and management should be linked to—and supportive of—strategic plans, human resource plans, human resource development plans, and other organizational planning activities.

Chapter 2
Trends Influencing Succession Planning and Management

Succession planning and management (SP&M) must be carried out against the backdrop of increasingly dynamic organizations.[1] Those organizations are responding, either proactively or reactively, to changes occurring in their external environments. As Leibman explains, "today's dynamic environment filled with global competition and business discontinuities defines the arena in which succession planning must flourish. To do so, a much more active orientation is required, one that is better characterized by succession management and its emphasis on ongoing and integrated processes."[2] For Leibman, succession management is more active than succession planning and must be carried out in a way that is tied to organizational strategy and responsive enough to deal with rapidly changing organizational settings. That is an accurate view. To be effective, SP&M programs must anticipate—and not just react to—the changes wrought by an increasingly dynamic business environment.

Many trends drive the future workplace and workforce. Among them:[3]

1. Changing technology
2. Increasing globalization
3. Continuing cost containment
4. Increasing speed in market change
5. The growing importance of knowledge capital
6. An increasing rate and magnitude of change

These trends demand a new role for managers. They also call for a new, more strategic role for HR practitioners.[4] Trends such as these frame the future of SP&M efforts, and effective SP&M programs are built to help organizations manage and even capitalize on the effects of these trends.

This chapter examines key trends influencing SP&M. The chapter opens with an activity for you to consider on the drivers of change and trends. It then focuses on answering this question: What trends are influencing SP&M? The chapter directs attention to five key trends exerting special influence on SP&M:

1. The need for speed
2. A seller's market for skills
3. Reduced loyalty among employers and workers
4. The importance of intellectual capital and knowledge management
5. The key importance of values and competencies

The chapter then offers conclusions about what these trends mean for SP&M.

Introductory Activity: Drivers of Change and the Trends

Take a moment to rate your organization on its handling of SP&M against the backdrop of the competitive environment. Complete the assessment questionnaire appearing in Exhibit 2-1. When you finish, score the results of your assessment. Then continue reading the chapter.

What Trends Are Influencing Succession Planning and Management?

While much has been written on trends shaping the future, it seems clear that at least five trends have special importance for SP&M programs:

- △ The need for speed
- △ A seller's market for skills
- △ Reduced loyalty among employers and workers
- △ The importance of intellectual capital and knowledge management
- △ The key importance of values and competencies

These trends are described below, followed by a discussion of their implications for succession planning and management.

Trend 1: The Need for Speed

Time has emerged as a key strategic resource.[5] If you doubt that, then consider how often the phrase "reduction in cycle time" is used in companies today. Also consider how fast the speed of processing time in computers is advancing.

Exhibit 2-1: An Assessment Questionnaire: How Well Is Your Organization Managing the Consequences of Trends Influencing Succession Planning and Management?

Directions: Use this questionnaire to structure your thinking about how well your organization is positioned to manage the *consequences* of key trends influencing SP&M. For each item listed in the left column below, rate how well you feel your organization is prepared to manage the consequences of the trends as they may influence SP&M.

Use the following scale to rate your opinions:

1 = *Not at all prepared* to manage the consequences of the trend as it influences SP&M

2 = *Very unprepared* to manage the consequences of the trend as it influences SP&M

3 = *Unprepared* to manage the consequences of the trend as it influences SP&M

4 = *Somewhat prepared* to manage the consequences of the trend as it influences SP&M

5 = *Prepared* to manage the consequences of the trend as it influences SP&M

6 = *Well prepared* to manage the consequences of the trend as it influences SP&M

7 = *Very well prepared* to manage the consequences of the trend as it influences SP&M

If you wish, ask decision-makers in your organization to complete this assessment questionnaire individually. Then compile the results and feed the results back to the decision-makers so that they may see their collective views.

The Questionnaire

	How Well Is Your Organization Positioned to Manage the Consequences of the Trend as It Influences SP&M?						
Trend	Not at All Prepared 1	2	3	4	5	Very Well Prepared 6	7
1. The need for speed	1	2	3	4	5	6	7
2. A seller's market for skills	1	2	3	4	5	6	7
3. Reduced loyalty among employers and workers	1	2	3	4	5	6	7

Exhibit 2-1: *(continued)*

4. The importance of intellectual capital and knowledge management	1	2	3	4	5	6	7
5. The key importance of values and competencies	1	2	3	4	5	6	7

Scoring

Add up the totals
of the columns above
and place the sum in
the box at right

Interpreting the Score

If your score is lower than *19*, then your organization is not well prepared to manage the consequences of the trends as they may influence SP&M.

Slashing the time it takes to get results is seen as a goal in its own right. This includes:

△ Finding faster ways to transform basic research into applied research so as to create new products or services and thereby beat competitors to production or service delivery
△ Entering new markets faster
△ Reducing unnecessary or redundant steps in the production process through process improvement to increase speed
△ Improving, through just-in-time inventory methods, the time match between the need for raw materials and their use in production so as to reduce inventory holding costs
△ Reducing the time it takes to fill an order or ship a product from producer to consumer

Speed is only likely to become more important in the future. That sensitivity to speed is affecting HR practices as well. Many companies keep statistics to see how long it takes to:[6]

△ Justify a position
△ Recruit for, and fill, a vacancy
△ Find talent wherever it might be for immediate use through virtual teams or concurrent work practices in which some work is performed twenty-four hours a day

△ Train people

In a more stable era, it might have been acceptable to permit a long lead time between the justification and filling of a position, the selection of a qualified person to do the work, and the realization of full productivity from a worker as he or she undergoes training and moves up the experience-learning curve. But stable times are gone. Time is a wasting resource, and people must be found and oriented so that they can become productive as quickly as possible.

Trend 2: A Seller's Market for Skills

Employers in the United States, as in many other parts of the world, have traditionally taken workers for granted. Many managers still assume that, if their organizations will only pay enough, they can always find the people they need to fill any position. But that assumption is not always valid anymore. There are several reasons why.

First, the U.S. population is aging.[7] Fewer workers are entering at the bottom of organizational pyramids because there are fewer workers of traditional entry-level age. Those new workers have a work ethic and values different from those of previous generations. Many prize a balance of work and personal life in a way that does not match up well to the frenetic pace in many organizations today, where hours of work for the average manager are on the rise.[8]

Second, more people are reaching traditional retirement ages. Some authorities contend that this will lead to a leadership shortage as senior managers, traditionally the oldest age group, take advantage of generous retirement plans.[9] Other authorities, however, caution against assuming that people will retire at traditional ages in the future, since retirement plans and other benefits are growing less secure than they once were.[10]

Third, the U.S. economy has sustained a broad expansion for the longest period in history. Many groups have benefited from this expansion. While there may be evidence that the rich are getting richer and the poor are getting poorer,[11] it is also true that (at least at the time this book goes to press) virtually anyone in America who wants a job can find one somewhere. This means that workers can afford to be more selective about where they work, which creates a seller's market for skills.

In response, many U.S. organizations have instituted retention programs to hold down turnover.[12] That is ironic, considering that many organizations in the 1990s implemented such staff reduction plans as downsizings, layoffs, reductions in force, employee buyouts, and early retirement programs to slash payroll and benefit costs. But, while downsizings continue in the wake of rapid market changes and corporate mergers, acquisitions, and takeovers, many decision-makers in organizations are now looking for ways to attract and retain talent. That is particularly true in information technology jobs, where a much-publicized labor shortage is thought to be a driver for future mergers and acquisitions.

The change in attitude has spawned increased interest in ways to give people hope for the future. An SP&M program is one such way, of course. A reinvented career planning and development program is another, and related, way.

Trend 3: Reduced Loyalty among Employers and Workers

There was a time when employees believed that they would get a job with one company and stay with that company until retirement. A stable employment record was considered an advantage during job interviews. Likewise, employers often assumed that, when they extended a job offer, they were establishing a long-term relationship with the worker. Even poor performers were tolerated, and sometimes moved out of the way and into harmless positions, to preserve workers' feelings of trust and security with their employers.

This, of course, is no longer the case. One result of the downsizing trend of the 1990s was that employers changed the employment contract.[13] As competitive conditions became more fierce and organizational conditions became less stable, no longer were employers making a long-term commitment.

A legacy of this change in common business practice is that employees have become more interested in short-term gains in pay, titles, development opportunities, and benefits. They want immediate rewards for good performance, since they distrust their employers' abilities to reward them in the future for hard work performed in the present.[14] They have changed from showing a willingness to tolerate delayed gratification to demanding immediate gratification, since they cannot be sure that they will be around with that employer to reap future rewards.

This change in the employment contract has profound implications for traditional SP&M practices. Employees can no longer trust their employers to make good on promises of future advancement. And, given that attitude, employers can no longer count on high potentials or exemplary performers patiently performing for long periods before expecting rewards, advancement, or professional development.

Speed is now as important in managing succession issues as it is in managing other aspects of organizational practice. Managers must manage against a backdrop of the possibility that they may lose valuable talent if they do not identify it quickly and offer prompt rewards and development opportunities to retain it.[15]

Trend 4: The Importance of Intellectual Capital and Knowledge Management

Intellectual capital can be understood, at least in one sense, as the collective economic value of an organization's workforce.[16] The effective use of intellectual capital is *knowledge management*.[17] It is important to emphasize that, as the speed in decision-making increases in organizational environments and operations, intellectual capital increases in value because it is essential for customers to deal with workers who know how to serve them quickly and effectively. This demands improved knowledge management of the workforce.

While land, capital, and information can be readily obtained from other sources—and, on occasion, leased, outsourced, or purchased—the organization's workforce represents a key asset. Without people who know what the organization does to serve its customers and how it does that, no organization could continue to function. In one example I like to use with my students, I ask them this question: What would a university be without its faculty, administrators, staff, and students? The answer is that it would be nothing more than assets ready for liquidation—land, buildings, equipment, and capital. Without the people, there would be no way to achieve the mission of the university by teaching, research, and service.

The same principle applies to all organizations. While traditional managers may view people as a cost of doing business, thought leaders realize that people represent the only asset that really matters in a competitive environment. People dream up new products and services. People make the leap from the results of basic research to the commercialization of applied research. People come up with technological advancements and use those advancements to achieve improved productivity and quality. People serve the customers, make the products, ship them to consumers, bill them, deposit the proceeds, and manage the organization's resources. Without people, the competitive game is lost. That is a lesson that is, unfortunately, too easy to forget at a time when many people are awed by rapid technological advancement. Of course, those impressive technological advancements are pointless unless people make use of them.

The implications of intellectual capital and knowledge management are important for SP&M. In a sense, succession planning and management is a means to an end. It is a tool of knowledge management, a means of ensuring that intellectual capital is properly serviced, retained, cultivated, and protected.

Trend 5: The Key Importance of Values and Competencies

People in organizations have high expectations of their leaders. These expectations are unlikely to diminish in the future. People want leaders who can get results and can, at the same time, model appropriate ethics. For these reasons, values and competencies have emerged as crucial to success in organizations.

As a later chapter will define them, values can be understood to mean deeply held beliefs. In the wake of high-profile scandals in the U.S. government, in other governments such as those of Japan and China, and in many businesses, values have emerged as a key issue of importance in organizational settings. Many multinational companies, for instance, have tried to address cultural differences by establishing core values honored internationally under one corporate umbrella.[18]

Competencies, while having different definitions,[19] have also emerged as key to management decision-making, human resource practice,[20] and SP&M programs. Values represent a moral dimension to the way leadership is exercised and work is performed.[21] Competencies can represent the distinguishing features between high performers and average or below-average performers. More flexible than work activities or tasks, competency models are the glue that holds together a succession planning effort. The use of competency models is a distinguishing characteristic between traditional and cutting-edge SP&M programs. As work becomes more dynamic and divorced from the traditional "boxes" found on organization charts, there must be a way to describe what performance is expected while being more flexible than traditional job descriptions, position descriptions, or task lists. Competency models have the advantage of providing that flexibility.

What Does All This Mean for Succession Planning and Management?

What will these trends mean for succession planning and management? The answer to that question is that, to be effective in the future, succession planning and management must be based on sensitivity to the need for speed,[22] align organizational with individual needs to be responsive to a seller's market for skills, emphasize a present orientation that will work in business settings where neither individuals nor organizations possess long-term loyalty, and recognize and cultivate the critical importance in competitive success of the organization's intellectual capital.

Summary

As noted at the opening of this chapter, succession planning and management must be carried out against the backdrop of increasingly dynamic organizations. This chapter examined five key trends exerting special influence on succession planning and management:

1. The need for speed
2. A seller's market for skills
3. Reduced loyalty among employers and workers
4. The importance of intellectual capital and knowledge management
5. The key importance of values and competencies

The chapter then offered conclusions about what these trends mean for succession planning and management.

The next chapter makes the case for a newer approach to succession planning and management, one that is responsive to—and helps organizations be more proactive to—new competitive realities.

Chapter 3
The Need for a Newer Approach

What are the characteristics of a state-of-the-art succession planning program (SP&M)? Read over the following case studies carefully to see how SP&M is handled by organizations in different industries. As you read, make a list on a separate sheet to answer this question: *What characteristics of a systematic SP&M program in these organizations have most contributed to their effectiveness, and why are organizations managing succession issues as they appear to be doing?* When you finish, compare your list to the list provided in the discussions following.

Case Study 1

Our everyday work with boards and on top-level assignments naturally leads to an interest and involvement in the CEO succession planning process. We see the good and the not-as-good: companies that have institutionalized a true and reliable process for developing their own leaders and those that have failed to "grow their own," or decide they need an outsider or different sort of leader for a variety of reasons.[1]

Until recently, CEO succession planning was something of a neglected area of responsibility at many companies. Not unlike individuals—even highly successful ones with significant assets who procrastinate when it comes to estate planning—CEOs have traditionally postponed confronting succession planning. Yet maintaining an uninterrupted flow of leadership remains one of the CEO's most important tasks and is certainly at the top of the board's list of essential duties.

The convergence of a number of factors has led to a growing urgency on the part of CEOs and directors to establish a systematic succession planning process, including:

△ Stronger, increasingly outsider-dominated boards that are more often taking the lead in the process on behalf of shareholders
△ The vulnerability of in-the-spotlight public companies that lack a succession plan

△ Such events as the 1996 airplane crash in Bosnia which killed Commerce Secretary Ron Brown and several corporate executives who were on a business development mission; the sudden death last year of Texas Instruments CEO Jerry Junkins; and the abrupt departure of President Alex Mandl of AT&T, all of which highlight the importance, very much like making a will, of having a clear succession plan in place

Those companies that have overcome their initial reluctance or inertia when it comes to succession planning often don't know where to start. Since we subscribe to the philosophy that it's best to learn from the successes, as well as the mistakes, of others, we decided it might be a valuable exercise to take a look inside some prominent companies that appear to have a handle on the process to find out what has and has not worked for them.

Learning from Leaders

With this agenda in mind, we invited some dozen companies—including MetLife, SmithKline Beecham, Mellon Bank, Caterpillar, Sunbeam, GTE, Hercules, Foster Wheeler, and HewlettPackard—to participate in our study. Companies invited to participate not only were leaders in their respective industries but had also demonstrated leadership in succession planning. In addition, we attempted to cover a variety of succession scenarios ranging from planned, orderly succession to the sudden death of the CEO. At the participating companies, we interviewed CEOs and top human resources executives.

One best practice that we have clearly inferred from our discussions with various companies is that a strong board is at the center of the process. While this has been a crucial factor in many of the companies we met with, for purposes of illustration here we'll briefly explain the board's role in succession planning at Hercules, a company many have recognized as having a strong and independent board. Just prior to his retirement a few months ago, Edward Carrington, then vice president of human resources, led us through succession planning Herculesstyle.

An Ongoing Dialog

Like everyone else at Hercules, the CEO (Tom Gossage at the time of our interview in October 1996 and, since January 1997, Keith Elliott) is held accountable to the board for performance against his defined and agreed-to goals, including succession planning, one of a few key responsibilities. At a dinner with the board, held once a year, the CEO is asked to evaluate inside candidates and their readiness to succeed to his or her position. The board will insist on one "ready now" or "drop in" candidate—someone who could step in and fill the CEO's shoes on a moment's notice in the event of a sudden tragedy—and will always want the CEO and other top managers to demonstrate that they are "two deep" in any position.

During this meeting, the board will also expect the CEO to present other candidates who may be ready to assume the top position according to a longer time frame (three to five years), and to describe what the organization is doing to help the candidates broaden their array of skills and experience. There is no succession committee per se as part of the board's structure (although there is a nomination committee, which would be involved in top management succession): all outside directors are involved in succession planning. While this once-a-year meeting deals with more than one issue, succession is clearly a top priority for Hercules' board and CEO.

The Role Is to Challenge

How much confidence does the board have in the CEO to determine the course of succession? "The board has a great deal of confidence in the CEO," says Carrington, "but we have a strong board and the role of the directors is to challenge the CEO's opinion." If there were some divergence of opinion regarding who the CEO viewed as his successor and who the board had in mind, particularly with regard to any immediate successor or "drop in" candidate, Hercules' board would not necessarily defer to the CEO. A dialog between the CEO and the board would ensue, and continue, until a resolution was reached that satisfied the board.

Currently, since the chairman and the CEO are the only insiders on Hercules' board, the company has established a mechanism, the management advisory board, to expose others on the top-management team to the outside directors in order to give those key managers a more global view of the business as seen from a director's perspective.

The management advisory board consists of a total of five people: the executive vice presidents (business heads), the chief legal counsel, and the chief financial officer. It is an important element in the grooming process for leadership in the company. The board has regular access to the group: The group members sit in on board meetings, though the board can ask them to leave. In this way, the board can tap the management advisory board's expertise without risking slipping into the role of managing the company. The board's job is to oversee the management of the company.

How Much Planning Is Enough?

How much time do the CEO and the board spend on succession planning? The amount of time regularly spent is related to how imminent a CEO's retirement is.

If the CEO is retiring, there would be a discussion, for perhaps an hour, regarding progress on a successor in a closed session (outside directors only) at every board meeting. Directors would want to know exactly what the CEO is doing to ensure a smooth transition and what they would need to do. As part of the grooming process for any CEO candidate, directors might introduce the candidate to people they know outside the company who could serve as mentors in various areas.

If the situation were less urgent, as with a CEO with no immediate plans to leave the company, the once-a-year board meeting might suffice. "In such a case, the emphasis would not be on rehashing candidates but on reviewing development plans against potential candidates in order to force an internal development discussion," explains Carrington.

One succession-related trend at a number of companies that Carrington finds "alarming" is that of directors taking over the CEO slot. "This indicates that the company had no real succession plan, no contingency plan, and in a public company, it can put the stock at risk," says Carrington, who views this approach as a band-aid solution at best.

Why do some companies, while acknowledging the importance of succession planning, find it so hard to actually accomplish? "Some boards are dominated by the CEO," says Carrington. "They leave it to him, and it doesn't happen."

In order for it to happen, it takes a tough board willing to confront the issue, continuously. Many boards, influenced by the pay and peer relationship with the CEO, are unable to take the initiative to tackle the issue of succession.

Hercules' philosophy seems to be that strong boards make for strong corporate management teams and solid succession plans. The company's board, which has often been cited as particularly strong and effective, puts together its own agenda and works with the CEO, but does not answer to him. In succession planning as in other areas of board responsibility, directors want to avoid "management capture" at all costs.

The most effective relationship between the CEO and the board, in Hercules' experience, is one in which issues are resolved at arm's length—a cordial relationship, but not too cozy. This relationship clearly pays off when it comes to succession planning, a process that is long on careful planning and short on unpleasant surprises.

Case Study 2

"When this department was organized in April 1988, our CEO, Joe Antonini, told me that one of my key responsibilities was to have replacements in line for him and all the officers of the company," says David Vine, senior vice president for executive resources at Kmart, himself, a former Kmart officer.[2]

(Since this interview, Vine has retired and been succeeded by Frederic M. Comins, Jr., vice president for executive resources, who also participated in the discussion.)

"The first thing I did was to interview some 30 of our officers here," Vine recalls. "I also went to all our regional offices and our subsidiaries to get to know all our people better.

"In addition, I visited some nonretailing companies, such as IBM and General Motors, which are known to have very good, formal, succession planning programs."

Annually, each corporate officer must submit his future business plan to the executive resources department as it relates to human resources and to the company's growth strategies. "We give them a chart," says Vine. "They must list their successors in rank order and say when they think these people will be ready. And we ask everyone who reports directly to an officer to do the same thing. Then, we meet with these people and discuss their recommended successors in detail."

Succession planning extends to all levels of the company. "While the formal succession planning meetings are certainly our main source of information, there are other sources," says Comins. "We have a total organization of some 350,000 people. Hopefully, there are many who are promotable, who will advance to the next level of responsibility and higher."

Train Fast and Early

"Competition is keen today. To be good you have to have the best people, and you have to train them early in their careers.

"Years ago," Vine points out, "our people stayed in the stores 20 to 25 years, and were then promoted to buyer jobs or higher. Today, the object is to identify our own promising people early and move them fast.

"We specifically ask our officers when they want to retire. Today, it's rare for a person to work until 65 years of age. Some leave at 55. They are obligated to tell us their retirement plans. It's line management's responsibility."

"One of our principal missions is to strengthen the bench—provide for high quality succession management," Comins adds. "Each executive has an obligation to prepare people to assume more responsibilities. Annually, we look at the organization through the succession planning process. At other times through related processes, we see how deep the bench is, where there are voids.

"It is every senior person's responsibility, whether an officer or not, to let us know when they see someone with extraordinary talent. We survey the whole field, reaching out as far as assistant store managers. When told of extraordinary talent, we try to validate that person's exceptional potential. First, we examine their present job performance. Then we interview them in a highly structured format, testing their cognitive abilities, their interpersonal strengths and weaknesses, and their job-related strengths and weaknesses. We call it a '360' because of the 360 degrees in a circle, within which we strive through a variety of tested tools to get as complete a picture of the person as possible."

Once individuals are designated, Comins reports, "We set up specific, developmental programs for them to speed up their growth."

"The programs extend all the way from the executive vice presidential level to the assistant store manager level," says Vine. "Generally, they are assistant store managers who have been with Kmart for at least two years. They are assigned to this office for 18 months with specific jobs. Not only do they have contact with the officers and other various people in the main office, they have to produce. We may move people horizontally to broaden them in other areas, to give them breadth of experience. We may assign them to special task forces or to committees with special assignments. These people we have identified from time to time sit in on executive committee meetings as observers. We want them to be familiar with all areas of the company—to know what's going on.

"Every month, they must also visit some of our out of town stores, and write reports on what they find in them and those of our competitors. These reports are sent directly to our CEO, with copies to this department."

"Fantastic" Meetings

"Every quarter, they meet with Joe Antonini and us to say what they have accomplished over the last three months, and what are their goals for the next three months.

"These quarterly meetings with Antonini are absolutely fantastic. He challenges them with specific questions, and they love it. They tell him what they've been doing. He may feel that they could improve in a certain area. He may challenge them, giving them something he wants them to work on, either individually or as a group by the next time they meet.

"You cannot imagine the number of times a week that we talk to Antonini by phone or in his office. We work with him regularly to make sure we keep everything in perspective—to maintain a vision based on today's realities and the future. Right now, we have charts mapping out our direction for five years down the road."

Since mid-1990, when Comins joined this department, there have also been round table discussions that Comins inaugurated. Each month, a company officer makes a presentation to the group. Prior to these meetings, members of the group are asked to submit questions to the particular officer. "They ask some very good questions," Comins reports, "specific to the job/function and maybe how it relates to other areas—finances or information systems, for example. These are very inquisitive people, asking very intelligent questions. The sessions last two or two-and-a-half hours. Occasionally, these special trainees put someone on the spot, causing an executive to think quickly on his feet. It's very exciting. They are not afraid to ask anything. The common thread is to constantly broaden their horizons."

What qualities are being sought for high-level positions? How will Kmart recognize the individual and individuals that will someday lead the company? "There are thousands of promotable people in a company this size," Comins acknowledges. "But there aren't thousands with the potential to necessarily be an officer of the company, or lead Kmart. We are looking for qualities that surpass what it takes to get just to the next job."

Antonini Recognized

Before the days of the executive resources department, what gauges were used to spot outstanding talent? "In talking to people in the past," Vine recalls, "I would say they recognized Joe Antonini as being very creative, very innovative. He was always a risk-taker both as a store manager, and as a district manager. He was not afraid to try something new. Those qualities were noticed. Most important, he made money for the store he managed and for the district he was in charge of. That said a lot.

"But someone may be an outstanding store manager for 20 or 30 years and advance no further. Our whole assessment process is designed to pick people with senior executive potential. We look for creative individuals, people with initiative, people who are willing to make decisions, to take risks. They should have a high energy level, be self-confident, and be able to sell their ideas. No matter how good they are at producing a profit, today they must have excellent human relations skills. If they are going to be leaders, they have to have goals, have to know how to get there, and must have others who want to go in the same direction. Today they can't use force, or threats, because management style is different. We are looking for leaders.''

In the executive succession process, there may be a tendency on the part of the present executive to pick a successor with less potential than himself. Addressing that possibility, Comins says, ''I don't think people feel threatened anymore. I think people at the highest levels understand that it is their responsibility to identify and develop talent. I don't think they view it as a threat in this organization.

''Joe Antonini has made a major impact on the whole thought process within the organization. Probably, we now embrace change more than ever before.''

Another tool to assure successful executive advancement is a formal mentor program. ''People I've talked to in the past tell me that most of them had a mentor, not formally designated,'' recalls Vine. ''We've thought long and hard about the mentor program. We try to match up people who will hit it off, where the protégé will learn from the mentor. Number one, we pick someone from a different functional area, not the person's boss. It's somebody they can go to and feel comfortable with, and somebody who can give the protégé understanding of another part of the company.''

''It doesn't just help the protégé,'' Comins adds. ''It helps the mentor as well. It's a nonthreatening relationship because the mentor is not his boss, nor his boss's boss. The mentor has no input in the protégé's performance appraisal. Assuming the relationship takes hold, it can be very intimate, like that of a coach or adviser. Obviously, it's up to both people to make the relationship work. When we match them up, we always say, '49 percent of this is the company's obligation, but 51 percent is your own.' They have to make things happen. They are in charge of their destiny. We are here to maximize their potential.

''These various programs are all designed to broaden the perspective of someone who someday will have a key role in leading the organization. It's like the story of three blind men who touch an elephant at different points: the trunk, a leg, and the tail, and define the elephant by only what they feel.

''Joe Antonini understands the entire elephant. And the people who will run major functions of this company, or one of its subsidiaries, will have to know they are dealing with an elephant.

"Kmart is not just a discount retail company. This is a world class corporation with a global impact that happens to be in retailing."

Case Study 3

Nursing departments not only are streamlining their organizational structures but also are reassessing their ability to develop and retain nursing personnel interested in management positions. A succession management program can provide the framework and resources for ensuring the development and retention of talent within the division.[3]

Demographic factors suggest that developing such talent will be more critical than ever to nursing's survival in the competitive decade ahead. According to *Workforce 2000,* the pivotal report published by the Hudson Institute for the Department of Labor, by the year 2000, the median age of the population will be 36, six years older than at any time in U.S. history.[4] This aging of the workforce has implications for nursing. In a recent study of local market competition, the experience and seniority of the nursing staff were associated with higher quality care and a competitive edge in the marketplace.[5] The authors concluded that "although nurse staffing and skill levels are highly visible items on hospital balance sheets, they are also highly visible indexes of hospital quality from the perspectives of patients, physicians and insurance plans."[6] A highly qualified staff is nursing's greatest resource— one that can be successfully nurtured by a succession planning and management program which develops talent, leadership, and experience within its nursing ranks.

Succession management can be defined as an organized method of identifying and developing talented individuals from within and providing them with opportunities for promotion and advancement.[7] More than a selection system, a succession planning and management program is a way to ensure continuity of leadership and involve all levels of the organization.[8]

Healthcare organizations invest resources in studying finance, planning, and marketing, but often they assume that the human resource skills critical for organizational success in these three areas will just appear. Also, they look outside their ranks for qualified consultants instead of looking for appropriately qualified professionals on their own staff. Sometimes, too, respected employees are placed in positions that don't match their skills or career goals.[9] SP&M programs can help healthcare executives avoid these pitfalls by providing a comprehensive analysis of the skills, talents, and personality characteristics of employees and matching these findings to the organization's current and future leadership needs.[10] Such a matching system can have significant benefits and the long delays that often occur in filling critical leadership positions through external searches can be avoided.

An SP&M management program can not only provide a management pool from which to draw immediate resources, but can lower employee turnover rates, improve staff morale, and most important of all, place the most qualified employees in key positions. These benefits ultimately reflect the organization's commitment to integrating employee development and job advancement into the corporate culture and work environment. Development of talent from within encourages stability in the organization, adherence to the corporate philosophy and mission and dedication to the attainment of strategic objectives. This leads to a sense of purpose and direction which permeates the institution from the personnel policies and procedures to more clearly defined job descriptions. Such outcomes benefit the employees as well as the institution.

Many articles in the nursing literature focus on organizational models which support and promote nursing leadership. Some focus on middle-level managers, others on the training of nursing executives, organizational restructuring, the role of business training in nurse executive upward mobility, and the relationship between succession patterns of nursing and those of other hospital executives.[11] All of these issues revolve around enhancing effectiveness, anticipating future resource needs, preparing staff for upward mobility and ultimately, achieving the best return on the institution's investment in human resources.

A Succession Management Model for Nursing

Since 1982, the Division of Nursing at the Washington Hospital Center (WHC), a 907-bed tertiary care facility located in Washington, D.C., has implemented a number of organizational transformations, beginning with streamlining the organizational structure.[12] During the first phase, the executive group was trimmed from fourteen to seven, one vice president for nursing and six assistant vice presidents. Each of the clinical nursing divisions was managed by an assistant vice president and the formerly centralized nursing education department was subdivided among the three 200- to 350-bed clinical divisions. This structure proved to be more efficient and an acceptable intermediate step in the long-term restructuring process.

The second stage of structural redesign occurred over a two-year period in preparation for a major hospital clinical service integration initiative. The number of clinical nursing divisions was reduced from four to two with an executive group of one senior vice president and three assistant vice presidents. At the same time, a new nursing division, Nursing Systems, was created to provide centralized administrative support to the clinical nursing divisions in the areas of financial management, analysis and budgeting, quality assurance, nursing personnel orientation and education, nursing research, computerized data systems design, administration of endowment fund awards, and development of nursing outreach programs.

This new division also produces a nursing newsletter and a professional nursing journal, *Nursing Connections.* Programs coordinated by the nursing systems division include graduate-level courses in nursing administration and finance; design and coordination of symposia; securing and coordinating guest lectureship and speaking engagements for clinical nurses and nurse executives at all organizational levels; achieving university recognition through securing graduate and undergraduate credits for Division of Nursing intensive care and specialty courses; and marketing nursing product lines. The systems division also assumes responsibility for coordinating the International Fellowships in Oncology and Critical Care Nursing and the Fellowship in Health Systems Management, a postgraduate program designed in cooperation with Harvard University School of Public Health to prepare nursing leaders for the future.

Creating Management Options for Nurses

The organizational restructuring presented the management hierarchy with some difficult questions about realigning the management structure and providing options for upwardly mobile, experienced nursing staff. What type of organizational structure would best serve an assistant vice president who leads a division of 300 to 400 beds—the size of many hospitals? And how could such an organization be structured so that it offered a variety of options to nurses interested in ascending the management ranks?

In the revised structure of each clinical nursing division, the new position of administrative director was established. This position is responsible for business elements such as decentralized finance, statistical analysis, and daily staffing readjustments which administratively support patient care. Qualifications for the position include a master's degree in nursing administration, a minimum of six years nursing experience in positions with progressive levels of responsibility, and at least three years experience in nursing administration. It is most important that the selected individual be qualified for and interested in assuming the role of assistant vice president.

Reporting to the administrative director is the management triumvirate of the clinical division: head nurses, clinical specialists, and clinical supervisors. This team assumes responsibility for clinical patient care and provides leadership in clinical practice, education, administration, and research. All enjoy department head status at WHC and work together to assure that the best possible patient care is delivered by nursing personnel twenty-four hours a day, seven days a week. The head nurse manages the department and assumes responsibility for all areas of clinical nursing practice and works with the clinical specialist, who covers several units, to identify the educational needs of patients and nursing personnel.

The clinical supervisor works with the head nurse and clinical specialist to ensure that the identified level of support is provided during non–prime time such as off-shifts and weekends. Qualifications for the clinical supervisor include a master's degree (preferably in nursing), a minimum of five years of clinical nursing practice and progressive clinical and/or administrative experience. Strong emphasis is placed on management expertise for head nurses, clinical and teaching expertise for clinical specialists, and a focus on clinical skills and administrative problem-solving for the clinical supervisor.

The position of clinical manager is the stepping stone from staff nursing into the management hierarchy. Staff nurses who aspire to one of the management roles can test their skills in the management area by moving into the clinical manager position. This position allows staff nurses to remain directly involved in patient care while learning management skills.

The clinical manager position is budgeted as 90 percent patient care provider and 10 percent selected managerial functions and tasks under guidance of the head nurse, clinical specialist, or clinical supervisor.

Interestingly, the benefits of the described succession management system extended throughout the nursing organization, including the top of the hierarchy. The experience gained over the years by the Senior Vice President of Nursing prepared her for successfully assuming a significantly more complex role as Senior Vice President for Nursing and Patient Care Services. This additional division was composed of some 10 departments as diverse as Environmental Services, Nutritional Services, and Facilities Management and Construction.

This system provides a proving ground for nurses to develop progressively and evaluate their management potential in a safe, well-supervised working environment. This system complements the four-level clinical progression program for staff nurses at WHC which recognizes the interrelationship of clinical practice, education, administration, and research in the professional role of nurses today. Each of the four levels is based on specific objectives in terms of clinical experience, performance, and continuing education, and each has concomitant rewards.

Measuring Program Effectiveness

A key consideration in designing an SP&M program is employee evaluation through monitoring performance standards. These should be objectively stated, easily measured, and designed by management with significant input from those being evaluated. It is important that the system of employee evaluation reflect a commitment to develop talent within the organization. A participative employee evaluation process which invites objective mutual goal setting can set the stage for identification of potential talent in each employee. Further, it provides the opportunity to support employees' areas of interest and expertise and match them with future strategic initiatives of the organization. Career guidance combined with sound educational support programs can provide the organization with stability while encouraging staff creativity and risk-taking through advanced leadership opportunities.

The Division of Nursing has had a participative employee evaluation process in place since 1982. Our process is based on performance standards which were developed with input from both management and staff nurses. Performance standards reflect the four major roles of nursing—clinical practice, education, administration, and research as integrated into our career progression program. Management personnel performance standards reflect an emphasis on clinical patient care outcomes and the business expertise expected of key nursing managers today.

Monitoring the pool of available talent is completed at least annually as vacancies occur or when organizational changes are anticipated. Candidates for increased levels of responsibility are targeted for upcoming opportunities such as clinical service reorganization. This proved to be extremely valuable several years ago when WHC opened a new 120-bed replacement tower. Existing medical and surgical patient care units were split, based on specialty, and moved to the new building wherein they were integrated with existing sister units. Periodic evaluation of our SP&M program has provided direction in selection of department heads, clinical specialists, and clinical managers who provide leadership while stabilizing the new environment within which the relocated employees delivered patient care.

Characteristics of Effective Succession Planning and Management Programs

What characteristics of the SP&M programs in the organizations described above have most contributed to their effectiveness? Compare your answer to that question with the list of characteristics appearing below. (The list is not necessarily complete and is not meant to be arranged in order of importance.)

Characteristic 1: Top Management Participation and Support

In the cases, top management participation and support are strongly evident. For instance, CEOs Tom Gossage and Keith Elliott at Hercules and Kmart's (former) CEO Joe Antonini personally participated in the succession planning program and thereby demonstrated strong personal support for it. Their involvement—and even that of the corporate board at Hercules—motivates participants and ensures that other members of the top management team devote time and effort to the succession planning program. Without the CEO's personal attention, SP&M will probably receive far less attention than it presently does in these companies.

Characteristic 2: Needs-Driven with External Benchmarking

The Kmart program began with top-level discussions about the specific business needs that the program would be designed to serve. The individual asked to coordinate the program also made benchmarking visits to organizations that have well-deserved reputations for effective SP&M practices. That helped tailor the Kmart SP&M program to the unique company culture while simultaneously taking advantage of state-of-the-art approaches that could be usefully adapted from organizations with more mature programs.

In the Hercules case, the board makes CEO succession a priority and holds the CEO accountable for making sure that some process is in place to address that need.

Characteristic 3: Focused Attention

As the cases illustrate, these companies are not content to allow succession planning to occur serendipitously on its own. A systematic effort is focused on accelerating the development of individuals with verified advancement potential.

Characteristic 4: Dedicated Responsibility

If a goal deserves attention, someone must be held responsible for achieving it. At Hercules, the board becomes actively involved. In the Kmart case, a special corporate officer is charged with high-level responsibility for SP&M, and that ensures that the issue is given full-time attention by someone with close access to the top management team.

Characteristic 5: Succession Planning and Management Extends to All Levels

Kmart is not content to restrict SP&M to the top rungs of the corporate ladder. Instead, it extends to all levels. Note that the greatest emphasis is placed at the *lowest* management levels where the most positions and people exist. In the other cases, attention is devoted to levels where business needs are greatest.

Characteristic 6: A Systematic Approach

The Hercules and Kmart cases emphasize that continuing processes are in place to focus attention on succession planning. At Kmart, each senior officer participates, forwarding completed forms to a central office. Those forms are, in turn, used to identify high-potential employees and operate a planned developmental program that is specifically geared to them.

Characteristic 7: A Comparison of Present Performance and Future Potential

Management succession in the cases is not a function of personal favoritism or seniority. Instead, the organizations possess some means by which to compare present job performance and future potential. The organizations identify individual developmental needs for top-level talent.

Characteristic 8: Clarification of High-Level Replacement Needs

At Kmart, the organization makes the effort to determine the retirement plans of key officers. (In this book the term *key job incumbent* refers to an individual presently occupying a key position.) In that way, the organization is better able to identify developmental time spans for specific key positions. At Hercules, the organization makes the effort to focus attention on CEO succession.

Characteristic 9: Each Executive Has an Obligation to Identify and Prepare Successors

Kmart emphasizes the obligation of each executive to identify and prepare successors. Hercules guarantees attention to the issue by holding regular, ongoing accountability meetings with the Board.

Characteristic 10: Specific Developmental Programs Are Established and Conducted

In the Kmart case, employees thought to have high potential participate in a planned developmental program.

Programs of this kind are often used in large corporations and may extend over many years.[13] Such programs may be viewed in three stages, which are based on the level of participants' experience with the organization. In stage 1, there is a relatively large pool of prospective high-potentials. They range from little experience through eight years with the organization. They are taught general management skills. Only 6 percent of those in stage 1 make it to stage 2, where they participate in tailor-made developmental experiences, intensive on-the-job development, and specialized courses, and occupy important positions. Only a smaller percentage of those in stage 2 progress to stage 3, where they occupy important positions while being carefully groomed for more senior positions.

Characteristic 11: High-Potentials Work While Developing

In the Kmart case, the organization does not emphasize classroom training or off-the-job development to the exclusion of action learning or learning from experience.[14] For this reason, high-potential employees are expected to produce while participating in the developmental program.

Characteristic 12: Developmental Programs Establish Familiarity with Who, What, When, Where, Why, and How

Large companies are so enormous that developmental experiences are, in part, established to familiarize future leaders with the corporate environment. That is a key emphasis of some developmental programs. As a result, participants become much more knowledgeable about the corporate culture—who does what, when they do it, where business-related activities are performed, why they are worth doing, and how they are accomplished. In this way, the internal development program emphasizes knowledge, skills, and abilities unique to the organization and essential to success in performing at higher organizational levels.

Characteristic 13: Developmental Experiences Encourage Critical Questioning

Top managers who address high-potential employees find that they are occasionally confronted with critical questions about "the way we have always done it." Critical questioning encourages creative thinking by top managers as well as by high-potential employees.

Characteristic 14: Succession Planning Emphasizes Qualities Necessary to Surpass Movement to the Next Higher-Level Job

Exemplary SP&M programs emphasize more than merely preparing individuals to move from one "box" on the organization chart to the next higher-level "box." Instead, they are geared to emphasize the building of competencies leading to advancement beyond the next job. They are thus long-term and strategic in scope and tend to build competencies in line with company values.

Characteristic 15: Formal Mentoring Emphasized

Mentoring and coaching have been the subject of growing attention in recent years as management writers have recognized that individual development is more heavily influenced by the on-the-job work environment than by off-the-job training, education, or development experiences.[15] (Indeed, as much as 90 percent of an individual's development occurs on the job.[16])

A mentor or coach provides advice about dealing with challenges presented by the work environment—including interpersonal problems and political issues. "Mentoring occurs when a talented junior person forms an attachment to a sensitive and intuitive senior person who understands and has the ability to communicate with the individual."[17] Mentors are thus teachers. They are not in positions of authority over their protégés or mentees. Nor do they necessarily serve as special advocates and cheerleaders for their protégés, as sponsors do. Mentors are typically chosen by the protégé or mentee. Hence, most mentoring occurs informally. Note in the Kmart case that the organization sponsors a formal mentoring program in which an effort is made to match up promising junior employees with more experienced, high-performing senior employees.

Other Characteristics

On your list, you may have identified other characteristics of an effective SP&M program. In reality, of course, there are no "right" or "wrong" characteristics. Indeed, "there isn't a foolproof formula for success. But there are certain essentials to any good plan and succession process:[18]

- △ A systematic (rather than anecdotal) way of identifying candidates
- △ Cross-divisional sharing of people and information
- △ Leadership that rewards managers for promoting (rather than holding on to) their best employees
- △ Career paths that move not just up a specialized ladder but across the company
- △ Frequent opportunities for employees to accept new challenges
- △ Recognition that employees have a stake in the company and share its successes"

In my survey of succession planning practices, I asked about the characteristics of effective SP&M programs. The survey results are presented in Exhibit 3-1. I have used those results to create a questionnaire, shown in Exhibit 3-2, which you can use to assess issues for inclusion in the SP&M program in your organization.

The Life Cycle of Succession Planning and Management Programs: Five Generations

In my consulting practice, I have discovered that many decision-makers in organizations that possess no SP&M program would like to leap in a single bound from no program to a state-of-the-art program. That is rarely possible or realistic. It makes about as much sense as trying to accelerate an automobile from a standing stop to 100 miles per hour in one second.

It makes much more sense to think in terms of a phased-in roll-out. The basis for this roll-out approach is my view that organizations go through a life cycle of development as they implement SP&M programs. At each generation, they gain sophistication about what to do, how to do it, and why it is worth doing.

The *first generation* of SP&M is a simple replacement plan for the CEO. This is easiest to sell if the organization does not have such a plan, since most CEOs realize what might happen to their organizations if they are suddenly incapacitated. (See Exhibit 3-3.) The target of the SP&M program in the first generation is the CEO only, and involving the CEO ensures that he or she properly assumes an important leadership role for the program and does not try to delegate it prematurely to Human Resources or to other groups.

As I tell my clients, the CEO is the real customer for most SP&M efforts—and my view is supported by the opinions of members of many

(Text continues on page 65.)

Exhibit 3-1: Characteristics of Effective Succession Planning and Management Programs

It is possible that effective succession planning programs share certain common characteristics across organizations. Review possible characteristics listed in column 1 below. Then, in column 2, check (√) yes or no to indicate whether your organization's succession planning program has that characteristic. Finally, in column 3, circle a code to indicate how important you believe the characteristic is for an effective succession planning program. Use the following scale: 1 = Not at all important; 2 = Not very important; 3 = Somewhat important; 4 = Important; 5 = Very important.

	Column 1	Column 2			Column 3				
	Characteristics of Effective Succession Planning Programs	Does Your Organization's Succession Planning Program Have This Characteristic?			How Important Do You Believe This Characteristic to Be for an Effective Succession Planning Program?				
		Y/N	Freq.	%	Mean	SD	Mode	Median	Response
A	Tied the succession planning program to the organizational strategic plans?	Yes	8	66.67	4.42	0.67	5	4.5	40.00%
		No	4	33.33					
B	Tied the succession planning program to individual career plans?	Yes	12	100	4.75	0.45	5	5	40.00%
		No	0	0.00					
C	Tied the succession planning program to training programs?	Yes	9	75.00	4	0.95	4	4	40.00%
		No	3	25.00					
D	Prepared a written purpose statement?	Yes	9	75.00	3.75	0.97	3,4	4	40.00%
		No	3	25.00					

E	Prepared written program goals to indicate what results the succession planning program should achieve?	Yes No	9 3	75.00 25.00	4.08	0.67	4	4	40.00%
F	Established *measurable* objectives for program operation (such as number of positions replaced per year)?	Yes No	2 10	16.67 83.33	3.75	1.06	4	4	40.00%
G	Identified what groups are to be served by the program, in priority order?	Yes No	7 5	58.33 41.67	3.92	1.38	5	4.5	40.00%
H	Established a written policy statement to guide the program?	Yes No	7 5	58.33 41.67	3.58	1.17	3	3	40.00%
I	Articulated a written philosophy about the program?	Yes No	10 2	83.33 16.67	3.83	0.94	4	4	40.00%
J	Established a program action plan?	Yes No	8 4	66.67 33.33	4.17	0.84	5	4	40.00%
K	Established a schedule of program events based on the action plan?	Yes No	6 6	50 50	3.92	1.08	5	4	40.00%
L	Fixed responsibility for organizational oversight of the program statement to guide the program?	Yes No	9 3	75.00 25.00	4.25	0.87	5	4.5	40.00%

(continues)

Exhibit 3-1: (*continued*)

	Column 1	Column 2			Column 3				
	Characteristics of Effective Succession Planning Programs	*Does Your Organization's Succession Planning Program Have This Characteristic?*			*How Important Do You Believe This Characteristic to Be for an Effective Succession Planning Program?*				
		Y/N	*Freq.*	*%*	*Mean*	*SD*	*Mode*	*Median*	*Response*
M	Fixed responsibility of each participant in the program?	Yes No	6 6	50.00 50.00	4.33	0.99	5	5	40.00%
N	Established incentives/rewards for identified successors in the succession planning program?	Yes No	1 11	8.33 91.67	2.25	0.97	2,3	2	40.00%
O	Established incentives/rewards for managers with identified successors?	Yes No	1 11	8.33 91.67	2.50	1.09	3	3	40.00%
P	Developed a means to budget for a succession planning program?	Yes No	2 10	16.67 83.33	3.25	1.14	3,4	3	40.00%
Q	Devised means to keep records for individuals who are designated as successors?	Yes No	8 4	66.67 33.33	4.00	0.85	3,4,5	4	40.00%

R	Created workshops to train management employees about the succession planning program?	Yes No	4 8	33.33 66.67	3.08	1.24	3	3	40.00%
S	Created workshops to train individuals about career planning?	Yes No	4 8	33.33 66.67	3.17	1.03	3	3	40.00%
T	Established a means to clarify *present position responsibilities*?	Yes No	7 5	58.33 41.67	3.33	1.37	3	3	40.00%
U	Established a means to clarify *future position responsibilities*?	Yes No	6 6	50 50	3.83	1.03	3,5	4	40.00%
V	Established a means to appraise individual performance?	Yes No	12 0	100 0.00	4.33	0.78	5	4.5	40.00%
W	Established a means to compare individual skills to the requirements of a future position?	Yes No	9 3	75.00 25.00	4.33	0.65	4	4	40.00%
X	Established a way to review organizational talent at least annually?	Yes No	11 1	91.67 8.33	4.5	0.67	5	5	40.00%
Y	Established a way to forecast future talent needs?	Yes No	6 6	50.00 50.00	4.25	0.87	5	4.5	40.00%

(continues)

Exhibit 3-1: (continued)

	Column 1	Column 2			Column 3				
	Characteristics of Effective Succession Planning Programs	Does Your Organization's Succession Planning Program Have This Characteristic?			How Important Do You Believe This Characteristic to Be for an Effective Succession Planning Program?				
		Y/N	Freq.	%	Mean	SD	Mode	Median	Response
Z	Established a way to plan for meeting succession planning needs through individual development plans?	Yes No	10 2	23.33 16.67	4.58	0.9	5	5	40.00%
AA	Established a means to track development activities to prepare successors for eventual advancement?	Yes No	7 5	58.33 41.67	4.25	0.75	4,5	4	40.00%
BB	Established a means to evaluate the results of the succession planning program?	Yes No	4 8	33.33 66.67	4.25	0.75	4,5	4	40.00%

Exhibit 3-2: Assessment Questionnaire for Effective Succession Planning and Management

Directions: Complete the following Assessment Questionnaire to determine how well your organization is presently conducting SP&M. Read each item in the Questionnaire below. Circle *(Y)* for *Yes, (N/A)* for *Not Applicable*, or an *(N)* for *No* in the left column opposite each item. Spend about 15 minutes on the questionnaire. When you finish, score and interpret the results using the instructions appearing at the end of the Assessment Questionnaire. Then share your completed Questionnaire with others in your organization. Use the Questionnaire as a starting point to determine the need for a more systematic approach to SP&M in your organization.

The Assessment Questionnaire

Circle your response below: *In your organization, would you say that SP&M:*

Y	N/A	N	1.	Enjoys top management participation, involvement and support?
Y	N/A	N	2.	Is geared to meeting the unique needs of the organization?
Y	N/A	N	3.	Has been benchmarked with best-in-class organizations?
Y	N/A	N	4.	Is a major focus of top management attention?
Y	N/A	N	5.	Is the dedicated responsibility of at least one high-level management employee?
Y	N/A	N	6.	Extends to all levels rather than being restricted to top positions only?
Y	N/A	N	7.	Is carried out systematically?
Y	N/A	N	8.	Is heavily influenced by a comparison of present performance and future potential?
Y	N/A	N	9.	Is influenced by identification of high-level replacement needs?
Y	N/A	N	10.	Has sensitized each executive to an obligation to identify and prepare successors?
Y	N/A	N	11.	Has prompted the organization to establish and conduct specific developmental programs that are designed to accelerate the development of high-potential employees?

Exhibit 3-2: (*continued*)

Circle your response below:				*In your organization, would you say that SP&M:*
Y	N/A	N	12.	Is guided by a philosophy that high-potential employees should be developed while working rather than by being developed primarily through off-the-job experiences?
Y	N/A	N	13.	Has prompted the organization to focus developmental programs on increasing the familiarity of high-potential employees with who does what, when they do it, where they do it, why they do it, and how they do it?
Y	N/A	N	14.	Has prompted the organization to focus developmental programs on the critical questioning of "the way things have always been done"?
Y	N/A	N	15.	Emphasizes the qualities or competencies necessary to surpass movement to the next higher-level job?
Y	N/A	N	16.	Has prompted your organization to examine, and perhaps use, formal mentoring?
Y	N/A	N	17.	Is conducted in a systematic way?
Y	N/A	N	18.	Encourages the cross-divisional sharing of people and information?
Y	N/A	N	19.	Is reinforced by a leadership that actively rewards managers for promoting (rather than holding on to) their best employees?
Y	N/A	N	20.	Is supported by career paths that move not just up a specialized ladder but across a continuum of professional competence?
Y	N/A	N	21.	Is supported by frequent opportunities for employees to accept new challenges?
Y	N/A	N	22.	Is driven, in part, by recognition that employees have a stake in the organization and share its successes?
Y	N/A	N	23.	Has prompted an explicit policy favoring promotion from within?

Total _____

Scoring and Interpreting the Assessment Questionnaire

Give your organization *1 point for each Y* and a *0 for each N or N/A* listed above. Total the points from the *Y* column and place the sum in the line opposite to the word *TOTAL* above. Then interpret your score in the following way:

Score

Above 20 points	Succession planning and management appears to be handled in an exemplary manner in your organization.
18–20 points	The SP&M efforts of your organization could stand improvement. However, SP&M is being handled effectively, for the most part.
14–17 points	Succession planning and management is a problem in your organization. It deserves more attention.
Below 14 points	Your organization is handling SP&M in a crisis mode. It is very likely that successors for critically important positions have not been identified and are not systematically developed. Immediate corrective action is desirable.

SOURCE: Jay L. Johnson, "How Kmart Plans for Executive Succession," *Discount Merchandiser,* 32:5 (1992), pp. 108–110. Reprinted with permission by *Discount Merchandiser.*

boards of directors. When the SP&M effort begins with the CEO, he or she understands what is involved in establishing a state-of-the-art SP&M program and is able to tailor it to suit his or her vision and strategy. Furthermore, he or she sets the example and sends a powerful message of personal commitment and support that is needed to make subsequent generations of such an effort successful.

It is worth noting that HR plays an important role. But it is essential to emphasize that HR does not "own" this effort. The "owner" is the CEO, and it is a position that (on this topic) he or she cannot delegate. HR leaders can certainly help: They can coordinate the effort, once leadership by the CEO has been exercised. They can provide advice and counsel about what to do, why it should be done, and how it should be done. But the CEO must lead the effort and be personally committed to it. *Lacking the CEO's personal support, commitment, and participation, SP&M efforts will usually fail.*

The *second generation* is a simple replacement plan for the CEO and his or her immediate reports—that is, the senior leaders of the organization, the senior executive team. By extending the SP&M effort to the management tier below CEO and by identifying the successors of that group, senior managers are involved firsthand in designing and implementing a succession effort. Since they are the targets of that effort, they understand it, have a chance to refine it, and develop ownership in it. By actively participating in the effort, they gain a thorough understanding of it that they can communicate to others in the third generation.

A key advantage of using the senior executive team as guinea pigs, so

Exhibit 3-3: A Simple Exercise to Dramatize the Need for Succession Planning and Management

For a dramatic and compelling exercise to emphasize the need for an SP&M program, ask your CEO or the managers in your organization what the following people had in common:

△ Donald Terner, President, Bridge Housing Corp., San Francisco, Calif.

△ Robert E. Donovan, President and Chief Executive Officer, Abb Inc., Norwalk, Conn.

△ Claudio Elia, Chairman and Chief Executive Officer, Air & Water Technologies Corp., Somerville, N.J.

△ Stuart Tholan, President, Bechtel-Europe/Africa/Middle East/Southwest Asia, San Francisco, Calif.

△ John A. Scoville, Chairman, Harza Engineering Co., Chicago, Ill.

△ Leonard Pieroni, Chairman and Chief Executive Officer, Parsons Corp., Pasadena, Calif.

△ Barry L. Conrad, Chairman and Chief Executive Officer, Barrington Group, Miami, Fla.

△ Paul Cushman III, Chairman and Chief Executive Officer, Riggs International Banking Corp., Washington, D.C.

△ Walter Murphy, Senior Vice President, AT&T Submarine Systems Inc., Morristown, N.J.

△ Robert A. Whittaker, Chairman and Chief Executive Officer, Foster Wheeler Energy International, Clifton, N.J.

△ Frank Maier, President, Ensearch International Ltd., Dallas, Tex.

△ David Ford, President and Chief Executive Officer, Interguard Corp. of Guardian International, Auburn Hills, Mich.

Answer: These were the people on board the plane with Commerce Secretary Ron Brown when it crashed in 1996. Don't you wonder if they had replacements ready in their organizations?

Used with permission from *Nursing Management*, June 1994 25(6): pp 50–56, © Springhouse Corporation (www.Springnet.com).

to speak, is that they are usually already well developed in their positions and are highly knowledgeable about what it takes to succeed in the business, industry, and corporate culture. By participating in the development of the SP&M effort, they ensure that it fits the corporate culture and aligns with organizational strategy. What is more, they set an example and, by doing that, send a powerful message to others in the organization that the SP&M effort is important and worthy of action, interest, and participation.

The *third generation* is an SP&M program for middle managers, who are usually the direct reports of the senior executive team, and perhaps (if the organization's leaders support it) for others on the organization chart as well. It is at this point that the model of SP&M, described later in this chapter (see Exhibit 3-5), is first widely used. Policies and procedures for SP&M are drafted if they were not already prepared formally in earlier generations; competency models by department or hierarchical level are first developed if they were not already prepared formally in earlier generations; value statements are crafted; and other key components of a modern SP&M program are designed, developed, and refined. By extending to this third tier and by identifying the successors of that group, middle managers are involved firsthand in designing and implementing an effort. Since they are the targets of the succession effort, they come to understand it and develop ownership in it. They also help refine it for their level and for those below them on the organization chart. The third generation is the most risky, since more people are involved and many new policies, procedures, and practices are first established, tested, and implemented.

The *fourth generation* moves beyond simple replacement plans to focus on the development of internal talent pools. *Internal talent pools* are groups of people inside the organization who are being developed for the future. Everyone is considered a possible successor for key positions and given such tools as career maps to help them prepare themselves for the future. In this generation, succession issues are divorced from the organization chart. Instead of targeting specific individuals to be successors, the organization's decision-makers use the many tools put in place in the third generation. It is possible in this generation to use competency models, performance appraisals, individual development plans, full-circle multi-rater assessments, and other sophisticated methods to help all workers develop to realize their potential.

The *fifth generation* focuses on the development of external as well as internal talent pools. *External talent pools* are groups of people outside the organization who are possible sources of talent for the future. Instead of waiting until key positions come open to source talent, the organization's decision-makers include in their talent pools temporary and contingent workers, retired workers, outsourcing agents, vendors, consultants, and even (perhaps) members of their organization's supply and distribution channels. In short, decision-makers look around the organization's external environment to see what talent exists outside as well as inside their organizations that could be tapped. In that way, they lead the target.

The fifth generation of SP&M is the most sophisticated. It is not easy—and usually not even possible—for an organization to make a single leap from no SP&M effort to a fifth-generation approach. Too much infrastructure and management support, not to mention the learning that occurs in generations one through four, are needed to make it work. The risks of failure are far too high. A better approach is to think in terms of a gradual phase-in, moving to a generation that meets the needs of the organization.

(Not all organizations need a fifth-generation approach.) That phase-in can occur fastest in organizations that are small, face a stable market, and possess low turnover in the management ranks. That phase-in occurs more slowly in organizations that are larger, face dynamic or fiercely competitive markets, and possess high turnover in the management (or high potential) ranks.

Identifying and Solving Problems with Various Approaches to Succession Planning and Management

The cases appearing at the opening of this chapter summarize several exemplary approaches to SP&M in organizations of varying sizes and industry categories. However, not all organizations handle SP&M as effectively or efficiently. Indeed, two experts speaking at an American Management Association Human Resources Conference indicated that succession planning is being woefully "ignored by a majority of American companies."[19]

Many problems bedevil current approaches to SP&M. Exhibit 3-4 summarizes the chief difficulties of using succession planning that were described by the respondents to my 1999 survey on succession planning

Exhibit 3-4: Chief Difficulties with Succession Planning and Management Programs

---

What are the chief difficulties that your organization has experienced with a succession planning program? (*Please describe them briefly below.*)

△ Getting the process completed well, evaluations, career discussion with candidates, and paperwork showing the outcomes
△ Focusing on what's important to get the program started
△ Different assessment standards
△ Full participation by all senior leaders
△ Ensuring that action plans are followed through
△ Measuring effectiveness of the program
△ Identifying true successor and high-potential employees
△ Communication of potential (or lack there of)
△ Lack of coordinated follow-through on development programs
△ Getting operational leadership to expect and produce more successors than they have in the past
△ Consistency from city to city
△ Time
△ Global, large organizations

---

*SOURCE: William J. Rothwell, *Results of a Survey on Succession Planning and Management Practices*, unpublished survey results (University Park, Pa.: The Pennsylvania State University, 2000).

practices. Additionally, I will review seven common problems affecting SP&M programs below.

Problem 1: Lack of Support

"One of the major drawbacks HR managers face in establishing a company succession plan is the lack of support from top company executives."[20] Indeed, "the attitude of too many corporation executives is 'why bother?' "[21] If top managers lack a sense of urgency, no SP&M program can be effective.

If top managers are unwilling to support a systematic approach to succession planning, it cannot succeed. If that is the case, the best strategy is to try to win over one or more credible *idea champions*. Especially promising for those roles are well-respected top managers who have recently—and, if possible, personally—experienced the work-related problems that stem from having no successor prepared to assume a critically important position when a vacancy occurs.

Problem 2: Corporate Politics

A second problem with succession planning is that it can be affected by corporate politics. Instead of promoting employees with the most potential or the best track record, top managers—or, indeed, any level of management employee—may "use the corporate ladder to promote friends and allies, while punishing enemies, regardless of talent or qualifications."[22] If allowed to operate unchecked, corporate politics can supplant performance and potential as an advancement criterion.

To solve this problem, decision-makers must insist on formal ways to identify work requirements and assess performance and potential rather than permit subjective judgments to prevail. (Methods of conducting formal assessments will be described in later chapters of this book.) Informal judgments are notoriously prone to numerous problems. Among them: *recency bias* (performance or potential is assessed with a heavier-than-desirable emphasis on recent and singular successes or failures); *pigeonholing* or *stereotyping* (supervisors develop impressions of individuals that are difficult to change); *the halo or horn effect* (supervisors are overly influenced in their judgments of individuals by singular events); *the Pygmalion effect* (supervisors see what they expect to see); and *discrimination* (treating people differently solely as a function of sex, race, age, or other factors unrelated to job performance). Left unchecked, informal judgments may also lead supervisors to pick successors like themselves.

Problem 3: Quick-Fix Attitudes

A third problem with the traditional approach to succession planning is that it can encourage quick-fix attitudes. Effectiveness is sacrificed to expediency. That can have far-ranging consequences, because ill-chosen leaders can prompt higher-than-normal turnover among their followers, create employee morale problems, and even bankrupt an otherwise sound business. Leadership *does* matter, and leaders cannot be cultivated quickly or easily.[23] Excellent leaders can only be cultivated over time.

Problem 4: Low Visibility

Top-level executives do not always see the fast, direct benefits of SP&M. The farther they are removed from daily operations—and numerous direct reports—the less valuable SP&M can seem to be to them. HR managers will propose and install various SP&M efforts, but they will often be replaced when top-level executives see no immediate benefits stemming from them.[24]

To solve this problem, succession *must* be made a high-visibility issue. Further, it must enjoy the active support—and direct participation—of workers *at all levels*. Without showing active support and participating directly, top managers will have no ownership stake in succession efforts.

Problem 5: The Rapid Pace of Organizational Change

Traditional replacement planning once worked well enough in stable environments and organizations. In those settings, vacancies could be predicted, candidates could be trained for targeted jobs, and a homogeneous workforce led to easy transitions and assured continuity.

But the rapid pace of organizational change has raised serious questions about the value of the traditional, fill-in-the-box-on-the-organization-chart approach to replacement-oriented succession planning. Indeed, one management consultant has asked, "is succession planning worth the effort?"[25] And he arrived at this conclusion: "The simple answer is no. Predicting succession (over, say, a three-to-five-year time frame) in an era of constant change is fast becoming an impossibility."[26]

To solve this problem, decision-makers need to look beyond a simple technological solution—such as the use of succession planning software for personal computers designed to accelerate the organization's ability to keep pace with staffing needs and changes. That can help, but more dramatic solutions are also needed. Possible examples: focus on work requirements, competencies, and success factors so as to maximize the value of developmental activities; use full-circle, multi-rater assessments; increase the use of job rotations to prompt management employees to become more flexible; use action learning and real-time education to equip management employees with the flexibility they need to cope with rapid change; establish team-based management so that key work requirements develop, and are spread across, different individuals; and move beyond a focus on "filling boxes on an organization chart" to "meeting work requirements through innovative means."[27]

Problem 6: Too Much Paperwork

Top managers in most organizations have a low tolerance for paperwork. A colleague of mine jokes that "top managers in my organization won't respond to a one-page survey or read beyond the first page of a memo." One reason for this is that top managers are often overburdened with paperwork, since they receive it from so many quarters. Technology, which was once seen as a blessed solution to information overload, now seems to be a contributing cause of it—as managers cope with burgeoning messages by electronic mail, cell phones, faxes, and other sources.

Hence, one problem with the traditional approach to succession planning is that it may require substantial paperwork to

- △ Assess present work requirements or competencies
- △ Appraise current individual performance
- △ Assess future work requirements or competencies
- △ Assess individual potential for advancement
- △ Prepare replacement charts
- △ Identify future career paths or career maps
- △ Identify key positions requiring replacements
- △ Establish Individual Development Plans (IDPs) to help individuals narrow the gap between their present work requirements/performance and future work requirements/potential
- △ Follow up on IDPs

While full-time specialists or part-time HR generalists can provide assistance in recordkeeping, they can seldom supply the details for every person, position, and requirement in the organization.

Perhaps the best approach is to minimize the amount of paperwork required. But that is difficult to do. Whenever possible, however, succession planning coordinators, management development professionals, or human resource professionals should supply information that is readily available from sources other than the immediate organizational superiors of employees participating in succession planning efforts. That way, the superiors can focus their attention on identifying the talent to implement business strategy, identifying critical positions and high-potential talent, and formulating and following through on developmental planning.

Problem 7: Too Many Meetings

Just as the traditional approach to succession planning can create resistance due to the massive paperwork it can generate, so too can it lead to resistance because it can require numerous and time-consuming meetings. For instance, to carry out SP&M, management employees may need to participate in:

△ *Kickoff meetings*. If an annual SP&M procedure is in place, management employees may be required to attend "kickoff meetings," conducted by the CEO, that are intended to reinforce the importance of the effort.

△ *Organizational, divisional, functional, or other meetings*. These meetings may focus on SP&M for each job category, organizational level, function, or location.

△ *Work requirements meetings*. If the organization makes it a policy to base succession on identifiable work requirements, competencies, success factors, or some other "objective criteria," then management employees will usually be involved in meetings to identify these criteria.

△ *Employee performance appraisal meetings*. In most organizations, management employees appraise the performance of their immediate subordinates as a part of the SP&M program.

△ *Career path meetings*. If the organization attempts to identify predictable, desirable, or historical relationships between jobs, then management employees may be asked to participate in that effort by attending meetings or training.

△ *Career planning meetings*. If the organization makes an effort to discover individual career goals and interests as a means to do a "reality check" on possible successors, then management employees may have to take time to meet with each employee covered in the succession plan.

△ *Potential assessment meetings*. Assessing individual potential is future-oriented and may require meetings different from those required for performance appraisal.

△ *Development meetings*. Planning for individual development, as a means of narrowing the gap between what individuals know or do presently and what they must know or do to qualify for advancement, may require time-consuming individual meetings.

△ *Training, education, and developmental meetings*. As one means by which succession plans may be realized, meetings centered around training, education, and development may demand considerable time.

While meetings can be consolidated to save some time, each meeting listed above serves an important purpose. Attending meetings can require a significant time commitment from management employees at all levels.

Requirements for a Fifth-Generation Approach

Minimum requirements for a fifth-generation approach to SP&M include:

△ A policy and procedure statement, in writing, to govern SP&M
△ A statement of values governing the effort (which may be included in the policy and procedure statement)
△ Competency models for the groups targeted
△ Full-circle, multi-rater assessment efforts (or other ways to assess individual potential)
△ Individual development plans
△ Skill inventories for talent pools inside and outside the organization

Of course, it goes without saying that senior management involvement and support are essential requirements—as are, particularly, the personal commitment and participation of the CEO.

Key Steps in a Fifth-Generation Approach to Succession Planning and Management

How should systematic SP&M be carried out in organizational settings? While the answer to this question may vary by national culture, organizational culture, and top management values, one way is to follow a "seven-pointed star model for systematic succession planning and management." That model is illustrated in Exhibit 3-5. The steps in the model, summarized below, provide the foundation for this book.

Step 1: Make the Commitment

As a first step, the organization's decision-makers should commit to systematic SP&M and establish an SP&M planning and management program. To some extent, this represents a "leap of faith" in the value of planned over unplanned approaches to SP&M. In this step the organization's decision-makers should:

Exhibit 3-5: The Seven-Pointed Star Model for Systematic Succession Planning and Management

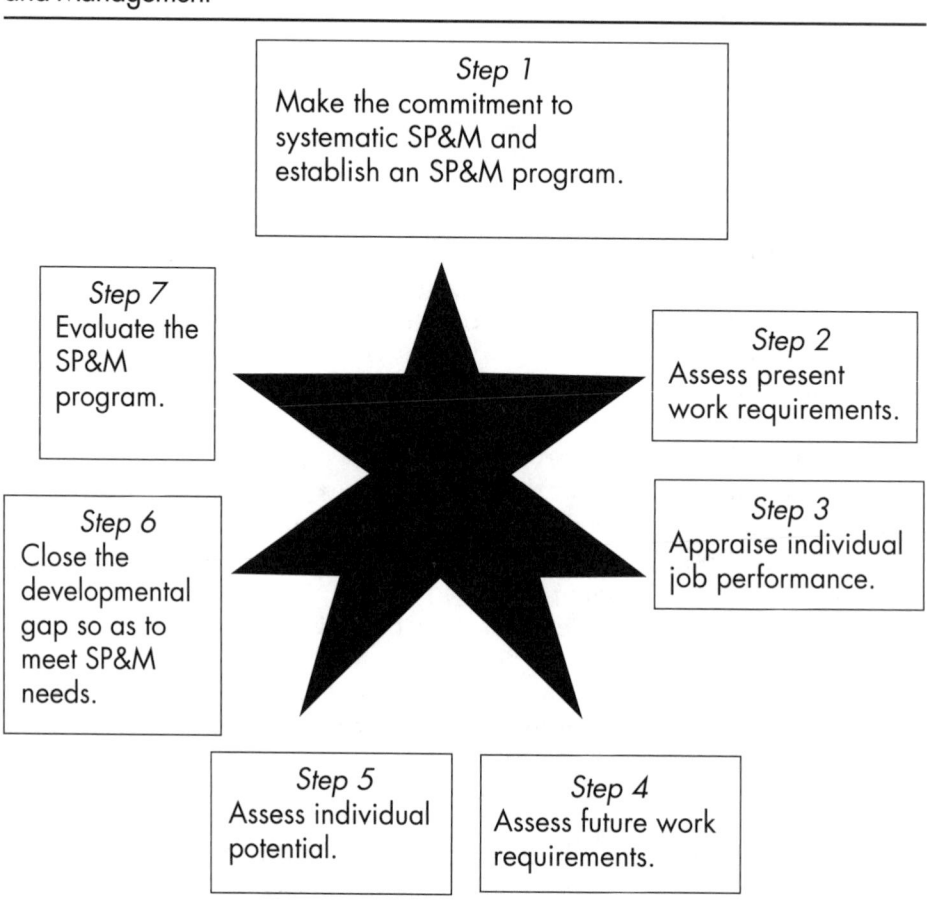

- △ Assess current problems and practices
- △ Assess and demonstrate the need for the program
- △ Determine the organization's exact SP&M program requirements
- △ Link the SP&M program directly to organizational and human resource strategic plans
- △ Benchmark SP&M practices in other organizations
- △ Clarify the roles of different groups in the program
- △ Formulate a program mission statement
- △ Write a policy and procedures to guide the program
- △ Identify target groups to be served by the program
- △ Establish program priorities
- △ Prepare an action plan to guide the program

- △ Communicate the action plan
- △ Conduct SP&M meetings as necessary to unveil the program and review progress continually
- △ Train those involved in the program as necessary
- △ Counsel managers about SP&M problems in their areas of responsibility

Step 2: Assess Present Work Requirements

As a second step, decision-makers should assess the present work requirements in key positions. Only in that way can individuals be prepared for advancement in a way that is solidly grounded on work requirements. In this step, decision-makers should clarify where key leadership positions exist in the organization and should apply one or more approaches to determining work requirements.

Step 3: Appraise Individual Performance

How well are individuals presently performing their jobs? The answer to this question is critical, because most SP&M programs assume that individuals must be performing well in their present jobs in order to qualify for advancement. As part of this step, the organization should also begin establishing an inventory of talent so that it is clear what human assets are already available.

Step 4: Assess Future Work Requirements

What will be the work requirements in key leadership positions in the future? To answer this question, decision-makers should make an effort to assess future work requirements and competencies. In that way, future leaders may be prepared to cope with changing requirements.

Step 5: Assess Future Individual Potential

How well are individuals prepared for advancement? What talents do they possess, and how well do those talents match up to future work requirements? To answer these questions, the organization should establish a process to assess future individual potential. That future-oriented process should not be confused with past- or present-oriented employee performance appraisal.

Step 6: Close the Developmental Gap

How can the organization meet SP&M needs by developing people internally or using other means to meet succession needs? To answer this question, the organization should establish a continuing program for leadership development to cultivate future leaders internally. Decision-makers should also explore alternatives to traditional promotion-from-within methods of meeting succession needs.

Step 7: Evaluate the Succession Planning Program

To improve, the SP&M program must be subjected to continual evaluation to assess how well it is working. That is the seventh and final step of the model. The results of evaluation should, in turn, be used to make program refinements and to maintain a commitment to systematic SP&M.

Summary

This chapter opened with case studies illustrating exemplary approaches to succession planning and management and a list of characteristics that are found in exemplary succession planning and management programs. It then summarized typical problems afflicting succession planning and management programs and suggested possible solutions to them. It also supplied a seven-pointed star model for systematic succession planning and management.

Chapter 4

Competency Identification and Values Clarification: Keys to Succession Planning and Management

Competency identification and values clarification are increasingly important foundations for an effective succession planning and management (SP&M) program. But what are competencies? How are competencies used in SP&M? How are competencies identified and used to guide SP&M efforts? What are values, and what is values clarification? How are values used in SP&M? How are values clarification studies conducted and used for SP&M? This chapter answers these questions.

What Are Competencies?

The word *competence* was first linked to a human trait in 1959.[1] Using that work as a starting point, David McClelland first focused attention on competencies in 1973.[2] McClelland noticed that standardized intelligence tests were not good predictors of job success, and he wondered why. Competencies as understood today stemmed from his initial questioning about reasons why standardized intelligence tests did not predict job success. Other authors and researchers, of course, contributed to the development of competency identification, modeling, and assessment as known and practiced today.[3]

Although the term *job competency* has different meanings, it can be understood to mean "an underlying characteristic of an employee (i.e., motive, trait, skill, aspects of one's self-image, social role, or a body of knowledge) which results in effective and/or superior performance in a job."[4] *Competency identification* is the process of discovering job competencies.[5] A *competency model* is the result of competency identification.[6]

Competency assessment is the process of comparing an individual to an existing competency model,[7] and that can be done by many means—including full-circle, multi-rater assessment.

Organizations have made extensive use of competency models in recent years, which have been widely accepted.[8] One reason is that competency models can help to clarify differences between outstanding (*exemplary*) and average performers—an increasingly important issue in a fiercely competitive global business environment. A second reason is that competency models are superior to work-based approaches, which rely on descriptions of work activities only, in pinpointing what people need to be successful. Increasingly, knowledge is only part of what is needed to be a successful performer. Also needed are appropriate attitudes and motivation, which are not well examined in traditional job descriptions or traditional performance appraisals.

How Are Competencies Used in Succession Planning and Management?

Competency models are essential building blocks on which to base an SP&M effort. Without them, it is difficult to:

△ Link and align the organizations's core competencies (strategic strengths) to job competencies

△ Define high-potentials or other broad categories of employees

△ Clarify exactly what present and future competencies are essential to success in the organization and in its various departments, jobs, or occupations

△ Provide a basis for performance management by creating a work environment that encourages high performance among all workers

△ Establish clear work expectations for the present and future

△ Create full-circle, multi-rater assessments that are tailor-made to the unique requirements of one corporate culture

△ Devise competency menus that describe how individuals might be developed for the future

△ Formulate Individual Development Plans (IDPs) to help individuals narrow the developmental gap between what competencies they need to be successful (as described by the competency model) and what competencies they presently possess (as identified by a full-circle, multi-rater assessment or other approaches to examining current performance or future potential)

Conducting Competency Identification Studies for Succession Planning and Management

Competency studies may have different goals. The goals must be clear before the resulting studies will be useful. Those who set out to conduct competency studies should be clear what they are trying to do, why they are doing it, and what their stakeholders (such as the CEO) are seeking. Elaborate studies do little good if nobody knows what they are for, nobody really wanted them, or nobody knows how to use them.

A *present competency study*, to define the term, focuses on one department, job category, or occupational group. In conducting a competency study of this kind, it is usually important to create two distinct groups—exemplary performers and average performers—for the department or other unit studied. The goal is usually to discover the difference between the highest performers in the group and the average performers in that same group. When completed, the present competency study clarifies what are the essential competencies for success at present.

A *future competency study* also focuses on one department, job category, or occupational group. But in conducting a competency study of this kind, it is usually important to start by describing the organization's strategic goals and objectives. What results will the organization seek in the future? Why will those results be sought? What competencies are necessary to realize those results? A different approach is needed from that in a present competency study. Often, there may be nobody in the organization who is an exemplary performer when compared to future requirements. It may thus be necessary to do scenario planning to discover the competencies needed in a future business environment. That also requires a level of sophistication that few internal practitioners possess—or have time to use if they do.

A *derailment competency study*, to define the term, focuses on the characteristics linked to failure—or to falling off the fast track—for those in one department, job category, or occupational group. In conducting a derailment study, it is usually important to identify individuals who have failed assignments, dropped off the high-potential list, have experienced career plateauing, or have otherwise become ineligible for a list of successors or high-potentials. The goal is to determine why people who were once considered high-potentials fell off the track or reached a career plateau. Once that is known, of course, strategies can be formulated to help them develop and surmount their failures—and help others avoid similar problems. Causes of derailment might include, among others, problems with morals (such as sexual indiscretions) or problems with health-related issues (such as alcoholism or drug-related ailments).

Different approaches to competency assessment have been devised.

The most thoroughly researched treatment available of these approaches is found in David Dubois's *Competency-Based Performance Improvement: A Strategy for Organizational Change* (Amherst, Mass.: Human Resource Development Press, 1993). While space is not available here to review each approach to competency assessment described at length by Dubois, those who are serious about SP&M will find the book to be a thoughtful treatment of the approaches currently available. Each may be applied to key positions and to high-potential individuals for purposes of SP&M. Summaries of these approaches appear in Exhibit 4-1.

Competency modeling offers a newer way to identify characteristics linked to exemplary job performance than traditional job analysis. An advantage of competency modeling is its rigor. Another is its ability to capture the (otherwise ineffable) characteristics of successful job performers and job performance. It can provide valuable information on key positions and high-potential employees on which to base SP&M practices.

Unfortunately, however, competency modeling does have disadvantages. One is that the term's meaning can be confusing. Another, more serious, disadvantage is that rigorous approaches to competency modeling usually require considerable time, money, and expertise to carry out successfully. Rarely can they be done internally except by the largest organizations. These can be genuine drawbacks when the pressure is on to take action—and achieve results—quickly.

Using Competency Models in Succession Planning and Management

Competency models have emerged as a foundation for state-of-the-art SP&M programs. Lacking them, organizations will rarely be able to proceed beyond a simple replacement approach to SP&M. They provide a blueprint for building competence needed at present or in the future, and they provide a norm or criterion against which to measure individual development requirements. They are especially important when an organization commits to developing talent pools, since they provide a standard against which all individuals may be assessed.

What Are Values, and What Is Values Clarification?

Simply stated, *values* are beliefs about what is good or bad. *Values clarification* is the process of making clear what values take priority over others, what is more important than other things. While competencies clarify differences between individual performers, values add an ethical dimension.

Exhibit 4-1: Approaches to Competency Identification

Approach	Brief Description	Steps in Applying the Approach
Job competence assessment method (JCAM)	"Relies on the use of a rigorous, empirical research procedure called job competence assessment, which helps determine what job competencies differentiate exemplary from average performance" (Dubois, 1993, p. 71).	1. Research the job components. 2. Research the attributes of the exemplary performers and construct the job competency model. 3. Validate the job competency model (Dubois, 1993, p. 73).
Modified job competence assessment method (MJCAM)	"Uses the JCAM research procedure, with the modification of having the exemplary and average performers write or otherwise record their critical behavior stories for use by the researcher" (Dubois, 1993, p. 71).	Replicate the steps for JCAM above.
Generic model overlay method (GMOM)	"Selects or obtains a prepared competency model and then overlays or superimposes it on a job within the organization" (Dubois, 1993, p. 71).	1. Complete the needs analysis, assessment, and planning step. 2. Research and develop a draft competency model. 3. Verify the draft competency model by having a group of exemplary job performers review the draft competency model. 4. Direct members of a focus group to review suggestions for modification to the model made by the exemplary performers (Dubois, 1993, p. 87).

Customized generic model method (CGMM)	The CGMM "relies on the researcher's tentative identification of a universe of candidate generic competencies that fully characterize the attributes of the exemplary and average performers of a job in the organization" (Dubois, 1993, p. 71).	1. Enlist initial client or client group support and develop a project plan. 2. Assemble and review all available information pertinent to the job. Prepare a job information paper or portfolio. 3. Research an initial set of job competencies. 4. Organize a focus group. 5. Convene the focus group and develop a draft, "best estimate" competency model. 6. Research the draft and develop the final competency model. 7. Brief the client or client group on project results (Dubois, 1993, p. 91).
Flexible job competency model method (FJCMM)	The FJCMM "relies on having a wide variety of comprehensive information sources for inclusion in the research base. A feature of this method is the identification and use of future assumptions about the organization and the job. . . . The use of this method results in the availability of job roles, job outputs, quality standards for the outputs, and behavioral indicators for each job competency" (Dubois, 1993, p. 72).	1. Assemble and review all available information that is pertinent to the job. Prepare a job information paper or portfolio. 2. Identify an expert panel consisting of senior organization leaders, managers, or exemplary subject-matter experts. 3. Develop present and future assumptions about the job in the context of the organization. 4. Develop a job outputs menu, including (optional) quality criteria for each output.

(continues)

Exhibit 4-1: (*continued*)

Approach	Brief Description	Steps in Applying the Approach
		5. Construct a job competencies menu and the behavioral indicators for each competency.
		6. Determine a menu of job roles through a cluster analysis of the job outputs.
		7. Construct one or more generic job competency models.
		8. Brief the client or client group on the project results. Prepare the final project products (Dubois, 1993, p. 100).

SOURCE: Adapted, with the publisher's permission, from David Dubois, *Competency-Based Performance Improvement: A Strategy for Organizational Change* (Amherst, Mass.: Human Resource Development Press, 1993). © 1993 Reprinted by permission of the publisher, HRD Press, Amherst, MA, (413) 253-3488.

They describe ethical expectations for those who live and work in one corporate culture.

Values have commanded increasing interest in organizational settings. Consider:[9]

> At a recent annual meeting of Eli Lilly and Company, Chairman and CEO Randall Tobias extended the meeting by over 2 hours to discuss the core values of the company and their importance to the future of the organization. Similarly, in a recent interview in *Organizational Dynamics*,[10] Herb Kelleher, Chairman and CEO of Southwest Airlines, discussed the central role that values play in that organization. Fortune magazine reported that over 50% of U.S. corporations have a values statement, more than double that of a decade ago.[11]

How Are Values Used in Succession Planning and Management?

Values statements and values clarification, like competency models, are essential building blocks on which to base a succession planning and management effort. Without them, it is difficult to add an ethical dimension to the development of people in various departments, job categories, or occupations. Much like competency models, they help to

△ Link and align the organization's core values to group and individual values
△ Define high-potentials or other broad categories of employees
△ Clarify exactly what present and future values are essential to success in the organization and in its various departments, jobs, or occupations
△ Provide a basis for performance management by creating a work environment that encourages value-based performance
△ Establish the values underlying work expectations for the present and future
△ Create full-circle, multi-rater assessments that are tailor-made to the unique requirements of one corporate culture
△ Provide another basis to formulate Individual Development Plans (IDPs) to help individuals develop themselves to meet present and future challenges

Conducting Values Clarification Studies for Succession Planning and Management

Many tools and techniques are available to help organizations clarify their values. Some organizations undertake values clarification through small group activities.[12] Others use unique approaches—such as teaching championship automobile racing.[13]

At least two other approaches may be used. One is simple; the other is more complicated.

A Simple Approach: Top Management Values Clarification

A simple way to clarify the values of the organization is to ask top managers what values are most important. To use this approach, provide a brief introduction to what values are, why they are important, and how they are used. Then ask senior executives—either in a meeting or online—to describe what they believe to be the most important values for the organization at present and in the future. When that list has been gathered from individuals, feed it back to them, allow them to discuss the list, and ask them to vote on the most important. When they finish this activity, ask them to define each value and state its importance to the organization and to individuals.

A More Complicated Approach: Values Clarification from Top Performers

A more complicated approach to carrying out values clarification is to ask top performers or high-potentials in the organization to describe their values. That can be done through behavioral event interviewing, a rigorous method used in competency modeling, in which individuals are asked to describe the most difficult ethical situation they have ever faced in their jobs in the organization and describe what they were thinking, feeling, and doing at each step as they faced that situation. The values statements should appear as part of their discussion. (If they do not, then the interviewer should be sure to ask probing questions to elicit comments about the values in which the high-potentials believe.) The values identified by individual high-potentials can then be summarized. What is important is not what one person says, but rather what thematic patterns surface from many respondents.

Once the values have been identified, then they can be fed back to high-potentials in focus groups for further discussion and refinement. When that process is completed, then the value statements can be given to top managers for approval or modification. In this way, the values clarified for the organization match up to the actual work-related beliefs of the best performers and are validated by top managers.

Using Values Clarification in Succession Planning and Management

Values clarification provides an additional, and increasingly important, dimension to SP&M. Without it, individuals may be equipped with sound competencies but may lack the ethical dimension that is so important to leadership in the future. Values can also be integrated with competency models so that it is possible to create a success profile or description of leadership requirements essential at all organizational levels, departments, job categories, or occupations in the future. Alternatively, it is possible to prepare values lists and assessment instruments against which to compare individuals. In other words, it is possible to use values as a driving force for building high-potentials and competence in organizations. Like competencies, then, values can be a glue that holds together all key aspects of a SP&M program.

Bringing It All Together: Competencies and Values

Organizations today need both competencies and values. It is just not enough to make people good performers. They must be ethical as well and possess a moral dimension that is consistent with the image the organization wishes to purvey. Lacking values, high-potentials cannot be successful in the long term and cannot bring credit on the organizations of which they are part.

Summary

As this chapter emphasized, competencies and values are increasingly important foundations for an effective succession planning and management program. The chapter defined competencies, explained how they are used in succession planning and management, defined values, and explained how values can be used in succession planning and management. A major point of the chapter was that, without competencies and values, creating a state-of-the-art succession planning and management program will be difficult.

The next chapter describes how to lay the foundation for a succession planning and management program by taking subsequent steps in planning and implementing a program that will be successful in one organizational setting or corporate culture.

Part II

Laying the Foundation for a Succession Planning and Management Program

The chapters in this part examine the means by which to lay the foundation for a systematic SP&M program in an organization by:

- △ Assessing current problems and practices
- △ Demonstrating the need for SP&M
- △ Determining organizational requirements
- △ Linking SP&M activities to organizational strategy and human resource strategy
- △ Benchmarking SP&M practices in other organizations
- △ Obtaining and building management commitment to systematic SP&M
- △ Clarifying program roles
- △ Formulating a mission statement
- △ Writing policy and procedures
- △ Identifying target groups
- △ Setting program priorities
- △ Addressing the legal framework in SP&M
- △ Establishing strategies for rolling out a SP&M program
- △ Preparing a program action plan
- △ Communicating the action plan
- △ Conducting SP&M meetings
- △ Training on SP&M
- △ Counseling managers about succession planning problems in their areas

Chapter 5
Making the Case for Change

For many years, introducing and consolidating change has been a center-piece of debate among managers and writers about management. Many believe that the essence of management's job is to be instruments for progressive change—or, at least, to create an environment suitable for change.

Establishing a systematic succession planning and management (SP&M) program in an organization that never had one is a major change effort. It requires a quantum leap from the status quo, what some call a "transformational change." Success depends on demonstrating, at the outset, a need for change. The only exception is the rare case in which decision-makers have already reached a consensus to depart radically from past practice.

To make the case for change in SP&M it will usually be necessary to:

△ Assess current problems and practices
△ Demonstrate the need
△ Determine organizational requirements
△ Link SP&M to the strategic plan and human resource plan
△ Benchmark SP&M processes in other organizations
△ Obtain and build management commitment to systematic SP&M.

These issues are the focus of this chapter. They may seem to be monumental issues—and sometimes they are—but addressing them is essential to lay a solid foundation on which to build a systematic SP&M program.

Assessing Current Problems and Practices

Information about current problems and practices is needed before it is possible to build a convincing case for change. Planning for the future requires information about the past and present.

Assessing Current Problems

Crisis is a common impetus for change. As problems arise and are noticed, people naturally search for solutions. As the magnitude and severity of the problems increase, the search for a solution intensifies.

The same principles apply to SP&M. If the organization has experienced no crises in finding qualified successors, retaining talented people, maintaining leadership continuity, or facilitating individual advancement, then few decision-makers will feel an urgent need to direct attention to these issues. On the other hand, SP&M is likely to attract increasing attention when any or all of the following problems surface:

△ Key positions are filled only after long delays.

△ Key positions can be filled only by hiring from outside.

△ Key positions have few people "ready now" to assume them (that is called *weak bench strength*).

△ Vacancies in key positions cannot be filled with confidence in the abilities of those chosen for them.

△ Key positions are subject to frequent or unexpected turnover.

△ Replacements for key positions are frequently unsuccessful in performing their new duties.

△ High performers or high-potential employees are leaving the organization in droves.

△ Individuals routinely leave the organization to advance professionally or to achieve their career goals.

△ Decision-makers complain about weak bench strength.

△ Employees complain that decisions about whom to advance are not based on who is best qualified but rather on caprice, nepotism, and personal favoritism.

△ Employees and decision-makers complain that decisions about whom to promote into key positions are adversely affected by discrimination or by expediency.

To build a case for a systematic approach to SP&M, ask decision-makers if they face the problems listed above. Additionally, focus attention on identifying the most important problems the organization is facing and reviewing how those problems are influenced by existing SP&M practices. If possible, document actual succession problems that have been experienced in the past—including "horror stories" (anecdotes about major problem situations) or "war stories" (anecdotes about negative experiences), if possible. Although anecdotes do not necessarily provide an accurate indication of existing conditions, they can be powerfully persuasive and can help convince skeptical decision-makers that a problem warrants investigation. Use them to focus attention on the organization's present SP&M practices—and, when appropriate, the need to change them from informal to systematic. Also, consider using approaches to identify and overcome objections to a SP&M program. (See Exhibit 5-1.)

In my 1999 survey, I asked the respondents to indicate whether SP&M had become more important to their organizations over the last few years. Their answers are revealing, indicating that many current problems have emerged that necessitate increased attention to SP&M. (See Exhibit 5-2.)

Assessing Current Practices

In large organizations using an informal approach to SP&M, nobody is aware of the methods being used *within* the organization. Nor should they be. After all, in those settings SP&M is handled idiosyncratically—or not at all—by each manager. As a consequence, nobody is aware of the organization's existing practices.

A good place to start, then, is to find out what practices are currently being used in the organization. Exemplary, albeit isolated, approaches may already be in use, and they may serve as excellent starting points on which to begin a systematic approach. They enjoy the advantage of a track record because they have already been tried out in the organization and probably have one or more managers who support them.

To emphasize this point, I am aware of one *Fortune* 500 corporation that uses an informal approach: Managers establish their own SP&M approaches as they feel they are warranted, and those activities vary dramatically. Most managers make no effort to conduct SP&M. As vacancies occur, replacements are frantically sought. Filling key positions is a crisis-oriented activity. (That is often true in organizations without systematic SP&M programs, as my 1999 survey revealed. See Exhibit 5-3.)

But even in this organization one major operating division has established a practice of circulating a confidential memo each year to department managers to request their nominations for their own replacements. No attempt is made to verify that the candidates possess the requisite knowledge and skills suitable for advancement; no attempt is made to verify that the candidates are willing to accept new assignments; and no attempt is made to ensure their availability, if needed, or to prepare them for advancement. However, the practice of circulating a memo is an excellent place to start a systematic approach to SP&M. It can be a focal point to direct attention to the issue—and to the need to adopt a systematic approach.

Use three approaches to assess the current status of SP&M in the organization: (1) talk to others informally; (2) send out an electronic mail question; or (3) conduct a written survey.

Exhibit 5-1: Strategies for Handling Resistance to Implementing Succession Planning and Management

Possible Cause of Resistance *Managers or employees resist a SP&M program because they believe it will:*	*Possible Strategies for Handling the Cause*
Mean that they have to give up something (such as a say in who is promoted)	△ Consider establishing a council to advise on matters related to the program △ Emphasize that organizational superiors of all individuals can and will be involved in making decisions
Require work for no reason (they see no need for it)	△ Start by describing how and why other organizations have used succession planning △ Show reasons for the program that go beyond mere replacement planning and include individual development
Do more harm than good	△ Try to find out why managers and employees feel this way and ask for their advice about how to prevent abuses of the program
Be managed by people who are not trustworthy or managed in a way that is not ethical	△ Hire an external consultant to establish the framework for the program and isolate the nature of the possible concerns
Require too much time, effort, or resources	△ Explain what information is required to make SP&M useful and then seek the advice of those who resist the program on this basis by asking for their suggestions about the best ways to get that information △ Double-check to determine whether you are recommending that the program be installed too quickly rather than gradually implemented

Exhibit 5-2: The Importance of Succession Planning and Management

Has succession planning become *more important* to your organization over the last few years? If "yes," briefly tell why; if "no," briefly tell why not.

All respondents answered "yes," and provided the following reasons:

△ Making sure we have talent we will need for the future
△ New Director of Organization has interest in having a program
△ Compelling need to develop internal candidates
△ Successors have occurred as the result
△ Succession Planning is more important now than in the past because our organization is taking steps to become a public company, and our organization's leadership will be scrutinized more closely than ever
△ New to company this year. Parent company is also focused on succession planning
△ Lack of talent in our industry; lack of available talent in market
△ Board interest, particularly for the senior management level
△ Competitive labor market
△ Employee recruiting and retention, competitive advantage as a successful company
△ Growth of our company as the workforce shrinks
△ Business expansion + aging current executive team

*SOURCE: William J. Rothwell, *Results of a Survey on Succession Planning and Management Practices*, unpublished survey results. (University Park, Pa.: The Pennsylvania State University, 2000).

Talk to Others Informally

Ask key decision-makers how they are handling SP&M practices. Begin by talking to the chairman or chief executive officer, if possible, because that person is likely to be more aware of the processes than others. Then discuss the matter with other top managers. Pose questions such as the following:

△ How is the organization presently handling SP&M? What is being done at the highest levels? at the lower levels? in different divisions? in different locales?
△ In your opinion, what should the organization be doing about SP&M—and why do you believe so?
△ What predictable losses of key personnel are anticipated in your area of responsibility? For example, how many pending retirements are you aware of? Will pending promotions lead to a *domino effect* in which a vacancy in one key position, filled by promotion from within, will set off a chain reaction that leads to a series of vacancies in many other positions?

Exhibit 5-3: Making Decisions about Successors (in Organizations without Systematic Succession Planning and Management)

How are decisions made about successors for positions in your organization? (*Circle all appropriate response codes below.*)

Decisions	Frequency	Percentage
We usually wait until positions are vacant and then scurry around madly to find successors.	4	22.22%
We "secretly" prepare successors.	5	27.78%
Whenever a position opens up, we rely on expediency to identify someone to fill it, hoping for the best.	8	44.44%
Other Methods	5	27.78%

△ We usually have someone in the background that can fill a position. If not, we do look outside for needed skills.
△ If the position cannot be eliminated or combined with others, then internal and external sources *are* utilized.
△ We use a system of logical #2's.

*Source: William J. Rothwell, *Results of a Survey on Succession Planning and Management Practices*, unpublished survey results (University Park, Pa.: The Pennsylvania State University, 2000).

△ What people or positions are *absolutely critical* to the continued successful operation of your division, function, department, or location? How would you handle the sudden and unexpected loss of a key person? several key people?

△ Have you experienced the loss of a key person in the last year or two? How did you handle it? If you had to do it again, would you handle it the same way? If so, why? If not, why not?

△ What regular efforts, if any, do you make to identify possible replacements for key people or positions in your part of the organization? (For example, do you discuss this issue as part of management performance appraisals, during business planning activities, or in other ways?)

△ What efforts, if any, do you make to identify individuals with the potential to advance beyond their current positions?

△ How do you prepare individuals to advance when you perceive they have potential? What systematic efforts are made to train, educate, or develop them for future positions?

△ What strongly held beliefs do you have about SP&M? For instance, do you believe the organization should inform possible successors of their status (and thereby risk creating a *crown prince problem*) or conceal that information (and risk losing high-potential employees who are tapped for better advancement prospects elsewhere, perhaps by other organizations or even by competitors)? How do you believe the organization should handle *plateaued workers*, who will advance no farther, and *blocked workers*, who are unable to advance beyond their current positions because they are blocked by plateaued workers above them?

When you finish interviewing decision-makers, prepare a summary of the results about SP&M practices in the organization. Cite individual names only if given explicit permission to do so. Include a summary of current information on effective SP&M practices obtained externally—from sources such as this book—and then ask if more attention can be devoted to the topic. The reactions you receive should provide valuable clues to how much interest and support exists among key decision-makers to explore a systematic approach to SP&M.

Send Out an Electronic Mail Question

A top manager in a large corporation focused attention on systematic SP&M merely by sending out an e-mail message to his peers. He posed this question:

Assume that you lost a key department manager on short notice through death or disability. (You can choose any department you wish.) Who is "ready" to assume that position? Name *anyone*.

That question provoked a flurry of responses. By merely posing this question, he served an important role as a *change champion*—and drew attention to *weak bench strength* in the organization's supervisory ranks.

Try the same approach in your organization—or find just one top manager who will pose a similar question to colleagues by e-mail. That will certainly draw attention to the issue. It may also open debate or create an impetus for change.

Conduct a Written Survey

A written survey may be used as an alternative to informal discussions. Unlike informal discussions, however, a written survey is a high-profile effort. Many people will probably see it.

For that reason, be sure to follow the organization's protocol for authorizing a written survey. That may mean discussing it, prior to distribution, with the CEO, the vice president of human resources, or others they suggest. Ask for their approval to conduct the survey—and solicit their input for questions of interest to them. In some organizations they may also wish to attach their own cover letters to the survey, which is desirable because it demonstrates their awareness and support—and may even increase the response rate.

Use the draft survey appearing in Exhibit 5-4 as a starting point, if you wish. It may save you time in developing your own survey, tailor-made to your organization's needs.

Once the survey has been completed, feed the results back to the decision-makers. In that way they can read for themselves what their peers have to say about the organization's current approach to SP&M. That can help them focus on specific problems to be solved and on achieving a consensus for action among themselves. However, conducting surveys is not without risk. They may, for instance, surface influential opposition to a systematic SP&M program. That will make it more difficult to make the case for that approach in the future.

Demonstrating the Need

Few decision-makers are willing to invest time, money, or effort in any activity from which they believe few benefits will be derived. It is thus essential to tie SP&M issues directly to pressing organizational problems and to the organization's core mission.

But exactly how is that done?

The answer to that question may vary across organizations. Each organization is unique; each organization has its own culture, history, and leadership group. But there are several possible ways by which to demonstrate the need for a systematic SP&M program. They are described below.

Hitchhiking on Crises

The first way to demonstrate need is to hitchhike on crises. As key positions become vacant or key people depart unexpectedly, seize that opportunity to poll decision-makers informally. Begin by summarizing the recent crisis. Contrast what happened with what could have happened if a systematic approach to SP&M had been used. Describe the impact of poorly planned SP&M on customers and employees, if possible. Then describe possible future conditions—especially future staffing needs that may result from recent downsizing, early retirement offers, or employee buyouts. Ask

Exhibit 5-4: A Questionnaire for Assessing the Status of Succession Planning and Management in an Organization

Cover Memo

To: Top Managers of _____ Corporation

From: _____

Subject: Survey on Succession Planning and Management Practices

Date: _____

Succession planning and management may be understood as *"any effort designed to ensure the continued effective performance of an organization, division, department, or work group by making provision for the development, replacement, and strategic application of key people over time."* It may be *systematic* or *informal*. In systematic SP&M, an organization's managers attempt to prepare successors for key positions; in informal succession planning, no effort is made to prepare successors—and, as vacancies occur in key positions, managers respond to the crises at that time.

Please take a few minutes to respond to the questions appearing below. When you are finished, return the completed survey to *(name)* by *(date)* at *(location)*. Should you have questions, feel free to call me at *(phone number)*.

Thank you for your cooperation!

The Survey

Directions: Please take a few minutes to write down your responses to each question appearing below. This questionnaire is intended to be anonymous, though you are free to sign your name if you wish. You will receive a confidential report that summarizes the key responses of all respondents and recommends action steps.

1. In your opinion, how well is this organization presently conducting SP&M? (*Circle your response in the left column*)

Very well   *Briefly explain why you feel as you do:*
Adequately
Inadequately
Very poorly

(continues)

Exhibit 5-4: *(continued)*

2. Should this organization establish/improve its approaches to SP&M?

Yes 　　　　　　　*Briefly explain why you feel as you do:*
No

3. In your area of responsibility, have you established
   (*Circle your response in the center column below*)

| | | Response | | |
Question		Yes	No	Your Comments
A. A systematic means to iden-tify possible replacement needs stemming from retire-ment or other predictable losses of people?		Yes	No	
B. A systematic approach to performance appraisal so as to clarify each individual's *current performance?*		Yes	No	
C. A systematic approach to identifying individuals who have the potential to advance one or more levels beyond their current positions?		Yes	No	
D. A systematic approach by which to accelerate the devel-opment of individuals who have the potential to advance one or more levels beyond their current positions?		Yes	No	
E. A means by which to keep track of possible replace-ments by key position?		Yes	No	

4. What special issues, if any do you believe that a systematic SP&M pro-gram designed and introduced in this organization should be careful to address?

5. What other comments do you have to make about a systematic SP&M program?

Please return the completed survey to (*name*) by (*date*) at (*location*). Should you have questions, feel free to call me at (*phone number*). You will receive a summary of the anonymous survey results by (*date*).

Thank You for Your Cooperation!

---

decision-makers whether they believe it is time to explore a systematic approach to meeting succession needs. Then be ready to offer a concrete proposal for the next steps to take.

Seizing Opportunities

A second way to demonstrate need is to *seize opportunities*.

In one organization, for example, the human resources department studied top managers' ages and projected retirement dates. The results were astonishing: *all* the top managers were due to retire within five years and *no* replacements had been identified or developed. In that case, the HR department detected a brewing crisis and helped avert it. The organization subsequently established a systematic SP&M program that enjoyed strong support—and great success.

Any major strategic change will normally create opportunities. For instance, as electrical utilities are deregulated, decision-makers realize that the future success (and even survival) of these organizations often depends on identifying and developing new leaders who can thrive in a highly competitive, market-driven environment. That raises questions about the developmental needs of successors who had been nurtured during a period of regulation. It also prompts developmental activities to increase the market-oriented skills of future leaders.

Use the Worksheet appearing in Exhibit 5-5 to focus attention on ways to hitchhike on crises and to seize opportunities.

Showing the "Bottom-Line" Value

A third way to demonstrate the need for a systematic SP&M program might be called "showing the 'bottom-line' " value. However, making that case for SP&M can be tough to do. As Jac Fitz-Enz writes:[1]

> One of the difficulties in trying to measure the work of planners is that their output is primarily a plan of the future. By definition,

Exhibit 5-5: A Worksheet for Demonstrating the Need for Succession Planning and Management

---

Directions: How can the need for a systematic SP&M program be demonstrated in an organization? Use the questions below to help you organize your thinking. Answer each question in the space appearing below it. Then compare your responses to those of others in the organization. Add paper if necessary.

---

1. What *crises*, if any, have occurred in placing high-potential individuals or filling key positions in recent years? Describe the situations and how the organization coped with them. Then describe what happened (the outcomes of those strategies).

   Make a list of the crises, if any, and briefly describe:

2. What *opportunities*, if any, have you noticed that may affect the knowledge, skills, and abilities that will be needed by workers in the organization in the future? (In particular, list strategic changes and then draw conclusions about their implications for knowledge, skills, and abilities.)

Make a list of strategic changes:	*Describe how those strategic changes are likely to affect the knowledge, skills, and abilities needed by workers in the organization in the future:*

---

we will not know for 1, 3 or perhaps 5 years how accurate their predictions were. In addition no one is capable of predicting future events, and therefore it is not fair to blame the planner for unforeseeable events. It is impossible to measure the value of a long-term plan in the short term. Planners thus often feel frustrated because they cannot prove their worth with concrete evidence.

Those involved in succession planning and management may feel that they face exactly the same frustrations to which Fitz-Enz alludes.

However, he has suggested ways to measure each of the following:

△ Workload (*How many positions need to be filled?*)
△ Speed of filling positions (*How long does it take to fill positions?*)
△ Results (*How many positions were filled over a given time span?*)

Succession planning and management may thus be measured by the number of key positions to be filled, the length of time required to fill them, and the number of key positions filled over a given time span. Of course, these measures are not directly tied to such bottom-line results for an organization as return on equity, return on investment, or cost-benefit analysis. But they are good places to start.

As Fitz-Enz rightly points out, the central questions to consider when quantifying program results are these:[2]

△ "What variables are really important to the organization?" and
△ "What results can be influenced by action?"

Meaningful, quantifiable results can only be obtained by focusing attention directly on answering these questions. Decision-makers must be asked what *they* believe to be the most important variables and actions that can be taken by the organization. This information, then, becomes the basis for establishing the financial benefits of an SP&M program.

When measuring SP&M results, decision-makers may choose to focus on such issues as these:

△ How long does it take to fill key positions? (Measure the average elapsed days per position vacancy.)
△ What percentage of key positions are *actually* filled from within? (Divide the number of key positions filled from within by the total number of key positions.)
△ What percentage of key positions are *capable* of being filled from within? (Divide the number of high-potential workers available by the number of expected key position vacancies annually.)
△ What is the percentage of successful replacements out of all replacements? (Divide the number of retained replacements in key positions by all replacements made to key positions.)

Of course, issues of importance to top managers, and appropriate measures of bottom-line results, will vary across organizations. The point is that these issues must be identified before appropriate criteria and bottom-line measures can be assigned.

Another way to view the bottom-line measure of a SP&M program is to compare the expenses of operating the program to the benefits accruing from it. That may be difficult—but is not impossible—to do.

As a first step, identify direct and indirect program expenses. Direct expenses result solely from operating a SP&M program. An example might be the salary of a full- or part-time SP&M coordinator. Indirect expenses result only partially from program operations. They may include partial salary expenses for managers involved in developing future leaders or the cost of materials to develop high-potentials.

As a second step, identify direct and indirect program benefits. (This can be tricky, but the key to success is involving decision-makers so that they accept and have ownership in the program benefits that are claimed.) Direct benefits are quantifiable and financially oriented. They might include savings in the fees of search firms. Indirect benefits might include the goodwill of having immediate successors prepared to step in, temporarily or permanently, whenever vacancies occur in key positions.

As a third step, compare the costs and benefits. Will the organization gain financially if a systematic approach to SP&M is adopted? In what ways? How can the relative effectiveness of the program be related directly to the organization's pressing business issues and core mission?

For additional information on cost-benefit analysis, review the numerous approaches that have been suggested for evaluating the bottom-line value of training programs.[3] Use those approaches to clarify costs and benefits of a systematic SP&M program.

Of course, other ways—apart from hitchhiking on crises, seizing opportunities, and showing the cost-benefit ratio for program operations—might be used to demonstrate the need for a systematic approach to SP&M. Consider: How has the need been successfully demonstrated for *other* new programs in the organization? Can similar approaches be used to demonstrate a need for a systematic SP&M program?

Determining Organizational Requirements

All organizations do not share identical requirements for SP&M programs. Differences exist due to the organization's industry, size, stage of maturity, management values, internally available expertise, cost, time, and other considerations. Past surveys confirm that these issues—and others—can affect the appropriate design of SP&M programs.[4]

However, top management goals are probably key considerations. What do top managers believe to be essential for a SP&M program? The most important questions on which to focus attention might include the following:

△ How eager are top managers and other decision-makers to systematize the organization's SP&M process(es)?

- △ How much time and attention are decision-makers willing to devote to assessing key position requirements? identifying leadership competencies? identifying success factors for advancement in the organization? conducting multi-rater assessments? appraising individual performance? preparing and implementing Individual Development Plans (IDPs) to ensure the efficient preparation of individuals for advancement into key positions?
- △ How stable is the current organizational structure? work processes? Can either—or both—be reliably used to plan for leadership continuity or replacements?
- △ How willing are decision-makers to devote resources to cultivating talent from within?
- △ How much do decision-makers prefer to fill key position vacancies from inside rather than from outside the organization?
- △ How willing are decision-makers to use innovative alternatives to simple replacements-from-within?

Begin determining the essential requirements of a SP&M program by interviewing top managers. Pose the questions appearing above. Add others as pertinent to the organization. (As a starting point, use the interview guide appearing in Exhibit 5-6 for this purpose.) Then prepare and circulate a written proposal for a SP&M program that conforms to the consensus opinion of key decision-makers.

Linking Succession Planning and Management Activities to Organizational and Human Resource Strategy

Succession planning and management should be linked to organizational and human resource strategy. However, achieving those linkages can be difficult.

Linking Organizational Strategy and Succession Planning and Management

Organizational strategy refers to the way in which a business chooses to compete. Important steps in the process include: (1) determining the organization's purpose, goals, and objectives; (2) scanning the external environment to identify future threats and opportunities; (3) appraising the organization's present strengths and weaknesses; (4) examining the range of strategies; (5) choosing a strategy that is likely to seize maximum advantage from future opportunities by building on organizational strengths; (6) implementing strategy, particularly through changes in struc-

Exhibit 5-6: An Interview Guide for Determining the Requirements for a Succession Planning and Management Program

Directions: Use this interview guide to help you formulate the requirements for a systematic SP&M program for an organization. Arrange to meet with top managers in your organization. Pose the questions appearing in the left column below. Record notes in the right column below. Then use the results of the interview as the basis for preparing a proposal for a systematic SP&M program for the organization. (You may add questions to the left column, if you wish.)

Questions	*Notes on Responses*
1. What are your thoughts about approaching succession planning and management in this organization *in a planned way?*	
2. How should we define *key positions* in this organization?	
3. How should we clarify the requirements for key positions?	
4. How should we assess current job performance?	
5. How stable do you believe the current organizational structure to be? Will it be adequate to use as the basis for identifying key positions requiring successors in the future?	

Questions	Notes on Responses
6. How do we determine the qualifications or requirements for each key position in the future?	
7. How do you feel that we can identify individuals who have the potential to meet the qualifications for key positions in the future?	
8. What do you believe are the essential resources that must be provided by the organization in order to accelerate the development of high-potential employees?	
9. How should we keep track of high-potential employees?	
10. What other thoughts do you have about the essential requirements for an effective succession planning and management program in this organization? Why do you believe they are essential?	

ture, policy, leadership, and rewards; and (7) evaluating strategy periodically to assess how well it is helping the organization to achieve its strategic goals and objectives.

Achieving effective linkage between organizational strategy and SP&M is difficult for three major reasons. First, while effective strategy implementation depends on having the right people in the right places at the right times, it is not always clear *who* the right people are, *where* the right places are, and *when* those people will be needed. Second, strategy is frequently expressed in a way that does not lend itself easily to developing action plans for SP&M. For instance, decision-makers may focus attention on "increasing market share" or "increasing return-on-investment"—without describing what kind of leadership will be needed to achieve those ambitious goals. Third, organizational strategy *as practiced* may differ from organizational strategy *as theorized*,[5] which complicates the process of matching leadership to strategy. That can happen when the daily decisions do not match written organizational strategy.

To overcome these problems, decision-makers must take active steps to build consideration of SP&M issues into the formulation of strategic plans. During the review of organizational strengths and weaknesses, for instance, decision-makers should consider the organization's leadership talent. What kind of expertise is presently available? During strategic choice and implementation, decision-makers should also consider whether the organization has the right talent to "make it happen." Who possesses the knowledge and skills that will contribute most effectively to making the strategy a reality? How can individuals be developed to help them acquire that knowledge and those skills? How can the organization establish an action plan to *manage* its human assets as effectively as its financial assets? Only by answering these questions—and taking active steps to narrow the gap between available and necessary talent—can the organization link its strategy and its succession planning and management.

Linking Human Resource Strategy and Succession Planning and Management

Human resource strategy is the means that the organization chooses to make the most effective use of its HR programs and activities to satisfy organizational needs. Important steps in this process parallel those in organizational strategy-making: (1) determining the purpose, goals, and objectives of the HR function; (2) scanning the external environment to identify future threats and opportunities affecting HR inside and outside the organization; (3) appraising the organization's present HR strengths and weaknesses; (4) examining the range of HR strategies available; (5) choosing an HR strategy that is likely to support the organizational strategy; (6) implementing HR strategy through changes in such programs as training, selection, compensation, benefits, and labor relations; and (7) evaluating HR strategy periodically for how well it supports organizational strategy.

Unfortunately, efforts to integrate HR strategy and organizational strategy have met with only mixed success. As Golden and Ramanujam write, "the lack of integration between human resource management (HRM) and strategic business planning (SBP) processes is increasingly acknowledged as a major source of implementation failures. It is often alleged that companies develop strategic plans based on extensive marketing and financial data but neglect the human resource requirements necessary to successfully implement them."[6] Numerous theories have been developed over the years to identify ways to link organizational and HR strategy.[7] However, little evidence exists to show that great strides have been made in this area.[8]

To link HR planning and SP&M, decision-makers should examine how well HR policies and practices help—or hinder—leadership continuity, individual advancement, and the cultivation of internal talent. More specifically:

△ How does the organization conduct recruitment, selection, and placement? How much consideration is given during this process to long-term retention and development of prospective or new employees?

△ How does the organization conduct training, education, and development? How much (relative) attention is given to the long-term cultivation of employee talent—as opposed to focusing attention on training individuals to meet immediate requirements?

△ How well do existing compensation and benefit practices support internal placement? transfers? promotions? Are actual *disincentives* established to dissuade employees from wanting to accept promotions or assume leadership roles?

△ How do existing labor relations agreements affect the organization's promotion, rotation, transfer, and other employment practices?

To integrate HR strategy and SP&M, examine existing HR program efforts—such as selection, training, compensation, and benefits—against succession planning and management needs. Identify HR practices that could encourage or that presently discourage effective SP&M. Then take active steps to ensure that HR practices facilitate, and do not impede, long-term efforts to groom talent from within.

Benchmarking Succession Planning and Management Practices in Other Organizations

Discussions with top managers and other key decision-makers in an organization should yield valuable information about the needs that an SP&M program should meet. But that information can be supplemented by benchmarking SP&M practices in other organizations. Moreover, the results of benchmarking may intensify the interests of key decision-makers in SP&M because they may demonstrate that other organizations are using better, or more effective, methods.

As Robert C. Camp explains:[9]

> Only the approach of establishing operating targets and productivity programs based on industry best practices leads to superior performance. That process, being used increasingly in U.S. business, is known as *benchmarking*.

Benchmarking has also surfaced in recent years as a powerful tool for improving organizational work processes and is frequently associated with Total Quality Management. Its primary value is to provide fresh perspectives, and points for comparison, from other organizations. It can thereby accelerate the process of introducing a state-of-the-art program by comparing existing practices in one organization to the best practices already in use elsewhere.

Although there are various means by which to conduct benchmarking, Camp suggests that it should be carried out in the following way:[10]

1. Identify what is to be benchmarked.
2. Identify comparative companies.
3. Determine a data collection method and collect data.
4. Determine the current performance "gap."
5. Project future performance levels.
6. Communicate benchmark findings and gain acceptance.
7. Establish functional goals (based on the results of the benchmarking study).
8. Develop action plans (based on the results of the benchmarking study).
9. Implement specific actions and monitor progress.
10. Recalibrate benchmarks.

Typically, then, benchmarking begins when decision-makers make a commitment. They clarify their objectives and draft questions to which they seek answers. Comparable organizations, often but not always in the same industry, are chosen. A suitable data collection method is selected, and written questionnaires and interview guides are frequently used for data collection. Site visits (field trips) are arranged to one or more organizations identified as being "best-in-class."

Benchmarking should not be pursued as a "fishing expedition"; rather, it should be guided by specific objectives and questions. Participants should start out with some familiarity with the process—such as succession planning and management practices. (That may mean that they have to be briefed before participating in a site visit.) Several key decision-makers should go on the site visits so they can compare practices in other organizations with their own. That is an excellent way, too, to win over skeptics and demonstrate that "the way we have always done it here" may not be the best approach.

Most Fortune 500 companies are well known for their effective succession planning and management practices. Blue-chip firms such as Motorola, Xerox, IBM, AT&T, General Electric, Coca-Cola, and General Motors—among others—are perhaps best known for conducting effective succession planning and management. They may rightly be considered "best-in-class" companies. Appropriate contacts at these organizations should be located through such professional societies as the Human Resource Planning Society (P.O. Box 2553, Grand Central Station, New York, NY 10163), the American Management Association (1601 Broadway, New York, NY 10019), the American Society for Training and Development (1640 King Street, Alexandria, VA 22313), or the Society for Human Resource Management (606 N. Washington Street, Alexandria, VA 22314).

Always develop questions *before* making a site visit. (See the list of possible questions in Exhibit 5-7.) Then contact representatives from two or three of those organizations and ask if benchmarking visits to their locations are possible. If so, send them the questions in advance of the visit so that they have time to prepare their responses. Sometimes they may wish to see the questions in advance before they commit to a visit.

It may be difficult to arrange benchmarking visits on SP&M. Many organizations consider the process sensitive to their operations—and revealing about their corporate strategies. Consequently, one approach is to seek access to organizations where you or others in your organization have personal contacts. If necessary, begin with local organizations that have successfully established SP&M programs. Identify them by talking to your peers in local chapters of the American Society for Training and Development (ASTD), the Society for Human Resource Management (SHRM), or other professional societies.

Exhibit 5-7: An Interview Guide for Benchmarking Succession Planning and Management Practices

Directions: Use this interview guide to help you prepare questions in advance of a benchmarking visit to another organization. Share these questions before your visit to an organization known for its effective SP&M practices. (Add questions as appropriate for your organization.) Pose the questions appearing in the left column below. Then record notes in the right column. Use the results in formulating a proposal for improving SP&M practices in your organization.

Questions	*Notes on Responses*
1. What mission statement has been established for succession planning and management in your organization?	
2. What goals and objectives have been established for succession planning and management in your organization?	
3. What policy and philosophy statement has been written to guide succession planning and management in your organization? (Would it be possible to obtain a copy?)	
4. How does your organization define *key positions*? What positions, if any, are given special attention in your succession planning program? Why are they given that attention?	

5. How does your organization identify, describe, or clarify the requirements of key positions? (For example, has your organization made an effort to identify job responsibilities, competencies, or success factors by level?)

6. How does your organization assess *current job performance* for succession planning and management purposes? (Do you use the organization's existing performance appraisal system—or something else?)

7. Does your organization use replacement charts based on the current organization chart? (If not, why?)

8. How does your organization determine the qualifications or requirements for each key position in the future?

9. How does your organization attempt to integrate succession planning and management with organizational strategy? with human resource strategy?

(continues)

Exhibit 5-7: *(continued)*

Questions	Notes on Responses
10. How does your organization identify successors for key positions?	
11. How does your organization identify high-potential employees (who are capable of advancing two or more levels beyond their current placement)?	
12. How does your organization establish Individual Development Plans (IDPs) to accelerate the development of high-potential employees?	
13. What special programs, if any, has your organization established to accelerate the development of high-potentials?	
14. What special computer software, if any, does your organization use in its succession planning and management activities?	
15. How does your organization evaluate succession planning and management activities?	

16. What special problems has your organi-
     zation encountered with succession plan-
     ning and management? How have those
     been solved?

Obtaining and Building Management Commitment to Systematic Succession Planning and Management

Securing management commitment to systematic SP&M may not occur rapidly. Skeptics are difficult to convince in short order. It will take time and proof of tangible evidence of success to win them over.

Opinions about Succession Planning and Management

My 1999 survey of SP&M practices revealed sharp disparities in opinions about systematic SP&M programs. Examine Exhibit 5-8. Then consider how you would answer those questions about top management opinions in *your* organization. Turn then to Exhibit 5-9 and consider how you would characterize your own opinions about systematic SP&M.

Understanding How to Secure Management Commitment

To understand how to secure management commitment, Diane Dormant's ABCD model remains a helpful tool.[11] ABCD is an acronym based on the first letter of several key words. Dormant's model suggests that large-scale organizational change—such as the introduction of a systematic SP&M program—can be understood by examining *adopters* (who is affected by the change?), *blackbox* (what is the change process?), *change agent* (who is making the change?), and *domain* (the change context).[12]

The most valuable feature of Dormant's model is her view that different strategies are appropriate at different stages in the introduction of a change. The change agent should thus take actions to facilitate change that are keyed to the adopter's stage in accepting an innovation.

Dormant believes that adopters progress through five identifiable stages in accepting an innovation.[13] During the first stage, *awareness*, adopters have little information about the innovation. They are passive and are generally unwilling to seek information. In that stage, change agents should advertise the innovation, making efforts to attract attention and provide positive information.

Exhibit 5-8: Opinions of Top Managers about Succession Planning and Management

How would you summarize the opinions of top managers in your organization about a succession planning program? (*Circle all response codes below that apply.*)

Opinions of Top Management	Frequency	Percentage
They don't believe succession planning is worth the time required for it.	2	6.67%
They have no clue why such a program might be worthwhile.	1	3.33%
They believe that a succession planning program is worthwhile but are not aware of how to manage it efficiently and effectively.	12	40.00%
They believe a succession planning program is worthwhile and that a formal program is better than an informal program.	15	50.00%
I don't know what they think about a succession planning program.	2	6.67%
Other comments △ Lack of resources compromises significant movement in this area. △ Managers are hesitant to spend time on strategic initiatives when daily issues seem so overwhelming. △ Managers want someone else to do the planning and development. △ We have reviewed an approach to implement a succession planning proposal for the fiscal year 1999–2000. △ They believe it is important to develop bench strength regardless of whether it is a formal or informal program. Our HR department provides a template for them to follow as a tool.	2	6.67%

*SOURCE: William J. Rothwell, *Results of a Survey on Succession Planning and Management Practices*, unpublished survey results (University Park, Pa.: The Pennsylvania State University, 2000).

Exhibit 5-9: Opinions of Human Resource Professionals about Succession
Planning and Management

How would you summarize *your* opinions about a succession planning program? (*Circle all response codes below that apply.*)

Your Opinions	Frequency	Percentage
I don't believe such a program is important.	0	0.00%
I believe that other methods work better in identifying and preparing possible succes-sors.	1	3.33%
I believe a succession planning program is worthwhile but other programs are more im-portant for this organization right now.	6	20.00%
I believe a succession planning program is important.	15	50.00%
Succession planning is critically important to this organization at this time.	13	43.33%
Other Opinions △ Succession planning is one type of pro-gram within the concept of people devel-opment for the future.	1	3.33%

*Source: William J. Rothwell, *Results of a Survey on Succession Planning and Management Practices*,
unpublished survey results (University Park, Pa.: The Pennsylvania State University, 2000).

In the second stage, *self-concern*, adopters are more active. They express concern about how they will be individually affected by a change and
pose questions about the consequences of an innovation. Change agents
in this stage should enact the role of counselor, answering questions and
providing relevant information.

In *mental tryout*, the third stage, adopters remain active and ask
pointed questions related to their own applications of an innovation.
Change agents should enact the role of demonstrators, providing relevant
examples and demonstrating to adopters how they may apply an innovation to their unique situations.

In *hands-on trial*, the fourth stage, adopters are interested in learning
how to apply an innovation to their own situations. Their opinions about
the innovation are being formed from personal experience. Change agents
should provide them with training and detailed feedback about how well
they are applying the innovation. Testimonials of success will be persuasive
during this stage, helping to shape the conclusions reached by the adopters about an innovation.

Adoption is the fifth and final stage. By this point adopters have integrated the innovation into their work and are interested in specific problem-solving that is related to their own applications. Change agents should provide personal support, help adopters find the resources they need to perform effectively, and provide rewards for successful implementation.

Applying these stages to the process of obtaining and building management support for systematic SP&M should be apparent. The appropriate strategies that change agents should use depend on the stage of acceptance. (See Exhibit 5-10.)

An important point to bear in mind is that a succession planning program will be effective only when it enjoys support from its stakeholders. Indeed, the stakeholders must perform SP&M for it to work. In short, they must *own* the process. Hence, obtaining and building management commitment to SP&M is essential for a systematic program to work.

Summary

When preparing to introduce a systematic succession planning program, begin by assessing the organization's current succession planning and

Exhibit 5-10: Actions to Build Management Commitment to Succession Planning and Management

Stage of Acceptance	Appropriate Actions
Awareness	△ Advertise SP&M to management employees. △ Provide general information about SP&M.
Self-concern	△ Answer questions. △ Provide relevant information.
Mental tryout	△ Provide relevant examples of applications of SP&M policy/practices to specific functions or activities within the organization. △ Demonstrate how SP&M may be used in each organizational area.
Hands-on Trial	△ Offer training on SP&M. △ Meet with top managers individually to discuss SP&M in their areas. △ Collect and disseminate testimonials of success.
Adoption	△ Provide personal support to top managers on applications of systematic SP&M. △ Help program users perform effectively through individualized feedback and counseling. △ Identify appropriate rewards for SP&M.

management problems and practices, demonstrating the business need for succession planning and management, determining the organization's unique succession planning and management requirements, linking the succession planning and management program to the organization's strategic plans and human resource plans, benchmarking succession planning and management processes in other organizations, and obtaining and building management commitment.

This chapter has reviewed these steps and thereby demonstrated ways by which to make the case for change.

The next chapter begins where this chapter ends. It emphasizes the importance of clarifying the roles of each level of management in the succession planning and management program, developing a program mission statement, policy, and philosophy, identifying target groups, and setting program priorities.

Chapter 6

Starting Up a Systematic Succession Planning and Management Program

An organization should be ready to start up a systematic succession planning and management (SP&M) program once the case has been persuasively made that one is needed. Starting up a systematic SP&M program usually involves taking such actions as clarifying roles in the SP&M program, formulating a mission statement, writing a program policy, clarifying procedures, identifying groups targeted for action, and setting program priorities. This chapter focuses on these issues.

Clarifying Program Roles

What are roles? How can roles in an SP&M program be clarified so that organizational members know what they should do to support the effort? This section answers these questions.

Understanding Roles

A *role* is an expected pattern of behaviors and is usually linked to a job in the organization. Although most organizations outline responsibilities in job descriptions, few job descriptions are sufficiently detailed to clarify how job incumbents should carry out their duties or interact with others. However, roles do permit such clarification. Indeed, "a role may include attitudes and values as well as specific kinds of behavior. It is what an individual must do in order to validate his or her occupancy of a particular position."[1]

Role theory occupies a central place in writings about management and organizations. Internalizing a role has often been compared to the communication process. (See Exhibit 6-1.) *Role senders* (role incumbents)

Exhibit 6-1: A Model for Conceptualizing Role Theory

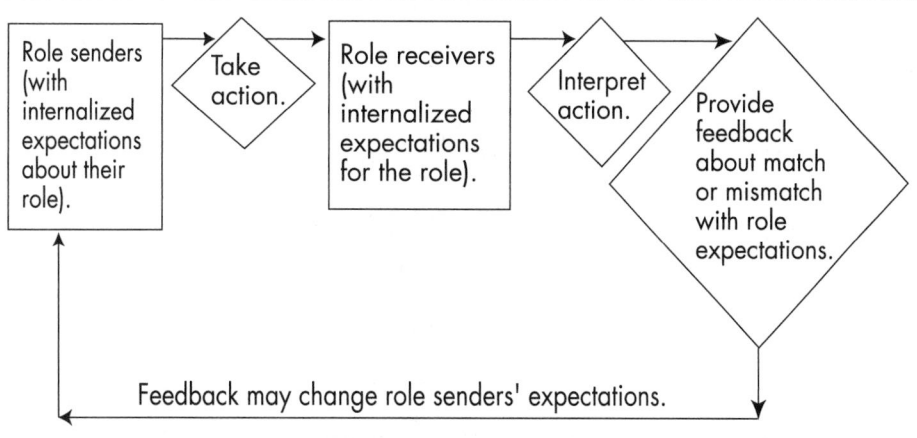

bring to their roles expectations about what they should do, how they should do it, and how they should interact with others. Their expectations are influenced by their previous education, experience, values, and background. They are also influenced by what they are told about the role during the recruitment, training, and selection process. *Role receivers*—others in the organization with whom role senders interact—observe these behaviors and draw conclusions from them based on their own expectations. They provide feedback to indicate whether the behavior matches what they expect. That feedback, in turn, may affect the role senders' expectations and behaviors.

To complicate matters, individuals enact more than one role in organizations. For instance, they may serve as superiors, colleagues, and subordinates. They may also enact roles outside the organization—such as spouse, parent, child, citizen, churchgoer, or professional. Each role may carry its own culturally bound expectations for behavior.

Multiple roles can lead to *role conflict*. For example, supervisors may be expected by their employers to act in the best interests of the organization. That means they must occasionally make hard-eyed business decisions. On the other hand, supervisors may also be expected to represent the interests and concerns of their subordinates to the employer. To cite another example: Human resource managers may perceive their own role to be facilitative and feel that they should provide advice to operating managers when they must reach decisions about HR issues. But operating managers may expect them to act forcefully and proactively on their own, spearheading new initiatives and taking steps to avert future HR problems that may arise in the organization. In both examples, conflicting expectations may lead role incumbents to experience pressure and frustration.

Effective performance is influenced by congruence in role expectations. Role senders can only achieve desired results when they know what they are expected to do *and* when role receivers make their expectations clear.

Applying Role Theory to Succession Planning and Management

As role theory indicates, performance is influenced by shared role expectations. As one step in establishing systematic SP&M, clarify program roles so that individuals throughout the organization are aware of what they are expected to do and how they are expected to behave.

At the outset, direct attention to the roles to be enacted by three important groups: (1) management employees; (2) program facilitators; and (3) program participants. These roles may overlap. In each case, however, it is important to surface what group members already believe about their roles in SP&M, feed that information back to them, provide information about alternative roles, and seek consensus on desirable roles.

Think of the roles of management employees as ranging along one continuum from active to passive and along another continuum from supporter to opponent. (See the grid in Exhibit 6-2 to help conceptualize those roles.) Management employees who take an active role believe that SP&M should occupy much of their time. They should be defining present work requirements, planning for future work requirements, appraising individual performance, assessing individual potential, planning for individual development, and participating in developmental activities. On the other hand, management employees who take a passive role believe that issues other than SP&M should occupy their time. A supporter sees systematic SP&M as a valuable activity; an opponent has reservations about it.

Think of facilitators' roles as ranging along a continuum from directive to nondirective. Facilitators who take a directive role indicate what they expect from those participating in a systematic SP&M program. They then attempt to enforce these expectations, providing briefings, training, or written directions to help others understand what they are supposed to do. Operating managers and top managers who are assigned responsibilities as SP&M coordinators may adopt that role—particularly during the start-up phase when many may be confused about what they are supposed to do.

On the other hand, facilitators who take a nondirective role attempt to identify what various stakeholders want from the program and what behaviors the stakeholders believe to be associated with those desired program results. They collect information from stakeholders, feed it back to them, and help them establish their own roles and action plans. Much time

Exhibit 6-2: Management Roles in Succession Planning and Management:
A Grid

		Supporter	Opponent
Level of Effort	Active	△ Champions succession planning efforts vigorously △ Views management's role as one geared to developing and motivating people	△ Opposes succession planning vigorously △ Views management's role as one geared to making profits—even when that means de-motivating people
	Passive	△ Expresses general support for succession planning, with reservations about some approaches △ Wishes more "study" and "analysis" to be conducted	△ Prefers to devote time to other activities

Level of Support

may be spent individually, helping managers and employees at different levels understand what their roles should be.

Participant roles range along one continuum from aware to unaware and along another continuum from organizationally focused to personally/individually focused. Participants are defined as those tapped by the organization to be involved in the SP&M process. They are usually designated to be developed for one or more future positions. They may be aware or unaware that they have been thus designated by the organization as possible successors. They may be focused on satisfying their personal needs in the future (an individual focus) or on satisfying the organization's needs (an organizational focus).

To clarify roles, ask managers, facilitators, and participants to answer the following questions:

△ What are you presently doing to help the organization meet its succession needs in the future?
△ What should you do to help the organization establish a systematic SP&M program to meet succession needs in the future?

△ What do you believe should be the role(s) of managers and employees in supporting an effective SP&M program in the organization?

Pose these questions in group or staff meetings or circulate written surveys as appropriate. (If neither approach will work due to a desire to keep an SP&M program "secret," then ask top managers these questions and ask how roles to support SP&M may be clarified at other levels in the organization.)

Formulating a Mission Statement

Why is an organization undertaking a systematic succession planning program? What outcomes do stakeholder groups desire from it? These questions should be answered during the program start-up phase in order to achieve agreement among stakeholders about the program's purpose and desired results.

The lack of a mission statement has been called the "Achilles' heel" of SP&M programs. As Walter R. Mahler and Stephen J. Drotter have pointed out, these programs have too often been established without careful thought being given to purpose or desired outcomes. "Company after company," they write, "rushed into program mechanics. Time went by and disillusionment set in. The programs did not live up to their promises."[2] The reason for this, they believe, is that the program mission was never adequately clarified at the outset.

What Is a Mission Statement?

A mission statement describes the purpose of a program or the reason for its existence. Sometimes it is called a "purpose statement." *Mission* and *purpose* may be regarded as synonymous.

Formulating a mission statement is a first step in organizational planning. Writers on organizational strategy suggest that formulating organizational mission should precede formulating strategy. An organizational mission statement answers such questions as these: *Why is the organization in business? What results is it trying to achieve? What market does it serve? What products or services does it offer?*

Mission statements may also be formulated for organizational functions (such as operations, finance, marketing, or personnel), divisions, locations, or activities. At levels below the organization, mission statements for functions, divisions, locations, or activities should answer such questions as these:

△ Why does the function, division, location, or activity exist?
△ How does it contribute to achieving the organization's mission? strategic plans?
△ What outcomes or results are expected from it?

Mission statements may also provide philosophical statements: (*What do we believe?*), product or service descriptions (*What is to be made or sold?*), customer descriptions (*Whose needs are to be served?*), and rationale (*Why is the mission worth performing?*).

What Questions about Succession Planning and Management Should Be Answered by a Mission Statement?

Like any organizational effort, an SP&M program should have a mission statement to explain why it exists, what outcomes are desired from it, why those outcomes are valuable, what products or services will be offered, who will be served by the program, and other issues of importance.

However, mission statements for SP&M programs will vary across organizations. After all, not all programs are designed to serve the same purpose, achieve the same results, or offer the same products or services. So what specific issues should be addressed in a mission statement for an SP&M program?

One way to begin to answer that question is to focus on issues of particular importance to the organization. In that way, decision-makers will formulate the program's mission. Such issues may include:

1. What is a key position?
2. What is the definition of a high-potential (HiPo)?
3. What is the organization's responsibility in identifying HiPos, and what should it be?
4. What is the definition of an exemplary performer?
5. What is the organization's responsibility in identifying and rewarding exemplary performers? What should it be?
6. How should the organization fill key positions?
7. What percentage of vacancies in key positions should be filled from within? from without? handled through other means?
8. What percentage of key positions should have at least one identifiable *backup* (successor)?
9. In what percentage of key positions should there be *holes* (that is, no designated successors)?
10. What is the maximum time that exemplary performers should remain in their positions?
11. What should be the maximum allowable percentage of avoidable

turnover among high-potentials? ~~exemplary performers?~~ What should be done to reduce it?

12. What should be the maximum allowable percentage of *failures* in key positions after individual advancement?

13. What percentage of key positions should be filled with employees from legally protected labor groups—such as women, minorities, and the disabled?

14. How desirable are international assignments for designated successors?

15. How should HiPos be prepared for advancement?

16. What should be the role and responsibility of each employee and the HR Department in the process of developing HiPos?

17. How much should individual career goals be surfaced, considered, and tracked in succession planning?

18. How openly should the organization communicate with individuals who are identified to be HiPos about their status?

Of course, additional questions may also be posed to help clarify program purpose. Use the Worksheet appearing in Exhibit 6-3 to help clarify the mission of SP&M in an organization.

How Is a Mission Statement Prepared?

Prepare a mission statement by using any one of at least three possible approaches: "ask, formulate, and establish"; "recommend and listen"; or "facilitate an interactive debate." In the "ask, formulate, and establish" approach, someone takes an initial step by "asking" questions about succession planning in the organization. That launches a dialog to establish program mission. Often that duty falls to human resource generalists, human resource development specialists, or management development specialists, although others—such as the CEO, a vice president of human resources, or a specially appointed SP&M coordinator—could function as *change champions* to focus attention on the need for change. As a second step, change champions should compile the answers received from different decision-makers. They should then "formulate" and circulate a proposal based on those answers. As a third and final step, decision-makers hammer out their own responses, using the proposal as a starting point. In so doing, they establish a mission statement for an SP&M program.

A key advantage of this approach is that it requires little initial effort from busy top managers. Others undertake the groundbreaking work to collect information about SP&M, compile it, and base recommendations on it. (That is what officers in the armed services call "staff work.") On the other hand, a key disadvantage of this approach is that executives do not

Exhibit 6-3: A Worksheet to Formulate a Mission Statement for
Succession Planning and Management

Directions: Use this Worksheet to help you formulate the mission of the succession planning and management (SP&M) program in your organization. For each question posed in the left column, write an answer in the right column. When you finish, circulate the Worksheet among decision-makers. Compile their responses and then feed them back as a catalyst for subsequent decision-making about the mission statement of the succession planning and management program in the organization. Add paper or questions appropriate to your organization as necessary.

Questions	*Answers*
1. What is a key position?	
2. What is the definition of a high-potential (HiPo)?	
3. What is the organization's responsibility in identifying HiPos, and what should it be?	
4. What is the definition of an exemplary performer?	
5. What is the organization's responsibility in identifying and rewarding exemplary performers? What should it be?	
6. How should the organization fill key positions?	
7. What percentage of vacancies in key positions should be filled from within? from without? handled through other means?	
8. What percentage of key positions should have at least one identifiable *backup* (successor)?	
9. In what percentage of key positions should there be *holes* (that is, no designated successors)?	

(continues)

Exhibit 6-3: *(continued)*

Questions	Answers
10. What is the maximum time that exemplary performers should remain in their positions?	
11. What should be the maximum allowable percentage of avoidable turnover among high-potentials? exemplary performers? What should be done to reduce it?	
12. What should be the maximum allowable percentage of *failures* in key positions after individual advancement?	
13. What percentage of key positions should be filled with employees from legally protected labor groups—such as women, minorities, and the disabled?	
14. How desirable are international assignments for designated successors?	
15. How should HiPos be prepared for advancement?	
16. What should be the role and responsibility of each employee and the HR Department in the process of developing HiPos?	
17. How much should individual career goals be surfaced, considered, and tracked in succession planning?	
18. How openly should the organization communicate with individuals who are identified to be HiPos about their status?	

19. Write a draft mission statement for the succession planning and management program of the organization in this space. Be sure to answer these questions: (1) Why does the program exist? (2) How does it contribute to achieving the organization's mission and strategic plans? and (3) What outcomes or results should be expected from it?

---

participate in the information-gathering process, so they will have no collective ownership in the results. A subsequent step is thus required to capture their support and thereby achieve consensus.

The "recommend and listen" approach is different. It relies on considerable expertise by the HR generalists, HRD specialists, or management and leadership development specialists who use it. To use this approach, they *must* start out with a thorough grasp of the organization's culture, top management desires and values, and state-of-the-art SP&M practices. From that perspective, they "recommend" a starting point for the program, providing their own initial answers to the key questions about program mission listed in Exhibit 6-3. They prepare and circulate their recommendations for a systematic SP&M program, usually in proposal form. They then "listen" to reactions from key decision-makers, using the initial proposal as a catalyst to stimulate debate and discussion.

The advantage of this approach is that it usually has a shorter cycle time than "ask, formulate, and establish." It also relies more heavily on expert information about state-of-the-art SP&M practices outside the organization, thereby avoiding a tendency to "reinvent the wheel." But these advantages exist only when those using the approach have a thorough grasp of the organization's current SP&M problems and practices, culture, decision-maker preferences, and state-of-the-art practices. Otherwise, it can provoke time-consuming conflicts among decision-makers that will only prolong efforts to achieve top-level consensus.

The most complex approach is to "facilitate an interactive debate." HR generalists, HRD specialists, management and leadership development specialists, or others who use it function as *group facilitators* rather than as *expert-consultants*.

The first step is to prepare a forum for key decision-makers to carry out an "interactive debate" about the SP&M program's mission. While the forum's *content* may be dictated by the CEO—or even by members of the board of directors—HR professionals set up the *process* for the debate. (*Content* refers to the issues on which the forum will focus; *process* refers to the means by which those issues will be examined.) That usually means that the CEO and the HR professional (or the CEO and an external facilitator) must work closely together to plot the best means by which to explore the most important succession planning and management issues facing the organization. Such a debate may take the form of an off-site retreat lasting several days or several meetings spread across several months. During the debate, top-level decision-makers work through numerous small group activities to clarify the mission, philosophy, and procedures governing the SP&M program.

The second step is to summarize results. Someone must prepare a written statement that contains key points of agreement after the retreat or after each meeting. That task usually falls to an HR professional or to an external facilitator, who prepares a presentation or handout. However, the CEO or other top-level decision-makers feeds these key points back to the retreat participants.

The third and final step is to conduct follow-up activities to ensure agreement. Follow-up activities may be conducted in several ways. One way is to hold a follow-up meeting with the participants to surface any points of confusion or disagreement. This can be done in small groups (at the end of a retreat) or individually with participants (after the retreat). Another way is to establish a top-level committee to govern SP&M in the organization and/or at various levels or locations of the organization.

An interactive debate does focus initial attention on key issues that should be addressed to formulate a clear program mission statement. That is an advantage of the approach. But it also requires much time and strong personal involvement from the CEO and others. That is its chief disadvantage.

Writing Policy and Procedures

Why is the organization undertaking an SP&M program? What results are desired from it? How can consistent program operations be ensured? Decision-makers may answers these questions by preparing written program policy and procedures.

What Is a Succession Planning and Management Policy, and What Are Succession Planning and Management Procedures?

Policy is a natural outgrowth of mission. Typically stated in writing, it places the organization on the record as supporting or opposing an approach to action.

Procedures flow from policy and provide guidelines for applying it. Writing a policy on SP&M clarifies what the organization seeks to do; writing procedures clarify how the policy will be applied. Typical components of an SP&M policy include a mission statement, philosophical statements, and procedures. A sample SP&M policy appears in Exhibit 6-4.

How Are Policies and Procedures Written?

Succession planning and management policy and procedures should usually be written only after decision-makers agree on program mission and goals. Crises, problems, or issues of importance should provide clues about what to include in the policy and procedures, and they will usually be implicit in the mission. As decision-makers prepare a mission statement they will typically consider what may be rightfully included in a written program policy and procedure.

In many cases the appropriate approach to use in writing policies and procedures stems from the approach used in preparing the mission statement. For instance, if an "ask and formulate" approach was used in formulating the mission statement, then prepare a draft SP&M policy and procedures to accompany the proposal submitted to executives. If a "recommend and listen" approach was chosen when preparing the mission statement, then draft an SP&M policy and procedures to accompany the mission statement in the initial proposal to management. If the approach chosen was to "facilitate an interactive debate," then committees in the organization will usually be the means by which to draft policy and procedures, oversee refinements, and issue updates or modifications to policy and procedures.

Identifying Target Groups

Who should be the focus of the SP&M program? Should the program be geared to top-level executive ranks only? Should it encompass other groups, levels, or parts of the organization? Answering these questions requires decision-makers to identify target groups.

Most of what has been written about SP&M programs has directed attention to replacing top-level executive positions. Substantial research has been conducted on SP&M for the CEO;[3] other writings have focused on the CEO's immediate reports. Relatively little has been written about SP&M for other groups, though many experts on the subject concede that the need has never been greater for effective SP&M efforts at lower levels. Indeed, interest in multiskilling, team-based management, and cross-training stems from the recognition that more time, resources, and attention

Exhibit 6-4: A Sample Succession Planning and Management Policy

Mission Statement

The purpose of the succession planning and management program in [*company or organizational name*] is to ensure a ready supply of internal talent for key positions at all times. This organization is fully committed to equal employment opportunity for all employees, regardless of race, creed, sex, national origin, sexual orientation, or disability.

Policy and Philosophy

It is the policy of the [*company or organizational name*] to help employees develop to the full extent of their potential and, to the extent possible for the organization, to help them achieve realistic career goals that satisfy both individual and organizational requirements.

This organization is firmly committed to promotion from within, whenever qualified talent is available, for key positions. This organization is also firmly committed to helping employees develop their potential so that they are prepared and qualified to assume positions in line with individual career goals and organizational requirements.

Procedures

At least once each year, the organization will sponsor:

△ *A replacement planning activity* that will assess how well the organization is positioned to meet replacement requirements by promotions or other personnel movements from within.

△ *Individual performance appraisal* to assess how well individuals are meeting their current job requirements.

△ *Individual potential assessment* to assess how well individuals are presently equipped for future advancement. Unlike performance appraisal—which is typically focused on past or present performance— the focus of individual potential assessment will be on the future.

△ *Individual development planning* to provide the means for action plans to help individuals narrow the developmental gap between what they already know or can do and what they must know or do to qualify for advancement.

The succession planning and management program will rely heavily on the processes listed above to identify individuals suitable for advancement. The program will work closely in tandem with an in-house career planning program, which is designed to help individuals identify their career goals and take proactive steps to achieve them.

must be focused on systematically developing human capabilities at all levels and across all groups.

The results of my 1999 survey on SP&M practices revealed that the respondents' organizations are not consistently identifying *and* developing successors. (See Exhibit 6-5.)

Exhibit 6-5: Targeted Groups for Succession Planning and Management

Succession planning may not be carried out with all groups in an organization. For each group listed below, indicate whether *your* organization makes a deliberate effort to identify and develop successors.

	Group	Does Your Organization Make a Deliberate Effort to Identify Successors in This Group?		Does Your Organization Make a Deliberate Effort to Develop Successors in This Group?	
		Frequency	Percentage	Frequency	Percentage
A	Executives (Yes)	12	100.00%	10	83.33%
	Executives (No)	0	0.00%	2	16.67%
B	Middle Managers (Yes)	10	83.33%	9	75.00%
	Middle Managers (No)	2	16.67%	3	25.00%
C	Supervisors (Yes)	5	41.67%	4	33.33%
	Supervisors (No)	7	58.33%	8	66.67%
D	Professionals (Yes)	5	41.67%	5	41.67%
	Professionals (No)	7	58.33%	7	58.33%
E	Technical workers (Engineers, computer specialists) (Yes)	4	33.33%	4	33.33%
	Technical workers (Engineers, computer specialists) (No)	8	66.67%	8	66.67%
F	Sales workers (Yes)	3	25.00%	1	8.33%
	Sales workers (No)	9	75.00%	11	91.67%
G	Clerical and secretarial workers (Yes)	3	25.00%	1	8.33%
H	Clerical and secretarial workers (No)	9	75.00%	11	91.67%

*Source: William J. Rothwell, *Results of a Survey on Succession Planning and Management Practices*, unpublished survey results (University Park, Pa.: The Pennsylvania State University, 2000).

Establishing Initial Targets

Where exactly is the organization weakest in bench strength? The answer to that question should provide a clue about where to establish initial targets for the SP&M program. (See the Activity in Exhibit 6-6. If necessary, circulate it to top managers—or ask them to complete it in an initial program kickoff meeting or mission statement retreat.)

Direct attention to three specific areas first, since they are a common source of problems: successors for top management positions; successors for first-line supervisory positions; and successors for unique, tough-to-fill technical or professional positions.

Top management positions are fewest in absolute numbers, but they are often critically important for formulating and implementing organizational strategy. They may grow weak in bench strength in organizations that experience significant employee reductions in the middle management ranks as a result of forced layoffs, employee buyouts, or early retirement offers.

Supervisory positions are largest in absolute numbers, so continuing turnover and other personnel movements leave these ranks subject to greatest need for replacements. As a port of entry to the management ranks, supervision is also critically important because many middle managers and executives start out in the supervisory ranks. Supervisors are often promoted from the hourly ranks, lacking management experience, or are hired from outside the organization. They are areas of weakness in organizations that have not planned management development programs or that provide little or no incentive for movement into supervision—such as organizations in which unionized hourly workers earn substantially more than supervisors, who are ineligible for overtime pay but must work overtime anyway.

Tough-to-fill technical or professional positions are often limited in number. Managers may be kept awake at night, tossing and turning, at the mere thought of losing a member of this group because recruiting or training a successor on short notice is difficult or nearly impossible.

Choose one group—or all three—as initial targets for the SP&M program if the results of Activity 6-6 demonstrate the need. Otherwise, use the results of Activity 6-6 to identify the initial targets for the program. Verify the groups chosen with decision-makers.

Expanding Succession Planning and Management to Other Groups

Although the organization may have neither the time nor the resources to establish a systematic SP&M program that encompasses all people and positions, decision-makers may agree that such a goal is worth achieving

Exhibit 6-6: An Activity for Identifying Initial Targets for Succession Planning and Management Activities

Directions: Use this activity to identify initial target groups for the SP&M program in an organization. For each job category listed in the left column below, indicate a priority (1 = highest priority) in the center column. Then, in the right column, briefly explain why the job category was assigned that level of priority. Circulate this activity to decision-makers and ask them to complete it. Compile the results and feed them back to decision-makers to emphasize what job categories were generally perceived to be the rightful target for the SP&M program. Add paper as necessary. (If appropriate, modify the list of job categories so they coincide precisely with any special labels/titles associated with them in the organization.)

Job Category	*Priority* *(1 = highest)*	*What is your reasoning?*
1. Executives	_____	
2. Individuals preparing for executive positions	_____	
3. Middle managers	_____	
4. Individuals preparing for middle management	_____	
5. Supervisors	_____	
6. Individuals preparing for supervision	_____	
7. Professional workers	_____	
8. Individuals preparing to be professional workers	_____	
9. Technical workers	_____	
10. Individuals preparing to become technical workers	_____	
11. Sales workers	_____	
12. Individuals preparing to become sales workers	_____	
13. Clerical workers	_____	

(continues)

Exhibit 6-6: *(continued)*

14. Individuals preparing to become clerical workers	_____
15. Hourly production or service workers	_____
16. Individuals preparing to become hourly production or service workers	_____
17. Other job categories	_____

eventually. For that reason, periodically administer Activity 6-6 to decision-makers to assess which groups should be targeted for inclusion and in what priority order.

Of course, decision-makers may wish to prioritize groups in ways other than by job category. For instance, they may feel that bench strength is weakest in any of the following areas:

△ Geographical locations
△ Product or service lines
△ Functions of organizational operation
△ Experience with specific industry-related or product/service-related problems
△ Experience with international markets

Ask decision-makers about where they perceive the organization to be weak in bench strength. Then target the SP&M program initially to improving bench strength at that level. While continuing efforts at that level, gradually extend the effort to include other groups.

Setting Program Priorities

Much work needs to be done to establish a systematic SP&M program. But rarely, if ever, can it be accomplished all at once. Someone has to set program priorities, both short-term and long-term. That may be done by top-level decision-makers, a full-time or part-time SP&M coordinator, or a committee representing different groups or functions within the organization.

Initial priorities should be set to address the organization's most pressing problems—and to rectify the most serious weaknesses in bench strength. Subsequent priorities should be set to reflect a long-term plan for systematic SP&M in the organization.

In addition to the activities already described in this chapter—such as clarifying roles, formulating a mission statement, writing a program policy, clarifying program procedures, and identifying the program's targeted groups—other actions will have to be undertaken. Priorities should be established on what actions to take—and when—depending on the organization's needs. These activities include:

△ Preparing an action plan to guide program start-up
△ Communicating the action plan
△ Training managers and employees for their roles in the systematic SP&M program
△ Organizing kickoff meetings and periodic briefing meetings to discuss the program
△ Counseling managers on handling unique succession planning problems—such as dealing with poor performers, managing high performers, grooming and coaching high-potentials, addressing the special problems of plateaued workers, and managing workplace diversity
△ Defining present and future work requirements, processes, activities, responsibilities, success factors, and competence
△ Appraising present individual performance
△ Assessing future individual potential
△ Providing individuals with the means by which to carry out career planning within the organization
△ Tracking performance and potential
△ Preparing and following through on Individual Development Plans (IDPs) to help close gaps between what people know or do and what they must know or do in the future to qualify for advancement and ensure leadership continuity
△ Tracking innovative efforts to meet replacement needs
△ Establishing effective approaches to evaluating the benefits of systematic SP&M
△ Designing and implementing programs geared to special groups (such as high-potentials, plateaued workers, high performers, or low performers) or to meet special needs (such as reducing voluntary turnover of key employees after downsizing, handling cultural diversity, using succession planning in autonomous work teams, and integrating SP&M with such other organizational initiatives as quality or customer service)

Depending on an organization's unique needs, however, some issues demand immediate attention—and action.

Take this opportunity to consider program priorities in the organization. Use the Activity that appears in Exhibit 6-7 to establish initial program priorities in the organization. (If you are the coordinator of the SP&M program, you may choose to circulate the activity to key decision-makers for their reactions, feed back the results to them, and use their reactions as a starting point for setting program priorities. Alternatively, share the activity with a standing committee on SP&M established in the organization, if one exists. Ask committee members to complete the activity and then use the results as a basis for setting initial program priorities.) Revisit the priorities at least annually. Gear action plans according to the program priorities that are established.

Addressing the Legal Framework in Succession Planning and Management

Legal issues should not be forgotten in SP&M. That is especially true because employee complaints filed with the Equal Employment Opportunity Commission have been on the increase in recent years. Those responsible for formulating and implementing an SP&M program should familiarize themselves with government laws, rules, regulations, and other provisions—both in the United States and, if they do business internationally, in other nations as appropriate—that may have a bearing on the program. Competent legal advice should be sought when the organization's decision-makers have reached agreement on the goals and objectives of the SP&M program. Additionally, employers should take special care to avoid real or perceived employment discrimination of all kinds based on race, age, sexual orientation, disability, and other non-employment-related issues in SP&M programs. Private sector employers should also take care to ensure that SP&M programs are consistent with company human resource policies and procedures as described in company documents (such as employee handbooks or policy and procedure manuals). Public sector employers falling under state or federal civil service rules should double-check their program descriptions to ensure that SP&M programs are consistent with policies and procedures governing hiring, promotion, training, and other policies.

A complex web of employment law exists at the federal government level in the United States. Key national employment laws are summarized in Exhibit 6-8. Under the supremacy clause of the U.S. Constitution, federal laws take precedence over local laws unless no federal law exists or federal law specifically stipulates that local laws may be substituted for federal law. In addition to national labor laws, each state, county, and municipality may enact and enforce special laws, rules, regulations, or ordinances affecting

Exhibit 6-7: An Activity for Establishing Program Priorities in Succession Planning and Management

---

Directions: Use this activity to help establish priorities for the succession planning program in an organization. For each activity listed in the left column below, set a priority by circling a number for it in the right column. Use the following scale:

1 = A top priority that should be acted on *now*

2 = A secondary priority that is important but that can wait awhile for action

3 = A tertiary priority that should only be acted on after items prioritized as *1* or *2* have received attention

Circulate this activity among decision-makers as appropriate. If you do so, compile their responses and then feed them back as a catalyst for subsequent decision-making. Add paper as necessary. (You may also wish to add other activities of interest.)

	Priority		
Activity	*Top* *1*	*Secondary* *2*	*Tertiary* *3*
1. Preparing an action plan to guide program start-up	*1*	*2*	*3*
2. Communicating the action plan	*1*	*2*	*3*
3. Training managers and employees for their roles in the systematic succession planning program	*1*	*2*	*3*
4. Organizing kickoff meetings and periodic briefing meetings to discuss the program	*1*	*2*	*3*
5. Counseling managers on handling unique succession planning problems	*1*	*2*	*3*
6. Defining present and future work requirements, processes, activities, responsibilities, success factors, and competence	*1*	*2*	*3*
7. Appraising present individual performance	*1*	*2*	*3*
8. Assessing future individual potential	*1*	*2*	*3*
9. Providing individuals with the means by which to carry out career planning within the organization	*1*	*2*	*3*

(continues)

Exhibit 6-7: *(continued)*

		Priority	
Activity	Top 1	Secondary 2	Tertiary 3
10. Tracking performance and potential	1	2	3
11. Preparing, and following through on, Individual Development Plans (IDPs)	1	2	3
12. Using, and tracking, innovative efforts to meet replacement needs	1	2	3
13. Establishing effective approaches to evaluating the benefits of systematic succession planning	1	2	3
14. Designing and implementing programs geared to meeting special needs	1	2	3
15. Other (specify)	1	2	3

employment in a local jurisdiction. The latter may influence succession planning and management practices.

Of special importance to SP&M programs is *The Uniform Guidelines on Employee Selection Procedures*. Private sector employers must ensure that all employment decisions are in compliance with these procedures. If they do not do so, they may risk a grievance under the Equal Employment Opportunity Commission or a "right to sue" letter when mediation efforts with the EEOC fail. Public sector employers may find themselves falling under different standards established by the applicable branch of government.

Establishing Strategies for Rolling Out a Succession Planning and Management Program

As an increasing number of employers begin to implement SP&M programs, they face dilemmas in how to roll them out. That is a frequent issue for consultants specializing in this area.

I advise my clients to start at the top, with the CEO. The CEO is the real "customer" who must be satisfied, and it is wise to "follow the generations" in a roll-out strategy. That means it is best to begin with the CEO and select his or her immediate successors first—a simple replacement

(Text continues on page 146.)

Exhibit 6-8: U.S. Labor Laws

Name of Law and Date of Enactment	Legal Citation	Brief Description of Key Provisions
Davis-Bacon Act (1931)	40 U.S.C. and sect; 276 et seq.	The Davis-Bacon Act applies to federal construction and repair contracts over $2,000. The Act requires contractors to pay their employees a specified minimum wage determined by the Secretary of Labor to be prevailing for similar work in that geographic area. Over 60 other federal laws make compliance with Davis-Bacon provisions a precondition for state and local contracts when a portion of the funding for those contracts comes from the federal government. The Act is enforced by the Wage and Hour division of the Department of Labor.
The National Labor Relations Act (Wagner Act and Taft-Hartley Act) (1947)	29 U.S.C. and sect; 151	The National Labor Relations Act protects the right of employees to choose whether to be represented by a union. The Act protects against coercion by employers or unions in making this choice and establishes the ground rules for union representation elections. The Act establishes collective bargaining between employers and unions. The Act is enforced by the National Labor Relations Board.
Fair Labor Standards Act (1938)	29 U.S.C. and sect; 201 et seq	The Fair Labor Standards Act provides minimum wage and overtime requirements. Under the FLSA all nonexempt employees are entitled to cash overtime for all hours worked over 40 in a workweek. The Act is enforced by the Wage and Hour Division of the Department of Labor and private lawsuits.

(continues)

Exhibit 6-8: *(continued)*

Name of Law and Date of Enactment	*Legal Citation*	*Brief Description of Key Provisions*
Labor-Management Reporting and Disclosure Act (Landrum-Griffin Act) (1959)	29 U.S.C. and sect; 401 et seq	The Labor-Management Reporting and Disclosure Act, or the Landrum-Griffin Act, establishes a set of rights for employees who are members of unions. They include the right to vote, attend meetings, meet and assemble with other members, and freely express views and opinions. The Act also requires all labor unions to adopt a constitution and bylaws, and contains certain reporting requirements for labor organizations, their officers, and employees. This Act is enforced by the Office of Labor Management Standards of the Department of Labor.
Contract Work Hours Safety Standards Act (1962)	40 U.S.C. and sect; 327 et seq	This Act sets a standard 40-hour workweek for employees of federal contractors and regulates work in excess of the standard week including the requirement to pay overtime. The Act is enforced by the Wage and Hour Division of the Department of Labor.
Equal Pay Act (1963)	29 U.S.C. and sect; 201 et seq	The Equal Pay Act prohibits discrimination in pay and benefits on the basis of sex for jobs in the same establishment that require equal skill, effort, and responsibility and which are performed under similar working conditions. The Act is enforced by the Equal Employment Opportunity Commission.
Title VII of the Civil Rights Act (1964)	42 U.S.C. and sect; 2000 et seq.	Title VII makes it unlawful for an employer with 15 or more employees to discriminate against individuals with respect to hiring, compensation, terms, conditions, and privileges of employment on the basis of race, color, religion, national origin, or sex. Title VII is enforced by the Equal Employment Opportunity Commission.

Executive Order 11246 (1965)	42 U.S.C.A. and sect; 2000e	Executive Order 11246 prohibits job discrimination by employers holding Federal contracts or subcontracts on the basis of race, color, sex, national origin, or religion and requires affirmative action to ensure equality of opportunity in all aspects of employment. The Order is enforced by the Office of Federal Compliance Contract Programs of the Department of Labor.
Service Contract Act (1965)	41 U.S.C. and sect; 351 et seq.	This Act is analogous to the Davis-Bacon Act in the area of service contracts performed by private companies doing work for the federal government. The Act requires contractors that provide services to the federal government to provide their employees a specified minimum wage and fringe benefits plan determined by the Secretary of Labor to be prevailing in the locality. The Act is enforced by the Wage and Hour Division of the Department of Labor.
Age Discrimination in Employment Act (1967)	29 U.S.C. and sect; 621 et seq.	The Age Discrimination in Employment Act, or ADEA, makes it unlawful for an employer with 20 or more employees to discriminate against individuals that are 40 years or older, with respect to hiring, compensation, terms, conditions, and privileges of employment on the basis of age. The Act is enforced by the Equal Employment Opportunity Commission.
Federal Coal Mine Health and Safety Act (1969)	30 U.S.C. and sect; 801 et seq.	This Act empowers the Secretaries of Labor and Health and Human Services to promulgate health and safety standards for the mining industry. The Act is enforced by the Mine Safety and Health Administration of the Department of Labor.

(continues)

Exhibit 6-8: *(continued)*

Name of Law and Date of Enactment	Legal Citation	Brief Description of Key Provisions
Occupational Safety and Health Act (1970)	29 U.S.C. and sect; 553, 651 et seq.	The Occupational Safety and Health Act, OSHA, requires all employers to provide a workplace that is free from recognized hazards that cause, or are likely to cause, death or serious physical harm to employees. The Act also establishes the Occupational Safety and Health Administration which is responsible for promulgating workplace safety standards and regulations for various industries. The Act is enforced by the Occupational Safety and Health Administration.
Rehabilitation Act (1973)	29 U.S.C. and sect; 701 et seq.	The Rehabilitation Act prohibits employers that receive federal grants, loans, or contracts from discriminating in their employment practices against individuals with disabilities. The Act is enforced by the Department of Labor.
Employee Retirement Income Security Act (1974)	29 U.S.C. and sect; 301, 1001 et seq.	The Employment Retirement Income Security Act, or ERISA, governs the operation of pensions and retirement benefits provided by private sector employers to their employees. The Act does not require that employers provide such benefits, but regulates the conduct of employers that do provide such plans. The Act is enforced by the Pension and Welfare Benefits Administration of the Department of Labor.
Vietnam Era Veterans' Readjustment Assistance Act (1974)	38 U.S.C. and sect; 4301	VEVRAA makes it unlawful for employers to discriminate against veterans of the Armed Forces in their employment practices. It also provides veterans with certain reemployment, seniority, health benefit, and pension rights with respect to prior employment. The Act is enforced by the Office of Veterans Employment and Training of the Department of Labor.

Black Lung Benefits Reform Act (1977)	30 U.S.C. and sect; 901 et seq.	This Act provides benefits to coal miners who are totally disabled due to pneumoconiosis and to the surviving dependents of miners whose death was a result of this disease. The Act is enforced by the Office of Workers' Compensation Programs of the Department of Labor.
Labor-Management Cooperation Act (1978)	29 U.S.C.A. and sect; 141 note, 173, 175a.	The Labor-Management Cooperation Act encourages the establishment and operation of joint labor-management activities designed to improve labor relations, job security, and organizational effectiveness. The Act authorizes the Federal Mediation and Conciliation Service to provide assistance, contracts, and grants to joint labor-management committees that promote these purposes.
Pregnancy Discrimination Act (1978)	42 U.S.C. and sect; 2000 et seq.	The PDA, a 1978 amendment to Title VII of the 1964 Civil Rights Act, makes it unlawful for an employer to discriminate on the basis of pregnancy or childbirth. The Act is enforced by the Equal Employment Opportunity Commission.
Multi-Employer Pension Plan Amendments Act (1980)	29 U.S.C. and sect; 1001a et seq.	This Act regulates the operation of multi-employer pension plans and provides protection and guarantees for the participants and beneficiaries of distressed plans. The Act is enforced by the Pension and Welfare Benefits Administration of the Department of Labor.
Job Training Partnership Act (1982)	29 U.S.C. and sect; 1501 et seq.	This Act creates Private Industry Councils composed of business owners and executives as well as representatives of organized labor to assist state and local governments in the development and oversight of job training programs. The Act is enforced by the Employment and Training Administration of the Department of Labor.

(continues)

Exhibit 6-8: *(continued)*

Name of Law and Date of Enactment	Legal Citation	Brief Description of Key Provisions
Migrant and Seasonal Agricultural Protection Act (1983)	29 U.S.C. and sect; 1801 et seq.	This Act governs the terms and conditions of employment for migrant and seasonal agricultural workers and regulates the employment practices of agricultural employers, agricultural associations, and farm labor contractors. The Act is enforced by the Wage and Hour Division of the Department of Labor and by private lawsuits.
Immigration Reform and Control Act (1986)	29 U.S.C. and sect; 1802 et seq.	The Immigration Reform and Control Act, or IRCA, requires employers to verify that applicants for employment are authorized to work in the United States. The Act provides civil and criminal penalties for knowingly employing unauthorized aliens and also prohibits discrimination based on national origin or citizenship if the alien is authorized to work. The Act is enforced by the Department of Justice and the Immigration and Naturalization Service.
Economic Dislocation and Worker Adjustment Assistance Act (1988)	29 U.S.C. and sect; 1651–53	This Act provides federal funds to the states for basic readjustment and retraining of workers who have been terminated because of layoffs or plant closures and who are unlikely to return to their previous occupations. The Act is managed by the Employment Standards Administration of the Department of Labor.
Employee Polygraph Protection Act (1988)	29 U.S.C. and sect; 2001 et seq.	This Act makes it unlawful for an employer to require, request, suggest, or cause an employee or applicant to submit to a lie detector test. In addition, it prohibits the employer from threatening or taking any adverse employment action against an employee or applicant

		who refuses to take a lie detector test. The Act is enforced by a private right of action in the federal district courts.
Worker Adjustment and Retraining Notification Act (1988)	29 U.S.C. and sect; 2101et seq.	The Worker Adjustment and Retraining Notification Act, or WARN, requires employers with 100 or more employees to give 60 days advance notice to employees of impending plant closings or layoffs involving 50 or more employees. The Act is enforced by private lawsuits.
Whistleblower Protection Statutes (1989)	10 U.S.C. and sect; 2409; 12 U.S.C.; 1831j; 31 U.S.C. and 5328; 41 U.S.C. 265.	The Whistleblower Protection statutes protect employees of financial institutions and government contractors from discriminatory and retaliatory employment actions as a result of reporting violations of the law to federal authorities. The Act is enforced by the Wage and Hour Division of the Department of Labor.
Americans with Disabilities Act (1990)	42 U.S.C. and sect; 12101 et seq.	The Americans with Disabilities Act, or ADA, makes it unlawful for an employer with 15 or more employees to discriminate against qualified individuals with disabilities with respect to hiring, compensation, terms, conditions, and privileges of employment. The Act is enforced by the Equal Employment Opportunity Commission.
Older Workers Benefit Protection Act (1990)	29 U.S.C. and sect; 623 et seq.	This amendment to the Age Discrimination in Employment Act makes it unlawful for an employer to discriminate with respect to employee benefits on the basis of age. It also regulates early retirement incentive programs. The Act is enforced by the Equal Employment Opportunity Commission.
Civil Rights Act (1991)	42 U.S.C. and sect; 1981 et seq.	The Civil Rights Act of 1991 amended the 1964 act, and the Americans with Disabilities Act (ADA), to allow compensatory and punitive damages, but places

(continues)

Exhibit 6-8: *(continued)*

Name of Law and Date of Enactment	Legal Citation	Brief Description of Key Provisions
		caps on the amounts that can be awarded. The Act also provides for jury trials in suits brought under these laws.
Family and Medical Leave Act (1991)	29 U.S.C. and sect; 2601 et seq.	The Family and Medical Leave Act requires that employers with 50 or more employees provide up to 12 weeks of unpaid leave, within any 12-month period, to employees for the care of a newborn or adopted child, for the care of a seriously ill family member, or for treatment and care of the employee's own serious medical condition. The Act is enforced by the Wage and Hour Division of the Department of Labor.
Congressional Accountability Act (1995)	2 U.S.C. and sect; 1301 et seq.	When many of the above laws were enacted, Congress was expressly exempted from compliance. The Congressional Accountability Act extends coverage of eleven laws to Congress in its capacity as an employer.

Source: Labor Policy Association (1997). U.S. Employment Laws. Website: http/www.lpa.org/lpa/laws.html. Washington, D.C.: Labor Policy Association.

strategy. Second, the CEO and his immediate reports—that is, the senior executive team—should be next. That, too, is a simple replacement plan. However, as an internal consultant from human resources or an external consultant works with the senior executive team, they begin to understand what issues are important in such a program and experience it firsthand. Their involvement and participation ensures their ownership and understanding. Third, middle managers are included. That is a third-generation plan. As middle managers are included, the program formulated by the senior executives is fire-tested with middle managers. That sets the stage for the talent pools and skill inventories that characterize generation-four and -five plans.

Of particular importance is the communication strategy. That is often an issue that should be addressed separately from the action plan. The CEO and senior executives should pay careful attention to how the SP&M

programs should be described to middle managers and other stakeholders inside and outside the organization. If they do not give special attention to the communication strategy so as to make the business goals clear and the policies and procedures clear, they risk a broad-scale failure of the plan when it is implemented. Human resource practitioners cannot do it all. They need to work with the CEO and senior executive team—and sometimes with external consultants as well—to craft a communication strategy to explain how the SP&M program works and why it exists.

Summary

Starting up a systematic SP&M program usually requires an organization's decision-makers to:

- △ Clarify the desired program roles of management, employees, facilitators, and participants
- △ Prepare a program mission statement
- △ Write a program policy and procedures
- △ Identify groups targeted for program action, both initially and subsequently
- △ Establish program priorities
- △ Address the legal framework in succession planning and management
- △ Plan strategies for rolling out a succession planning and management program

The next steps in starting up the program are covered in the next chapter. They include: preparing a program action plan, communicating it, training management and employees for enacting their roles in the program, conducting program kickoff meetings, conducting program briefing sessions, and conducting counseling sessions.

Chapter 7
Refining the Program

Beyond start-up, some additional steps will usually need to be taken before a systematic succession planning and management (SP&M) program becomes operational. These steps include:

- △ Preparing a program action plan
- △ Communicating the action plan
- △ Conducting SP&M meetings
- △ Training on SP&M
- △ Counseling managers to deal with SP&M issues uniquely affecting them and their work areas

This chapter briefly reviews each topic listed above, providing tips for effectively refining an SP&M program in its early stages.

Preparing a Program Action Plan

Setting initial program priorities is only a beginning. Turning priorities into realities requires dedication, hard work, and effective strategy. Preparing a program action plan helps conceptualize the strategy for implementing systematic SP&M in the organization.

The Value of an Action Plan

An *action plan* activates and energizes an SP&M program. It is a natural next step after setting program priorities because it indicates how they will be met.

Components of an Effective Action Plan

An action plan is akin to a project plan. It answers all the journalistic questions:

- △ *Who* should take action?
- △ *What* action should they take?
- △ *When* should the action be taken?
- △ *Where* should the action be taken?
- △ *Why* should the action be taken?
- △ *How* should action be taken?

In this way, an action plan provides a basis for program accountability.

How to Establish the Action Plan

Take several steps when establishing an action plan. First, list priorities. Second, indicate what actions must be taken to achieve each priority. Third, assign responsibility for each action. Fourth, indicate where the actions must be performed. Fifth and finally, assign deadlines or time indicators to indicate when the actions should be completed—or when each stage of completion should be reached. The result of these steps should be a concrete action plan to guide the SP&M program. (Fill in the Worksheet appearing in Exhibit 7-1 to clarify the program action plan.)

Communicating the Action Plan

Few results will be achieved if an action plan is established and then kept secret. Some effort must be made to communicate the action plan to those affected by it and to those expected to take responsibility for participating in its implementation.

Problems in Communicating

Communicating about an SP&M program presents unique problems that are rarely encountered in other areas of organizational operations. The reason: many top managers are hesitant to share information about their programs widely inside or outside their organizations.

They are reluctant to share information outside the organization for fear that succession plans will reveal too much about the organization's strategy. If an SP&M program is closely linked to, and supportive of, strategic plans—and that is desirable—then revealing information about it may tip off canny competitors to what the organization intends to do.

They are reluctant to share information inside the organization for fear that it will lead to negative consequences. High-performing or high-potential employees who are aware that they are designated successors for key positions may:

Exhibit 7-1: A Worksheet for Preparing an Action Plan to Establish the Succession Planning and Management Program

Directions: Use this Worksheet to help you formulate an action plan to guide the start-up of an SP&M program in your organization. In column 1, list program priorities (*what* must be done first, second, third, and so on?) and provide a rationale (*why* are these priorities?). In column 2, list what tasks must be carried out to transform priorities into realities (*how* will priorities be achieved?). In column 3, assign responsibility for each task. In column 4, indicate (if applicable) special locations (*where* must the tasks be accomplished or the priorities achieved?). In column 5, assign deadlines or time indicators.

Circulate this Worksheet among decision-makers—especially top-level managers who are participating on an SP&M committee. Ask each decision-maker to complete the Worksheet individually. Then compile their responses, feed them back, and meet to achieve consensus on this detailed action plan. Add paper and/or priorities as necessary.

Column 1	Column 2	Column 3	Column 4	Column 5
Program Priorities and Rationale	*Tasks*	*Responsibility*	*Location(s)*	*Deadlines/ Time Indicators*
(By when should each task be completed? What must be done in order of importance, and why are these priorities?)	(How will priorities be achieved?)	(Who is responsible for each task?)	(Where must tasks be accomplished, if that is applicable?)	(Assign deadlines or time indicators)

- △ Become complacent because they think advancement is guaranteed. This is called the *crown prince phenomenon*.
- △ Grow disenchanted if organizational conditions change and their status as successors is no longer assured.
- △ "Hold themselves for ransom" by threatening to leave unless they receive escalating raises or advancement opportunities.

Of course, the opposite can also happen: If high-potentials are kept unaware of their status, they may seek advancement opportunities elsewhere. Equally bad, good performers who are *not* presently identified as successors for key positions may grow disenchanted and demotivated, even though they may already be demonstrating that they have that potential. A poorly handled communication strategy can lead to increases in avoidable or critical turnover, thereby costing the organization precious talent and driving up training costs.

Choosing Effective Approaches

As part of the SP&M program, decision-makers should review how the organization has historically communicated about succession issues—and consider how it should communicate about them. Establishing a *consistent* communication strategy is vital.

Valuable clues about the organization's historical communication strategy may be found in how key job incumbents were treated previously and how wage and salary matters are handled. If key job incumbents did not know that they were designated successors before they were eligible for advancement or if the organization's practice is not to publish salary schedules, then it is likely that a "closed" communication strategy is preferred. That means information is kept secret, and successors are not alerted to their status. On the other hand, if key job incumbents did know that they were designated successors before they were promoted or if salary schedules are published, then an "open" communication strategy is preferred. That means people are treated with candor.

Choose an approach to communication based on the preferences of decision-makers. If their preferences seem unclear, ask questions to discover what they are:

△ How, if at all, should employees be informed about the SP&M program? (For instance, should the mission statement and/or policy and procedures on SP&M be circulated?)

△ How should the organization characterize the roles of employee performance appraisal, individual potential assessment, and individual development planning in SP&M?

△ How should decisions about individual selection, promotion, demotion, transfer, or development in place be explained to those who ask?

△ What problems will result from informing individuals about their status in succession plans? from not informing them?

△ What problems will result from informing employees about the SP&M program? What problems will result from *not* informing them?

Ultimately, the organization should choose a communication policy that is consistent with the answers to the questions above. Often the best approach is to communicate openly about the SP&M program in general—but conceal the basis for individual personnel actions in line with good business practice and individual privacy laws. Individuals should be encouraged to develop themselves for the future—but should understand, at the same time, that nothing is being "promised"; rather, qualifying is a first step but does not, in itself, guarantee advancement.

Conducting Succession Planning and Management Meetings

It is a rare organization that does not need at least one meeting to lay the foundation for a systematic SP&M program. Often, four meetings are necessary during start-up: one of top decision-makers to verify the need for the program; a second, larger meeting to seek input from major stakeholders; a third, smaller committee meeting of change champions to hammer out a proposal to guide program start-up; and a fourth meeting to introduce the program and reinforce its importance to management employees who will play critical roles in cultivating, nurturing, coaching, and preparing the leaders of the future at all levels. Later, periodic meetings are necessary to review program progress and ensure continuous improvement.

Meeting 1: Verifying the Need

In the first meeting, a handpicked group—usually limited to the "top of the house"—meets to verify that a genuine need exists to make SP&M a more systematic process. In this meeting it is common to review current practices and problems that stem from an informal approach to SP&M. This meeting usually stems directly from a crisis or from the request of one who wants to introduce a new way to carry out SP&M.

Meeting 2: Seeking Input

In the second meeting, a larger group of key decision-makers is usually assembled to surface SP&M problems and to galvanize action. This meeting may take the form of an executive retreat. Executives should properly be involved in the program formulation process, since—regardless of the initial targeted group for the SP&M program and its initial priorities—such a program has important strategic implications for the organization. Despite recent moves to involve employees in organizational decision-making, it has long been held that executives bear chief responsibility for organizational strategy formulation. That is borne out by numerous research studies of executive roles.[1] It is also consistent with the common-sense view that someone must assume leadership when beginning new initiatives.[2]

Planning an executive retreat focused on SP&M should usually be a joint undertaking of the CEO and a designated coordinator for the SP&M program. (The coordinator may be the vice president of personnel or human resources, a high-level staff generalist from the HR function, the training director, an OD director, or a management development director.) A designated coordinator is needed because busy CEOs, while they should maintain active personal involvement in the SP&M program if it is to work, will seldom have the necessary time to oversee daily program operations. That responsibility should be assigned to someone or it will be lost in the shuffle of daily work responsibilities. Hence, naming a program coordinator is usually an advisable choice.

While a designated coordinator may be selected from a high level of the line (operating) management ranks—and that will be a necessity in small organizations not having an HR function—the individual chosen for this responsibility should have a strong commitment to SP&M, considerable knowledge about the organization's HR policies and procedures as well as applicable HR laws, expertise in state-of-the-art management and leadership development and human resource development practices, in-depth knowledge about the organization's culture, and credibility with all levels of the organization's management. (It doesn't hurt, either, if the individual chosen for this role is perceived to be a high-potential in his or her own right.)

The CEO and the SP&M coordinator should meet to hammer out an action plan for the executive retreat focused on collecting input. The retreat should be held soon after the CEO announces the need for a systematic SP&M program and names a program coordinator. Invitations should be extended to the CEO's immediate reports. The retreat should usually be held off-site, at a quiet and secluded location, to minimize interruptions. The focus of the retreat should usually be on:

△ Explaining the need for a more systematic approach to SP&M
△ Formulating a (draft) program mission statement
△ Identifying initial target groups to be served by the program
△ Setting initial program priorities

An executive retreat is worthwhile because it engages the attention—and involvement—of key players in the organization's strategic planning activities, thereby creating a natural bridge between SP&M and strategic planning. The retreat's agenda should reflect the desired outcomes. Presentations may be made by the CEO, the SP&M coordinator, and the vice president of HR. Outsiders may be invited to share information about SP&M—including testimonials about succession programs in other organizations, war stories about the problems that can result when SP&M is ignored, and descriptions of state-of-the-art SP&M practices. An important component of any retreat should be small group activities geared to surfacing problems and achieving consensus. (Many of the activities and worksheets provided in this book can be adapted for that purpose.) In many cases, a retreat will end when the CEO appoints a standing committee to work with the succession planning coordinator to report back with a detailed program proposal.

In some organizations, the CEO or the SP&M coordinator may prefer that the retreat be facilitated by third-party consultants. That is desirable if the consultants can be located and if they possess considerable expertise in SP&M and in group facilitation. It is also desirable if the CEO feels that third-party consultants will increase the credibility and emphasize the importance of the program.

Meeting 3: Hammering Out a Proposal

A standing SP&M committee should be established to continue the program formulation process begun in the executive retreat. A committee format is really the best approach to (1) maintain high-level commitment and support, (2) conserve the time required to review the fruits of the committee's investigations, and (3) provide a means for senior-level involvement in SP&M.

The SP&M coordinator should be automatically named a committee member, though not necessarily committee chair. If the CEO can be personally involved—and that is highly desirable—he or she should be the chair. Committee members should be chosen for their interest in SP&M, their track records of exemplary performance, their proven ability to develop people, and their keen insight into organizational culture.

In most organizations, a committee of this kind should meet frequently and regularly during program start-up. Initial meetings should focus on investigating organizational SP&M needs, benchmarking practices in other organizations, and drafting a detailed proposal to guide the SP&M program.

Meeting 4: The Kickoff Meeting

In the fourth meeting, the program is introduced to those previously involved in the second meeting and any others, as appropriate. This is typically called a kickoff meeting.

In most cases, this meeting should focus on program details—and the part that the meeting participants should play to ensure program success. In short, a kickoff meeting should seek answers to two questions: (1) What is the SP&M program in the organization? and (2) What do the participants need to do to make the program successful?

When organizing a kickoff meeting, pay attention to the following questions:

1. *Who* will be invited?
2. *What* exactly should participants know or be able to do upon leaving the meeting?
3. *When* should the kickoff meeting be held? For instance, would timing it to follow a strategic planning retreat be desirable?
4. *Where* should the kickoff meeting be held? If maximum secrecy is desired, an off-site location is wise.
5. *Why* is the meeting being held? If the aim is to reinforce the importance of this new effort, then the CEO should usually be the keynote presenter.
6. *How* will the meeting be conducted?

Specific training on program details can then be offered later on establishing work requirements, appraising individual performance, assessing individual potential, establishing career goals, establishing Individual Development Plans (IDPs), and using training, education, and development to help meet succession needs.

Meeting 5: Periodic Review Meetings

Conduct periodic review meetings after the succession planning program has been established. These meetings should focus on such issues as:

△ The linkage between SP&M and organizational strategic plans (that may be handled during strategic planning retreats)
△ The progress made in the SP&M program
△ Any need for revisions to the program's mission statement, governing policy and procedures, target groups, priorities, action plans, communication strategies, and training relevant to the succession planning program
△ The status of succession issues in each organizational component, including periodic meetings between the CEO and senior executives.

The last of these should be familiar to executives in most major corporations. Once a quarter, senior executives from each part of the corporation meet with the CEO and a top-level committee to review the status of SP&M in that part of the corporation. Common topics in such meetings include: (1) reviewing employee performance; (2) identifying and discussing high-potentials; (3) discussing progress made on Individual Development Plans; and (4) addressing critical strengths and weaknesses having to do with individual development. Such meetings serve to keep the SP&M program on target and to emphasize its importance to senior executives, who should be held accountable for "people development" as much as for "market development" or "financial development."

Training on Succession Planning and Management

Implementing a systematic approach to SP&M requires new knowledge and skills from those expected to cultivate the organization's internal talent. Some means must be found to *train* them so that they are the most efficient and effective in their new role.

Matching Training to Program Planning

Training to support SP&M should be designed to match program priorities. Indeed, to plan training on SP&M, examine program priorities first, and use them as clues for designing initial training efforts.

In most cases, when organizations establish systematic SP&M, training should be undertaken to answer the following questions:

- △ What is the organization's SP&M program? What are its mission, policy, procedures, and activities?
- △ What are the desirable roles of management employees, succession planning and management facilitators, and individual employees in the SP&M program?
- △ What is the organization's preferred approach to clarifying present and future work requirements? How should it relate to SP&M as a source of information about activities, duties, responsibilities, competencies, and success factors in key positions?
- △ What is the organization's performance appraisal system, and how should it relate to succession as a source of information about individual job performance?
- △ What is the organization's formally planned individual career planning program (if one exists), and how does it relate to succession as a source of information about individual career goals and aspirations?
- △ What is the organization's high-potential assessment program (if

one exists, as it should), and how does it relate to succession as a source of information about individual potential for future advancement?

△ How do the organization's training, education, and development programs relate to preparing individuals for succession and advancement?

△ What is an Individual Development Plan? Why is planning for individual development important? How should programs for individual development be designed? implemented? tracked?

△ How does the organization keep track of its human talent?

△ How should the organization evaluate its SP&M program?

△ How should the organization handle special issues in SP&M—such as high performers, high-potentials, and plateaued workers?

△ How should the SP&M program be linked to the organization's strategy? to HR strategy? to other plans (as appropriate)?

Refer to the draft training outlines appearing in Exhibit 7-2 as a starting point for developing in-house training sessions on SP&M. Note that such training should be tailor-made to meet organizational needs.

As an alternative, decision-makers may prefer to contract with qualified external consultants to design and deliver training on SP&M for the organization. Such consultants may be located through word-of-mouth referrals from practitioners in other organizations, those who have written extensively on SP&M, or such sources as *The ASTD's Buyer's Guide and Consultant Directory*. They are especially appropriate to use when in-house expertise is limited, external consultants will lend initial credibility to the program, the pressure is on to obtain quick results, or in-house staff are unavailable. If decision-makers decide to use external assistance, then the consultants should be invited in for a day or two to discuss what assistance they can provide. They should be asked for references from previous organizations with which they have worked. Before their arrival, they should also be given *detailed* background information about the organization and its existing SP&M programs and problems.

Many external consultants will begin by meeting individually with key decision-makers and will then provide a brief group presentation about SP&M issues. Both can serve a valuable purpose. Individual meetings will emphasize the importance of the issue. Group meetings will help to informally educate participants about state-of-the-art practices outside the organization, which can create an impetus for change.

Ensuring Attendance at Training: A Key Issue

Perhaps the single most challenging aspect of offering training on SP&M is securing the critical mass necessary to ensure consistent approaches

(Text continues on page 162.)

Exhibit 7-2: Sample Outlines for In-House Training on Succession Planning and Management

---

Purpose

To provide an opportunity for skill-building on employee performance appraisal, potential assessment, and individual development planning

Targeted Participants

Individuals, such as key position incumbents and immediate organizational superiors of high-potentials, who have important roles to play in implementing the action plan governing the succession planning program

Objectives

Upon completion of this training, participants should be able to:

1. Explain the organization's business reasons for establishing an SP&M program and the relationship between SP&M and strategic planning and human resources planning.
2. Describe the mission, policy, procedures, and activities of the SP&M program.
3. Review the roles and responsibilities of managers in preparing their employees to assume key positions in the organization.
4. Explain how the organization clarifies work requirements and identifies key positions.
5. Explain the role of employee performance appraisal in SP&M and describe the organization's performance appraisal procedures.
6. Conduct effective employee performance appraisal interviews.
7. Explain the role of employee potential assessment in SP&M and describe the organization's procedures for potential assessment.
8. Conduct effective employee potential assessments.
9. Explain the role of individual development planning in SP&M and describe the organization's procedures for individual development planning.
10. Select and oversee appropriate internal development approaches.
11. Explain when promotion from within is—and is not—appropriate for filling key vacancies.
12. Review the organization's approach to inventorying human talent.

Outline—Session 1
"Introducing Succession Planning and Management"

I. Introduction
    A. Purpose of the session
    B. Objectives of the session
    C. Organization (structure) of the session
II. Defining Succession Planning and Management (SP&M)
    A. What is it?
    B. Why is it important generally?
III. Relating SP&M to the Organization
    A. What are present organizational conditions?
    B. What are the organization's strategic plans/goals?
    C. What are the organization's human resources plans and goals?
    D. What is the need for SP&M, given organizational strategy and human resource plans?
IV. The Purpose of the SP&M Program
    A. Mission
    B. Policy
    C. Procedures
    D. Activities
V. Roles in SP&M
    A. What should be the role of the immediate organizational superior?
    B. What should be the individual's role in SP&M?
VI. Defining Work Requirements
    A. Job Analysis
    B. Job Descriptions and Specifications
    C. Other Approaches
VII. Identifying Key Positions
    A. How are they defined?
    B. Where are they located?
    C. How will key positions change in the future—and why?
VIII. Conclusion
    A. Summary
    B. Action planning for on-the-job action
    C. Session evaluations

(continues)

Exhibit 7-2: *(continued)*

Outline—Session 2
"Conducting Effective Employee Performance Appraisals for
Succession Planning and Management"

   I. Introduction
      A. Purpose of the session
      B. Objectives of the session
      C. Organization (structure) of the session
  II. Defining Employee Performance Appraisal
      A. What is it?
      B. Why is it important generally?
 III. Relating Employee Performance Appraisal to SP&M
      A. Approaches
      B. Current method
      C. Relationship between appraisal and SP&M
 IV. Reviewing the Organization's Performance Appraisal Procedures
      A. Overview
      B. Step-by-step description of procedures
  V. Conducting Effective Performance Appraisal Interviews
      A. Overview
      B. Using the form to structure the interview
 VI. Role Plays (practice appraisal interviews)
VII. Conclusion
      A. Summary
      B. Action planning for on-the-job action
      C. Session evaluations

Outline—Session 3
"Conducting Effective Employee Potential Assessment for
Succession Planning and Management"

   I. Introduction
      A. Purpose of the session
      B. Objectives of the session
      C. Organization (structure) of the session
  II. Defining Employee Potential Assessment
      A. What is it?
      B. Why is it important generally?
 III. Relating Employee Potential Assessment to SP&M
      A. Approaches
      B. Current method
      C. Relationship between potential assessment and SP&M

IV. Reviewing the Organization's Potential Assessment Procedures
    A. Overview
    B. Step-by-step description of procedures
V. Conducting Effective Potential Assessment
    A. Overview
    B. Using existing forms and procedures
    C. Gathering individual career planning information for use with potential assessment
VI. (*Optional*) Role Plays (practice assessment interviews)
VII. Conclusion
    A. Summary
    B. Action planning for on-the-job action
    C. Session evaluations

Outline—Session 4
"Conducting Effective Individual Development Planning"

I. Introduction
    A. Purpose of the session
    B. Objectives of the session
    C. Organization (structure) of the session
II. Defining Individual Development Planning
    A. What is it?
    B. Why is it important generally?
III. Relating Individual Development Planning to SP&M
    A. Approaches
    B. Current method
    C. Relationship between individual development planning and SP&M
IV. Reviewing Approaches to Individual Development Planning
    A. Overview
    B. Step-by-step description of approach
V. Facilitating Effective Individual Development Planning
    A. Overview
    B. Approaches to individual development planning
    C. Relating individual career planning to individual development planning
VI. Conclusion
    A. Summary
    B. Action planning for on-the-job action
    C. Session evaluations

throughout the organization. It is particularly difficult to ensure that key managers will attend group training—and they are precisely the most important to reach because they exert the greatest influence on SP&M issues. But no matter what is done, some key managers will claim that they have too much work to do and cannot spare valuable time away from work to attend. Others will not attend and will offer no explanation. But it may prove to be impossible to fit them into any group training schedule that is established.

No magic elixir will solve these problems. It amounts to a matter of commitment. If members of the board of directors and the CEO are genuinely committed to ensuring effective succession planning, then they will become personally involved to ensure the attendance of the targeted training participants. They will also attend themselves—and perhaps help deliver the training—and thereby demonstrate hands-on interest and support. Their participation and involvement will exert a powerful, but subtle, inducement for others to attend. But if they are unwilling to be involved, no amount of cajoling or threatening is an effective substitute. Moreover, *they* must set the example and follow the policies established for the organization.

Here are a few tips for securing attendance at group training on SP&M, assuming that adequate top management commitment exists:

△ Draft a memo for the chairman or CEO to initial to go out with training invitations. Stress who will be in attendance, what issues will be discussed, and why the training is important.

△ Pick an opportune time. Check dates to make sure that the dates chosen for training do not conflict with other, predictable dates.

△ If possible, tie the training on succession planning to other events— such as strategic planning retreats—in which the targeted participants are already scheduled to attend.

△ Field-test the training materials on a small, handpicked group of supportive managers. Be sure that all time is effectively used and that every training activity relates directly to SP&M practices in the organization.

△ If possible, videotape a well-rehearsed practice session and share it before the session with the chairman, CEO, or other key management personnel. Ask for their suggestions about revision before the session.

Other Approaches to Training Management Employees for Enacting Their Roles in Succession Planning and Management

There will always be some management employees who will be unable to attend group training on SP&M, even when vigorous steps are taken to ensure attendance. They will have legitimate reasons for not attending. But that will not alter the fact that they missed the training. They are the group most likely to operate in a way inconsistent with organizational policy because they missed the opportunity to learn about it firsthand.

Deal with this audience through a form of "guerrilla warfare." Make sure that it is clear who they are. Then use any of the following tactics to train them:

△ Meet with them individually, if their numbers are small enough to make that practical and if they are not so geographically dispersed that traveling to their locations is prohibitively expensive. Deliver training personally.
△ Videotape a practice session of the training and send it to those unable to attend. Then follow up with them later for their questions and reactions.
△ Ask another manager who did attend—such as the CEO—to describe to them the key lessons of the training in his or her own words. (That should reinforce the importance of the message.)

Training Participants in Succession Planning and Management

Training for participants in SP&M will be greatly affected by the organization's communication strategy. If decision-makers do not wish to inform individuals of the organization's SP&M practices, then no training will typically be given; on the other hand, if the organization adopts a policy of openness, then training on SP&M may be offered.

There are three general ways of offering such training: (1) direct training; (2) training integrated with other issues; and (3) training tied to career planning.

Direct Training

In direct training, employees are informed of the organization's SP&M policy and procedures. They are briefed in general terms, usually without specific descriptions of how the program is linked to existing organizational strategy. They learn how the SP&M program is linked to defining work requirements, appraising employee performance, assessing individual potential, and establishing Individual Development Plans.

Training Integrated with Other Issues

When training on SP&M is integrated with other issues, employees are told how their training, education, and development efforts factor into qualifying for advancement. No promises are made; rather, the value of planned learning activities is stressed as one means by which the individual can take proactive steps to qualify as a successor for leadership positions.

Training Tied to Career Planning

Organizational succession planning and individual career planning represent mirror images of the same issue. Succession planning and management helps the organization meet its HR needs to ensure that it is equipped with the talent needed to survive and succeed. On the other hand, individual career planning helps the individual establish career goals and prepare for meeting those goals—either inside or outside the organization.

When training on SP&M is tied to training on career planning, individuals are furnished with information about work requirements at different levels and in different functions or locations. They also learn about performance requirements in different job categories and about future success factors. With this information, they can establish their own career goals and take active steps to prepare themselves for advancement by seeking appropriate training, education, and development experiences.

Counseling Managers about Succession Planning Problems in Their Areas

Succession planning and management coordinators should make a point of meeting periodically with managers to discuss SP&M issues in their work areas and to offer individualized counseling about how to deal with those problems. If that counseling is requested, it indicates that executives have accepted SP&M, they value advice about people management issues, and they are making honest efforts to meet the SP&M needs of their organization.

The Need for Individual Counseling Sessions

Executives sometimes have need of third-party advice. In some cases they will be reluctant to share those problems with anyone—including the CEO—for fear that they will be perceived as unable to manage tough-to-handle management situations. Individual counseling with these executives by the SP&M coordinator can serve an invaluable purpose for improving SP&M practices. For this reason, the CEO and other decision-makers in the organization should actively encourage such sessions.

Who Should Conduct the Sessions?

The SP&M coordinator should arrange to meet with senior executives to conduct individual counseling sessions on a regular basis. However, the coordinator must first seize the initiative to arrange the meetings until the coordinator has gained sufficient credibility to be sought out for help by executives.

The SP&M coordinator should call each senior executive periodically and ask when they can meet. Although these individual meetings can be time-consuming, they are the best way to demonstrate commitment to the effort—and get real payoffs from it. Individual meetings are usually best timed sometime *ahead* of periodic SP&M meetings, such as those held quarterly in many corporations. By meeting ahead of time, the SP&M coordinator and the executive in charge of that work area can discuss sensitive personnel issues that executives may be reluctant to bring up in group meetings—or share over the phone or by mail.

Essential Requirements for Effective Counseling Sessions

To conduct effective counseling sessions, follow these general guidelines:

1. Send questions in advance, making the purpose of the session clear.
2. Tailor the questions to issues that will be treated in regularly scheduled group meetings with the CEO so that their relevance is immediately apparent.
3. Keep the meeting short and on target unless asked to offer advice on specific issues.
4. Always assume that everything is said in strictest confidence. (This point deserves strong emphasis.)
5. Be alert to casual remarks or questions that may indicate problems, probing with additional questions to learn more as appropriate.

Common Succession Planning and Management Problems—and Possible Solutions

Succession planning and management coordinators who meet to counsel managers on "people problems" unique to their areas should be prepared to deal with complex problems. Many events may derail the progress of otherwise high-potential employees, and an SP&M coordinator should be prepared to offer advice on what to do about those problems. Reclaiming high-potential employees on the verge of derailing their careers is an important role, and one that is often informally loaded on the SP&M coordinator.

Over the years I have been asked to offer executives advice on how to counsel high-potentials experiencing the following problems that threatened to derail their futures:

△ An executive engaged in a high-profile extramarital affair with a subordinate
△ An executive accused of blatant sexual harassment—but where the accusation could not be substantiated
△ An executive, slated for the CEO spot, who was recognized as an alcoholic by everyone except himself
△ A male executive who was grossly insubordinate to his female superior
△ An executive renowned for her technical knowledge who was notorious for her inability to work harmoniously with her peers
△ An executive who experienced a major personality conflict with his immediate superior

These are merely samples of the problems about which the SP&M coordinator may be asked to offer advice.

Although few SP&M coordinators are trained psychologists or psychiatrists, they should be able to apply the following steps, which I have found helpful when advising executives about "people problems."

Step 1: Ask for information about the present situation

What is happening now? Where is the executive obtaining information? When and how was this information revealed? Was the information obtained firsthand, or is the executive relying on intermediaries, rumors, or speculation? What steps have been taken to separate fact from fancy?

Step 2: Ask for information about corrective actions already attempted

What efforts, if any, have already been made to correct the problem? What were the results of those actions? What efforts have been made to alert the affected individual to the problem or to clarify desired behavior or performance?

Step 3: Determine the problem's cause, if possible, and assess whether it can be solved

What does the executive believe is the cause of the problem? Does the person who is experiencing the problem know what to do? (If not, it may indicate a training need.) Is the person engaging in undesirable behavior deliberately and maliciously? (If so, it may indicate a disciplinary problem.)

Has anyone asked the person experiencing the problem to identify its cause and possible solution(s)? Can the individual avoid derailing his or her career, or have matters already gone so far that others have lost all confidence for improvement?

Step 4: Establish an action plan

Emphasize the importance of properly managing the organization's human resources to the executive who is receiving the counseling. Express strong confidence in the executive's ability to deal with the problem. Offer to help in any way possible. Suggest such steps as these: (1) Put the problem in writing and meet with the person having the problem so as to make it as clear as possible; (2) Encourage the executive to clarify, in writing, what needs to be done, how it should be done, and what will happen if it is not done.

Step 5: Follow up

After meeting with the executive who has had a problem, the SP&M coordinator should make a point of following up later to see how the problem was resolved.

By following the five steps outlined above, SP&M coordinators should be able to identify and resolve "people problems." That is a valuable service in its own right to an organization, and it can help get people who are in danger of derailing get "back on track."

Summary

This chapter focused on refining the succession planning and management program. It summarized what was needed to prepare a program action plan, communicate the action plan, and counsel managers on succession planning and management problems—particularly those having to do with "people problems"—unique to their areas of responsibility.

To be successful, however, any succession planning and management program should be based on systematic analyses of present job requirements, future job requirements, present individual performance, and future individual potential. Conducting such analyses is not for the fainthearted, the ill-prepared, or the uncommitted. These processes require hard work and diligence, as the next section of this book will show.

Part III

Assessing the Present and the Future

To be effective, succession planning and management should be based on reliable information about the organization's requirements and about individual performance and potential. To obtain that information, most organizations must establish the means by which to:

- △ Identify key positions
- △ Use approaches to determine work requirements in key positions
- △ Use full-circle, multi-rater assessment
- △ Appraise performance
- △ Create talent pools
- △ Identify key positions for the future
- △ Use approaches to determine future work requirements in key positions
- △ Assess individual potential

Only by approaching these activities systematically can the organization ensure planned succession. These issues are treated in Chapters 8 and 9, which comprise Part III.

Chapter 8

Assessing Present Work Requirements and Individual Job Performance

Leaders must know the present before they can plan the future.[1] They must be realistically aware of the organization's strengths and weaknesses before they can navigate around future external threats and seize the advantages presented by external opportunities. That can be a daunting task because leaders are biased observers: they are, after all, accountable in large measure for an organization's strengths and weaknesses. It is thus easy for them to overlook weaknesses, since the cause(s) may be rooted in their own past decisions; it is easy for them to overlook strengths, which they may take for granted. Managers, it has been shown,[2] will persist in an ill-fated course of action because they fall prey to the *gambler's fallacy*, based on the logic that "more effort will lead to a big payoff." But some efforts never pay off; rather, they merely lead to mounting losses. That is why organizations replace leaders after a repeated string of failures.

Many of the same basic principles apply to succession planning and management (SP&M). Before leaders can effectively plan for succession, they must be aware of the organization's work requirements and the strengths and weaknesses of its available leadership talent. Indeed, having the right person for the right job at the right time is a strategic issue of key importance that has long presented a major challenge to top managers. But to know who those people are and what they must do, the organization must first be able to furnish answers to such questions as these:

△ What are the organization's key positions?
△ What are the work requirements in key positions?
△ How should individual performance be appraised?

This chapter focuses on answering these questions. It thus emphasizes examining *present* conditions. The next chapter focuses on anticipating *future* conditions. Taken together, they are a starting point for long-term and systematic SP&M.

Identifying Key Positions

To achieve maximum benefits from a systematic succession planning program, begin by first identifying *key positions*. The reason: Key positions underscore and dramatize important work processes that must be carried out and important work results that must be continuously accomplished by the organization. Key positions warrant attention because they represent strategically vital leverage points affecting organizational success. When they are left vacant—or when the work is left undone for whatever reason—the organization will not be able to meet or exceed customer expectations, confront competition successfully, or follow through on efforts of crucial long-term significance.

What Is a Key Position?

A *key position* exerts critical influence on organizational activities—operationally, strategically, or both.

Identifying Key Positions

Key positions have traditionally been viewed as those at the pinnacle of the organization's chain of command. The most obvious reason is that important decision-making has been done at the top of most organizations and imposed downward. But, as decision-making has become more decentralized as a result of increasing employee involvement and the application of principles linked to high-involvement work organizations, key positions have become diffused throughout organizations. Hence, they may reside at many points on the organization chart.

Key positions are not identical across organizations. There are several reasons why. One reason is that all organizations do not allocate work in exactly the same way. Positions sharing job titles in different organizations do not necessarily perform identical duties. A second reason is that top managers in different organizations do not share the same values. As a result, they may vest job incumbents with more or less responsibility, which is influenced by their own perceptions (and values) about which activities are most important. A third reason is that organizations do not share identical strengths and weaknesses or face identical environmental threats and opportunities. Hence, a key position in one organization may not be a key position in another. Key positions are thus unique to a single organization.

Let's focus on six ways to identify key positions.

By the Consequences/Uproar Resulting from a Pending or Existing Vacancy

When the organization lacks a *key position incumbent*—defined as someone occupying a key position at any level, in any function, or at any location—it is apparent because important decisions cannot be reached, orders cannot be shipped, production cannot proceed, customers' needs cannot be satisfied, or bills are left unpaid. In short, a vacancy in a key position creates an uproar because an important activity is placed "on hold" while the right talent is lacking to make an informed decision, complete a process, or achieve results. This delay can prove costly, placing an organization at risk to competitors who do not face such a handicap. Possible results include loss of customers, market share, and (in the worst cases) bankruptcy.

One way, then, to recognize a key position is by the consequences of—or uproar caused by—not filling a vacancy when it exists or is expected. I call this *the uproar method* of identifying key positions. Generally, the greater the uproar created by an existing or a pending vacancy, the greater the importance of that key position and the work process(es) over which it exerts influence.

By Organization Charting

Prepare a current organization chart. Show all functions. List the leader's name in each function, if the organization is sufficiently small to make that possible. Then list the number of people assigned to carry out the function. Pose these questions:

1. What does this function uniquely contribute to the organization's mission? and
2. Could this function operate effectively if the leader were gone?

The answer to the first question provides valuable clues about organizational processes. It should be expressed in terms of the *inputs, transformational processes,* and *outputs* of that function relative to the organization's work. That tells *why* the function is important—and what it does to accomplish the results desired from it.

The answer to the second question yields clues about key positions.

If the answer is "no," then the next question to ask is *Why is that leader so valuable?* What is it that makes him or her important—and potentially tough to replace? Does he or she possess specialized expertise or carry out specialized work duties? (If so, then it is a key position.) Do the staff members collectively assigned to that function lack the ability to achieve results in the absence of a leader? (If so, then a potential *replacement need* has been identified that should be shored up.)

If the answer is "yes," then ask *Why is the function able to operate without the leader?* Are others particularly key to its operation? If that is the case, then the leader does not occupy a key position, but one or more workers do.

If this activity is carried to its natural conclusion, key positions should be easily identified on the organization chart. Each key position is tied to a critically important organizational function, result, or work process. A vacancy in any key position will represent a *hole*, a gap between an organizational requirement and the human talent needed to meet that requirement.

By Questioning

Most senior executives have a keen grasp of their areas of responsibility. Ask them what they regard as *key positions* within their own areas. Do that by posing a question like this: "What positions in your area of responsibility are so important that, if they suddenly became vacant, your part of the organization would face major problems in achieving results?" Ask for the titles of the positions to be listed—not the names of job incumbents. Then ask "Why are these positions so important?" Don't provide clues; rather, allow executives to furnish their own rationales. (That tactic is likely to lead to the best information.)

By Historical Evidence

Has the organization experienced crises or uproars in the past resulting from unexpected departures by key job incumbents? Use evidence of past uproars as indicators of where key positions are located. Scan personnel records to obtain the names and job titles of people who departed in the last few years. Then contact their former supervisors in the organization to find out *which* departures posed the greatest problems for the organization and *why* they posed problems. Were they in tough-to-fill positions? Did they possess unique, tough-to-replace knowledge and skills? What was it *exactly* that made these losses so important? How was the uproar handled? If a vacancy occurred in the same position again, would it still cause an uproar? Why? Compile the answers to these questions as evidence of key positions.

By Network Charting

Network charting is a technique of communication analysis that has recently been used in identifying employment discrimination.[3] But its applications are potentially much more powerful in charting the decision-making process in organizations. The idea is a simple one: trace the path of communication flows during one or more decisions to answer such questions as "who is included?", "who is excluded?", and "why are some individuals included or excluded?"

A key assumption of network charting is that decision-makers will seek information only from individuals who occupy important positions and/or who are viewed as credible, trustworthy, and knowledgeable about the issues on which decisions are required. Significantly, it has also been shown that decision-makers prefer to include people like themselves—and exclude people unlike themselves—from decision-making processes. Hence, communication flows in the same way that succession decisions are often made—that is, through *homosocial reproduction*,[4] the tendency of leaders to perpetuate themselves by sponsoring people who are in some way like themselves. As Rosabeth Moss Kanter describes the process:[5] "Because of the *situation* in which managers function, because of the position of managers in the corporate structure, social similarity tends to become extremely important to them. The structure sets in motion forces leading to the replication of managers as the same kind of social individuals. And the men who manage reproduce themselves in kind."

Network charting can be carried out by interviewing people or by retracing communication flows. But the best way, though time-consuming, is to shadow a key decision-maker to determine firsthand *what positions* and *what individuals* are included—and why. In this application of network charting, the aim is not to uncover employment discrimination; rather, it is to determine which positions are considered key to decision-making in each part of the organization. The results should yield valuable information about key positions in—and the route of work processes through—the organization.

By Combination

A sixth and final approach is to combine two or more other approaches listed above. Academic researchers call this *triangulation*,[6] since it involves verifying information by double-checking it from multiple sources. Radar and sonar operators originated the approach, I believe, as a way to obtain a definite fix on an object. Practically speaking, however, many organizations have neither time nor resources to double-check key positions. Often, only one approach is used.

What Information Should the Organization Maintain about Key Positions?

Once key positions have been identified, additional questions will present themselves:

△ *Who* occupies those key positions now? What are their qualifications? What background, education, experience, or other specialized knowledge did they bring to their positions?

△ *What* are the work requirements in key positions? (*See the next section below.*)

△ *When* are those key positions likely to become vacant? Can some key vacancies be predicted based on the announced retirement or career plans of key position incumbents?

△ *Where* are key positions located in the organization? (Answer that question based on the organization's structure, job categories, and geographical locations.)

△ *How* is performance appraised in the organization? How well do performance appraisal practices match up to information about work requirements by position?

△ *How well* are the key position incumbents presently performing? Did their backgrounds, education, and experience properly equip them to perform? If not, what are they lacking?

△ *How* did key job incumbents secure their positions? Were they groomed to assume their positions, recruited from outside, transferred from within, or did they reach their positions through other means?

By answering these questions, the organization can begin to establish an *information system* to track key positions, key position incumbents, and individual performance.

Three Approaches to Determining Work Requirements in Key Positions

Once key positions have been identified, direct attention to determining the work requirements in those positions. After all, the only way that individuals can be prepared as replacements for key positions is to clarify first what the key position incumbents *do*. At least three ways may be used to do that. They are described below.

1. Conducting Job and Task Analysis

Job analysis summarizes or outlines the activities, responsibilities, duties, or essential functions of a job. *Task analysis* goes a step beyond job analysis to determine what must be done to carry out each activity or meet each responsibility, duty, or essential function. The result of a job analysis is called a *job description*; the result of a task analysis is called a *task inventory*.

Some authorities distinguish between the terms *job* and *position*:

> A *job* consists of a group of related activities and duties. Ideally, the duties of a job should consist of natural units of work that are similar and related. They should be clear and distinct from those of other jobs to minimize misunderstanding and conflict among employees and to enable employees to recognize what is expected of them. For some jobs, *several* employees may be required, each of whom will occupy a separate position. A *position* consists of different duties and responsibilities performed by only *one* employee.[7]

It is thus important to distinguish between a job description, which provides information about an entire job category (such as supervisors, managers, or executives) and a position description, which provides information unique to one employee. In most cases, the focus of determining work requirements for SP&M is on *positions*, since the aim is to identify work requirements unique to key positions.

What Is a Position Description?

A position description summarizes the duties, activities, or responsibilities of a position. Hence, it literally *describes* a position in one organizational setting. It answers this question: *What are incumbents in the position expected to do in the organization?*

No universally accepted standards exist either for job descriptions or for position descriptions.[8] In most organizations, however, position descriptions list at least the title, salary or wage level, location in the organization, and essential job functions. An *essential job function*, a legal term used in the Americans with Disabilities Act, is an activity that must be conducted by a position incumbent. More specifically, it "is [a job activity] that's fundamental to successful performance of the job, as opposed to marginal job functions, which may be performed by particular incumbents at particular times, but are incidental to the main purpose of the job. If the performance of a job function is only a matter of convenience, and not necessary, it's a marginal function."[9]

Some organizations add other features to job descriptions, and the same features may be added to position descriptions as well. These additions may include, for instance, the approximate time devoted to each essential job function, the percentage of a position's total time devoted to each essential job function, the relative importance of each essential job function to successful performance, and a *job specification* listing the minimum qualifications required for selection.

How Is Position Analysis Conducted?

Position analysis is conducted in the same way as job and task analysis. As Carlisle notes, "the process of analyzing jobs and tasks involves at least three key steps. First, the job or task is broken down into its component parts. Second, the relationships between the parts are examined and compared with correct principles of performance. Third, the parts are restructured to form an improved job or task, and learning requirements are specified."[10]

Use the Worksheet appearing in Exhibit 8-1 as a guideline for preparing a current key position description. For ideas about what essential job functions to list, see *The Dictionary of Occupational Titles* (published by the U.S. Department of Labor), works on the Americans with Disabilities Act,[11] and works about management job descriptions.[12]

Advantages and Disadvantages of Position Descriptions

Position descriptions are advantageous for identifying work requirements for three reasons. First, most organizations have at least job descriptions, which can be an important starting point on which to base more individualized position descriptions. Second, position descriptions can be the basis for making and justifying many personnel decisions—including selection, appraisal, and training—and not just decisions linked to succession planning and management. Third and finally, legislation—particularly the Americans with Disabilities Act—has made written expressions of work requirements important as legal evidence of what is necessary to perform the work.[13]

However, position descriptions are by no means foolproof. First, they tend to focus on activities, not so much on results. Second, they may leave out important personal characteristics that are crucial to successful job performance. Third, they date quickly. Keeping them updated can be a time-consuming chore.

Exhibit 8-1: A Worksheet for Writing a Key Position Description

Directions: Give careful thought to the process of writing this position description, since it can be critically important in recruiting, selecting, orienting, training, appraising, and developing a job incumbent for a key position. The best approach is to ask the key position incumbent to write the description and then to review it several levels up, down, and across the organization. (In that way, it should be possible to obtain valuable information about the desired results necessary for this position at present—some of which even the current position incumbent may be unaware of.) For now, focus on what the position incumbent is *presently doing* and what others in the organization *want the key position incumbent to be doing in the future*. Add paper if necessary.

Title: (*Fill in the position title:*) _____

Salary Level: (*Note the present pay grade:*) _____
Organizational Unit/Department: (*Note the present placement of the position in the organizational structure:*) _____

Immediate Supervisor: (*Note to whom the position incumbent presently reports on the organization chart by title:*)

_____

Position Summary: (*In one or two sentences, summarize the purpose—or mission statement—for this position. Answer this question: why does it exist?*)

_____

_____

Position Duties/Responsibilities/Activities/Key Results/Essential Functions: (*Make a list in the left column below of the most important position duties, responsibilities, activities, key results, or essential functions. If necessary, use a separate sheet to draft the list and then record the results of your deliberations in priority order in the space below. Be sure to list the most important duty, responsibility, activity, key result, or essential function first. Begin each statement with an action verb. Then, in the right column, indicate the approximate percentage of time devoted to that activity.*)

List of position duties/ responsibilities/activities/ key results/essential functions:	*Approximate % of Time Devoted to Each:*

2. Identifying Competencies and Developing a Competency Model

Competency identification is a possible step beyond job and task analysis as a means of clarifying key position requirements. In this context, *competency* refers to "an underlying characteristic of an employee (that is, motive, trait, skill, aspects of one's self-image, social role, or a body of knowledge) which results in effective and/or superior performance in a job";[14] *competency identification* pinpoints competencies; and a *competency model* "includes those competencies that are required for satisfactory or exemplary job performance within the context of a person's job roles, responsibilities and relationships in an organization and its internal and external environments."[15]

Competency models have emerged as the mainstream approach used in many organizations to integrate all facets of human resource management. Competency identification was described at greater length in Chapter 4. Most well-known companies have based their succession programs on competency models.

3. "Rapid Results Assessment"

A new approach to competency modeling is needed to maximize the strengths and minimize the weaknesses of traditional approaches. Such a new approach may involve the marriage of a traditional approach to competency assessment, such as McLagan's Flexible Approach (see Exhibit 4-1),[16] with the so-called DACUM method.

DACUM is an acronym formed from letters in the phrase *Developing A Curriculum*.[17] It has been widely used in job and task analysis for technical positions and in establishing occupational curricula at community colleges. Seldom, however, has it been described as a means by which to determine work requirements in management or professional positions.

To use DACUM in its traditional sense, select a facilitator who is trained in the approach. Convene a panel consisting of eight to twelve people who are expert in the job. Then take the following steps:[18]

1. Orient the committee to DACUM
2. Review the job or occupational area of concern
3. Identify the general areas of responsibility of the job
4. Identify the specific tasks performed in each area of responsibility
5. Review and refine task and duty statements
6. Sequence task and duty statements
7. Identify entry-level tasks

The result of a typical DACUM panel is a detailed matrix illustrating work activities. They are arranged in order of difficulty—from the simplest to the most complex activities. In DACUM's traditional application, panel members approach descriptions of "personality characteristics" as an additional activity. For instance, at the conclusion of the DACUM session panel members may be asked a question such as this: "What personal characteristics describe an effective job incumbent?" That question should elicit such responses from panel members as "punctuality," "good attendance," "ability to work harmoniously with coworkers," or "dresses appropriately." Rarely are such characteristics linked to specific, measurable behaviors—though they may be critical to successful job performance.

In practice, a DACUM panel usually meets in a quiet room for one or more days. The facilitator asks panelists to list work activities, in round-robin fashion, in no particular order. Each activity is written with Magic Marker on a sheet of paper and posted on a blank wall at the front of the room. Because panelists can list activities quickly, most DACUM facilitators need one or two confederates to assist them by writing the activities and posting them on the wall. Panelists who are unable to think of an activity are skipped. The process continues until all the panelists exhaust activities to list.

At that point, the facilitator calls a break. With the help of confederates—and perhaps one or more panelists or other job experts—the facilitator devises descriptive categories for the activities and groups related activities together. When finished, the facilitator reconvenes the panel. Panelists add, subtract, or modify categories and verify activities. Finally, they sequence categories and activities from most simple to most complex. These steps closely resemble classic brainstorming, which consists of two steps: *idea generation* and *idea evaluation*.[19]

To use DACUM as a tool for competency assessment, facilitators should take additional steps. Once a DACUM job matrix has been completed and verified, facilitators should adjourn the panel and plan to convene at another time. Once the panel is reconvened, facilitators should present panelists with the DACUM job matrix—either as an individualized handout or as a large wall chart. Facilitators should then progress around the room, focusing panelists' attention on each cell of the job matrix, and asking panelists to (1) list underlying motives, traits, aspects of self-image, social roles, or body of knowledge that effective job incumbents should exhibit to carry out that activity, and (2) work outputs or results stemming from each activity. The answers should be written inside each cell.

Once again, the panel should be adjourned briefly. As in the first panel meeting, facilitators should make an effort to eliminate duplication and economically list personal characteristics and work outputs for *each* activity. When facilitators are finished, they should again reconvene the panel and seek verification and consensus on the results. If the meeting runs too long, facilitators may adjourn and follow up by written survey, thereby turning traditional brainstorming into a modified delphi process.[20]

The value of this approach should be apparent. First, it is much faster than traditional competency modeling. (That is a major advantage, and it is worth emphasizing.) Second, this approach—like traditional DACUM—has high face validity because it uses experienced job incumbents (or other knowledgeable people). It should gain ready acceptance in the organization. Third, it permits the personal involvement of key decision-makers, thereby building the ownership that stems from participation. Fourth and finally, it enjoys the key advantage of a competency-based approach in that the modified DACUM moves beyond the traditional focus on work activities or tasks to include descriptions of underlying characteristics and/ or outputs.

Of course, this new approach—which I have chosen to call *rapid results assessment*—does have its disadvantages. The results do not have the research rigor of other competency assessment approaches. Hence, rigor is sacrificed for speed. Second, the results of the approach will depend heavily on the credibility of the individual panelists. If inexperienced people or poor performers participate, the results will be viewed with suspicion.

Rapid results assessment can provide valuable information for succession planning and management. If the assessment process is focused on key positions—and DACUM panels include immediate superiors, peers, incumbents, and even subordinates—it can yield powerful information about role expectations for incumbents in these positions. It can also provide the basis, as DACUM does, to select, appraise, train, reward, and develop people who are being groomed for key positions.

Using Full-Circle, Multi-Rater Assessments

Since the publication of the first edition of this book in 1994, many organizations have begun to use full-circle, multi-rater assessments as a means to appraise an individual's present performance or assess an individual's future potential.[21] Such assessments—sometimes called *360-degree assessments* because they examine an individual from a full circle around him or her—are useful ways to collect much data from organizational superiors, subordinates, peers or colleagues, and even customers, suppliers, distributors, and family members. They usually indicate how well an individual is performing (or has the potential to perform) when compared to competency models or work requirements. Many full-circle, multi-rater assessment questionnaires can be purchased from commercial vendors or accessed online.

But many questions arise when decision-makers contemplate using full-circle, multi-rater assessments. Among them:

1. *Who* will be assessed, and by whom will they be assessed?
2. *What* will be assessed? Will it be present performance, future potential, or both?
3. *When* will the assessment occur?
4. *Why* is the assessment being conducted? Since full-circle, multi-rater assessment is expensive, will the benefits in improved accuracy and credibility of results outweigh the costs?
5. *How* will the assessment be conducted? Will it be conducted online, on paper, or by a combination? What will be done with the results, how will the results be interpreted and fed back to the individuals, and how will they be used?

These questions should be answered before the organization undertakes the use of full-circle, multi-rater assessments. (Use the Worksheet appearing in Exhibit 8-2 to consider these questions.)

There are many advantages to full-circle, multi-rater assessments. They consolidate feedback from many people surrounding an individual about his or her present performance or future potential. The feedback alone is powerful in creating an impetus for change and individual development. Moreover, the ratings have much power in tapping into multiple perspectives, since (as the old saying goes) "what you think depends on where you sit in the organization."

But there are disadvantages to full-circle, multi-rater assessments, and they should be considered before the organization incurs the expense of using them. First, these assessments can be expensive and are thus worthwhile only when decision-makers know what they want and why they want it. Second, if individuals are rated against criteria such as competencies or work requirements that are not unique to the corporate culture (as is true if off-the-shelf or online instruments are used without modification), the results may not be too useful or meaningful. In fact, the results may be misleading in the end. After all, performance and potential are influenced by the organizational context in which individuals perform. Third, when large numbers of people are subjected to these assessments, the task of data analysis can be daunting. (Consider: one person may have as many as 12 raters. If 100 people are subjected to assessment, that means 1200 ratings must be compiled and fed back individually.)

It is likely that full-circle, multi-rater assessment will only be used more frequently in organizations in the future. For that reason, those managing SP&M programs should become familiar with sources that describe how to establish and use them.[22]

Exhibit 8-2: A Worksheet for Considering Key Issues in Full-Circle, Multi-Rater Assessments

Directions: When decision-makers begin thinking about using full-circle, multi-rater assessment, there are many issues they should clarify at the outset.

Use this Worksheet to guide their thinking. For each question appearing in the left column below, take notes about their answers in the right column. There are no "right" or "wrong" answers in any absolute sense, of course. But it is important to clarify the answers to these questions.

Questions	Answers
1. Who will be assessed, and by whom will they be assessed?	
2. What will be assessed? Will it be present performance, future potential, or both?	
3. When will the assessment occur?	
4. Why is the assessment being conducted?	
5. How will the assessment be conducted? (Will it be conducted online, on paper, or by a combination?)	
6. What will be done with the results, how will the results be interpreted and fed back to the individuals, and how will they be used?	

Appraising Performance

For an SP&M program to be effective, it must be based on information about work requirements in key positions *and* about the performance of incumbents and prospective successors. Hence, employee performance appraisal should be an important source of information for SP&M. But what is performance appraisal, and how should it be linked to SP&M?

Defining Performance Appraisal

Performance appraisal is the process of determining how well individuals are meeting the work requirements of their jobs. Just as most organizations prepare job descriptions to answer the question *what do people do?*, most organizations also prepare performance appraisals to answer the question *how well are people performing?* It is important to emphasize that performance appraisals are properly viewed within the context of *performance management*,[23] which is the process of creating a work environment in which people want to perform to their peak abilities and are encouraged to develop themselves for the future. (See Exhibit 8-3.)

Performance appraisals are commonly used to justify pay raises, promotions, and other personnel decisions. They are also critically important for SP&M, since few organizations will advance individuals into key positions when they are not performing their present jobs adequately.

While a fixture of organizational life, employee performance appraisal has not been immune to criticism. Indeed, it is rare to find managers who

Exhibit 8-3: The Relationship between Performance Management and Performance Appraisal

Performance management addresses this question: *What is necessary to encourage performance now and in the future?*

Performance Management
(focuses on all aspects of the work environment, work, and worker that impact on performance and can be past, present, or future-oriented)

Performance Appraisal
(usually focuses on past job performance and is used to make decisions on pay, promotion, and other job changes)

Performance appraisal addresses this question: *How well are people performing their jobs?*

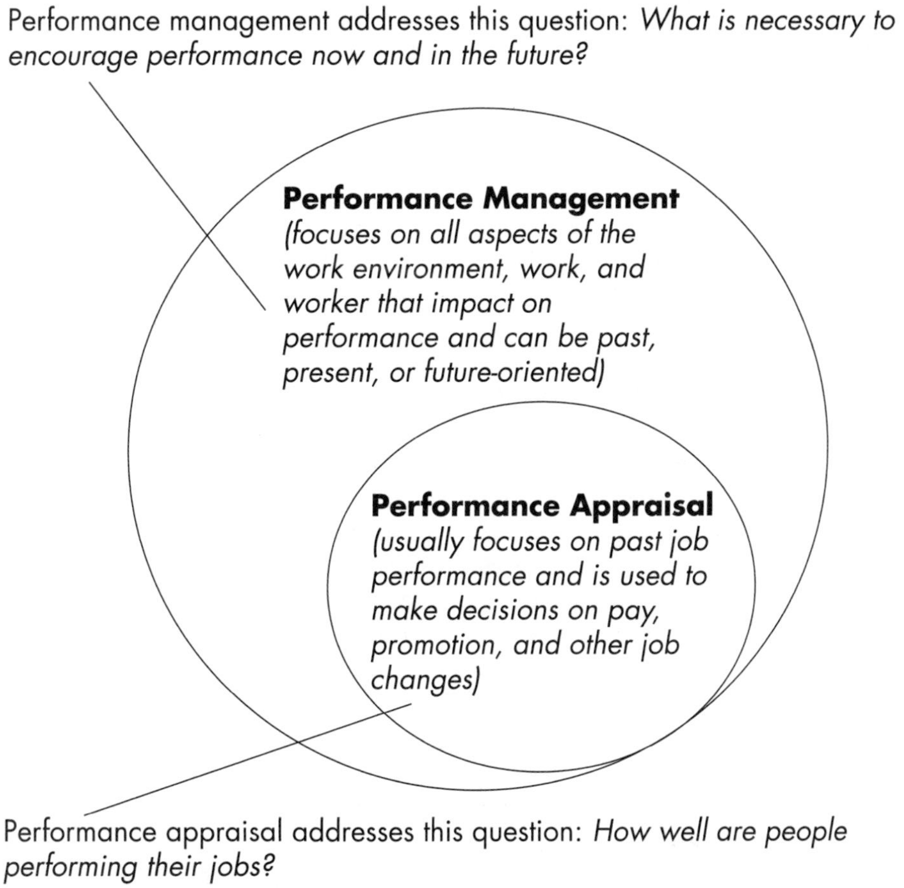

will enthusiastically champion the performance appraisal practices of their organizations. In recent years, appraisals have been increasingly prone to litigation.[24] Moreover, appraisals have been attacked by no less than the late curmudgeonly guru of Total Quality Management, W. Edwards Deming. Deming faulted employee performance appraisal for two primary reasons. First, Deming believed that performance appraisal leads to management by fear. Second, appraisal "encourages short-term performance at the expense of long-term planning."[25] It prompts people to look good in the short run, with potentially devastating long-term organizational effects.

The central point of Deming's argument is that people live up to the expectations that their superiors have for them. That is the *Pygmalion effect*, which takes its name from the ancient artist who fell in love with his own sculpted creation of the woman Galatea. The Pygmalion effect asserts that managers who believe that their employees are performing effectively will create a self-fulfilling prophecy. The underlying assumption, then, is that the world is influenced by viewers' beliefs about it.

When performance appraisal is conducted in a highly critical manner, it has the potential to demotivate and demoralize people. Indeed, research evidence indicates that performance appraisal interviews focusing on "what people are doing wrong" can actually lead to *worse* performance.

How Should Performance Appraisal Be Linked to Succession Planning and Management?

Despite harsh attacks from critics, performance appraisal is likely to remain a fixture of organizational life. One reason is that, despite their flaws, written appraisals based on job-related performance criteria are superior to informal, highly subjective appraisals at a time when employees are increasingly prone to litigate. In the absence of written forms and formal procedures, managers do not cease appraising employees; rather, they simply do it in a less structured fashion. Worse yet, they may face no requirement to provide employees with feedback—with the result that they can never improve. Indeed, few can dispute that employees will not improve their performance—or develop in line with succession plans—if they have received no timely, concrete, and specific feedback on how they are doing or what they should do to improve. While annual performance appraisals are no substitute for daily feedback, they should be used together to help employees develop.[26] Otherwise, the organization will have no records of employee performance—other than the faulty memories and unarticulated impressions of supervisors and other employees—on which to base pay, promotion, transfer, or other decisions affecting workers' lives.

There are many approaches to performance appraisal, and much has been written on the subject.[27] (Different types of appraisals are summarized in Exhibit 8-4.) To be effective, however, performance appraisal should be based as closely as possible on the work that employees do. Used in conjunction with *individual potential assessments*—which compare individuals to *future job assignment possibilities* or *future competencies*—they can be a powerful tool for employee improvement and development. For that reason, the best appraisal is one that examines employee performance point-by-point to present responsibilities.

One way to do that is to begin with a position description. Employees should then be appraised against each activity. In this way, the organization can maintain precise and detailed records of employee performance in each facet of the individual's job; and the individual will receive specific feedback about how well he or she is performing.

The problem is that such appraisals can be time-consuming to write and conduct. And, in the case of individuals who are performing poorly, their immediate organizational superiors must take the time to explain what needs to be improved and how it should be improved. To save time, some organizations attempt to develop simple, easy-to-fill-out appraisals to ease the paperwork burden on supervisors. Unfortunately, the easier an appraisal is to fill out, the less useful it is in providing feedback to employees.

To solve that problem, try developing free-form appraisals that use job descriptions themselves—or competencies—as the basis for appraisal. (See Exhibit 8-5 for a Worksheet to help prepare such an appraisal.) Another approach is to develop appraisals so that they are geared only toward future improvement rather than past performance. In that way, they are focused less on what employees are doing wrong and more on what they can do right. If that approach is followed consistently, it can provide useful information to employees about what they should do to prepare themselves for the future—and qualify for succession.

Creating Talent Pools: Techniques and Approaches

A *talent pool* is a group of workers who are being prepared for vertical or horizontal advancement. *Vertical advancement* usually means promotion up the organization's chain of command. Of course, in recent years, promotions have been diminishing in number. *Horizontal advancement* usually means that the individual's competencies are enhanced so that he or she has a broader scope of knowledge, skills, and abilities in keeping with the organization's direction or his or her occupation.

To create talent pools, organizations should possess competency models by departments, job categories, hierarchical levels, or occupations. The competency models may describe present competencies or desired

(Text continues on page 191.)

Exhibit 8-4: Approaches to Conducting Employee Performance Appraisal

Approach	Focus	Brief Description
Global rating	Focuses on the individual's overall job performance.	The appraiser is asked to characterize an individual's overall job performance on a single scale or in a single essay response.
		Chief advantage: Appraisers can make responses quickly.
		Chief disadvantage: Performance is more complex than a single rating can indicate.
Trait rating	Focuses on traits related to the individual's performance. Examples of traits might include "initiative" or "timeliness."	Appraisers are asked to characterize an individual's job performance over a specific time span using a series of traits. Often, trait ratings are scaled from "excellent" through "unacceptable." The appraiser is asked to check an appropriate point on the scale. However, traits can also be assessed by an essay response in which the appraiser is asked to write a narrative about the individual's performance relative to the trait.
		Chief advantage: Appraisers can make responses quickly.
		Chief disadvantage: Traits can have different meanings, so consistency of rating and job-relatedness of traits may be critical issues to deal with.

Dimensions/ Activity Rating	Focuses on each job activity, duty, responsibility, or essential function.	Think of a dimensional rating as a "job description that has been given scales to assess performance." Appraisers are asked to rate individual performance on *each* job activity, duty, responsibility, or essential job function. Responses may be provided by checking a mark on a scale or by writing an essay. *Chief advantage:* This approach to appraisal makes a deliberate effort to tie performance appraisal to job duties, thereby ensuring job-relatedness. *Chief disadvantage:* To work effectively, both appraiser and performer must agree in advance on the duties. That means job descriptions must be updated regularly, and that can become time-consuming.
Behaviorally anchored rating scales (BARS)	Focuses on job behaviors—observable activities—distinguishing exemplary from average performers.	A BARS performance appraisal typically consists of 5 to 10 vertical scales that are developed through a critical incident process to distinguish effective from ineffective performance. Each scale represents actual performance. A BARS rating system is compatible with a competency-based approach to job analysis. *Chief advantage:* Since each BARS is tied directly to job activities, this approach to performance

(continues)

Exhibit 8-4: (*continued*)

Approach	Focus	Brief Description
		appraisal enjoys high face validity. It can also lead to improved job performance by clarifying for performers exactly what behavior is desirable and undesirable.
		Chief disadvantage: To work effectively, BARS requires considerable time and effort to devise. That can exceed the resources—or commitment—of many organizations.
Management by objectives (MBO)	Focuses on the results of job performance rather than processes to achieve results.	Before the appraisal period begins, the appraiser and performer jointly agree upon job results desired. At the end of the appraisal period, the results are compared to the objectives established at the outset of the appraisal period.
		Chief advantages: The focus is on results rather than on methods of achieving them. Both appraiser and performer are involved in establishing performance objectives.
		Chief disadvantages: For the appraiser and performer to reach agreement, much time may be required. Writing performance objectives can turn the process into a "paper mill."

Exhibit 8-5: A Worksheet for Developing an Employee Performance Appraisal Linked to a Position Description

Directions: Use this Worksheet to develop a "free-form" employee perform-ance appraisal that is based specifically on the position description. In the left column below, indicate what the position description indicates are the duties, activities, responsibilities, key result areas, or essential job functions. Then, in the right column, indicate how performance in the position may be measured.

What are the position's activities, duties, responsibilities? (List them from an up-to-date position description.)	*How should performance be measured for each activity, duty, or responsibility? (Indicate appropriate ways to measure successful performance.)*

future competencies. Also important, as described in Chapter 4, are value statements that indicate desired values.

Begin the process of creating a talent pool by clarifying targeted groups. Answer such questions as these:

△ Who is included?
△ What is a talent pool? How many talent pools should exist in the organization?
△ When is each talent pool to be formed?
△ Where is each talent pool to be located? (What is its geographical scope?)
△ Why is each talent pool desirable?
△ How will the talent pool be analyzed for current bench strength, and desired future bench strength, and how will the status of each talent pool be tracked and assessed?
△ How will individuals in the talent pool be developed for the future?

There are as many ways to define talent pools as there are to define competency models. In other words, it is possible to have talent pools by department, by hierarchical level on the organization's chain of command, by job category, by region, by occupation, and by other means.

It is worth emphasizing that, if talent pools are formed, no one person should be designated as a successor for key positions. Instead, the logic is that all people in the talent pool will be prepared in line with present and future organizational and individual needs. To be effective, a talent pool should be paired with competency models, appropriate performance management practices to encourage individual development and performance, appropriate assessment strategies, and appropriate developmental efforts.

Summary

This chapter has emphasized present conditions. More specifically, it addressed the following questions:

△ What are the organization's key positions?
△ What are the work requirements in key positions?
△ How should individual performance be appraised?
△ What methods should be used to keep track of the organization's work requirements and individual performance?

The next chapter focuses on anticipating *future* conditions as essential in succession planning and management. It thus discusses how to identify future work requirements in key positions and how to assess individual potential.

Chapter 9

Assessing Future Work Requirements and Individual Potential

Having information about present work requirements or competencies and individual job performance provides only a one-dimensional picture. To make the picture more complete—and thus provide the basis for systematic succession planning and management (SP&M)—information is also needed about future work requirements and individual potential.[1] Hence, this chapter focuses on assessing future work requirements and individual potential. More specifically, this chapter addresses these questions:

- △ What key positions are likely to emerge in the organization's future?
- △ What will be the work requirements in those positions?
- △ What is individual potential, and how should it be assessed?

Identifying Key Positions for the Future

Neither key positions nor their work requirements will remain forever static. The reason, of course, is that organizations are constantly in flux in response to pressures exerted internally and externally. As a result, SP&M coordinators need to identify future key positions and determine future work requirements if they are to be successful in preparing individuals to assume key positions. They must, in a sense, cope with a *moving target effect* in which work requirements, key positions, and even high-potential employees are changing.[2]

But how can they be certain what positions will be key to the organization in the future? Unfortunately, the unsettling fact is that no foolproof way exists to predict key positions with absolute certainty. About the best that can be done is to conduct careful reviews of changes in work and people and draw some conclusions about the likely consequences of change.

Applying Environmental Scanning

As a first step in predicting key positions in the future, begin by applying *environmental scanning*. This can be understood as a systematic process of examining external trends.[3] Focus attention on economic, governmental/legal, technological, social, geographical, and other issues and trends affecting the organization's external environment. (Use the Worksheet in Exhibit 9-1 for this purpose.) For best results, involve decision-makers in this process, since key positions in the future should reflect the organization's strategic plans and changing work processes.

Applying Organizational Analysis

As a second step in predicting key positions in the future, turn next to *organizational analysis*. This is the systematic process of examining how an organization is positioning itself to address future challenges.[4] It can also be understood as any effort made to assess an organization's strengths and weaknesses. Consider the following questions:

- △ How well positioned is the organization presently to respond to the effects of future trends?
- △ What action steps can the organization take to meet the threats and opportunities posed by future trends?
- △ How can the organization maximize its strengths and minimize its weaknesses as the future unfolds in the present?

As these questions are answered, pay particular attention to likely changes in

- △ *Organizational structure* (What will be the reporting relationships? How will divisions, departments, work units, and jobs be designed?)
- △ *Work processes* (How will work flow into each part of the organization? What will be done with it? Where will the work flow to?)

Structure and processes are important issues because key positions result from decisions made about how to structure responsibility and organize the work process.[5] To direct attention to likely key positions in the future, then, decision-makers should examine how the organization will respond to external pressures by structuring responsibility and organizing work processes. Key positions will emerge—and old ones will fade—based on the way the organization chooses to respond to environmental demands. Use the Activity appearing in Exhibit 9-2 to help decision-makers address these issues.

Exhibit 9-1: A Worksheet for Environmental Scanning

Directions: What trends evident in the external environment will affect the organization in the future? Answering that question should prove valuable in strategic business planning, human resource planning, and succession planning. Environmental scanning attempts to identify those trends—and, more important, to predict their effects.

Use this simple Worksheet to structure your thinking about trends that will affect your organization in the future and what their effects are likely to be. Answer each question appearing in the Worksheet below. Then compare your responses to what other decision-makers in the organization have written.

---

1. What trends outside the organization are most likely to affect it in the next 1–5 years? Consider economic conditions, market conditions, financial conditions, regulatory/legal conditions, technological conditions, social conditions, and other trends that might uniquely affect the organization.

   List of trends likely to affect the organization:

---

2. For *each* trend you listed in response to question 1 above, indicate *how* you think that trend will affect the organization. Describe the trend's possible consequence(s), outcome(s), or result(s). (*While you may not be able to do that with complete certainty, try to gaze into the crystal ball and predict what will happen as a result of a trend.*)

   List effects/consequences:

Exhibit 9-2: An Activity on Organizational Analysis

Directions: How will your organization respond to the trends evident in the external environment that will likely affect it in the future? Use this Worksheet to help you structure your thinking about how external environmental trends will affect work in the organization.

Obtain answers to the activity appearing in Exhibit 9-1. Then answer each question appearing in the Worksheet below. Finally, compare your responses to what other decision-makers write. Use the responses to consider future work requirements in the organization.

1. For each consequence, outcome, or result you listed in response to question 2 in Exhibit 9-1, indicate *what functions/positions in the organization are most likely to be affected* and *how* you think those functions/positions will be—or should be—affected.

List each consequence, outcome, or result.	*Describe what functions/positions are most likely to be affected and how you think they will be—or should be—affected.*

2. How should the organization respond to future trends? Should workflow change? Should work methods change? Should the organization's structure change? Are any changes likely as a response to increasing external competitive pressure? How does the organization's strategic plan indicate that those challenges will be met? Will new key positions emerge as a result of changes to organizational strategy? Will old key positions fade in importance while new ones become more important?

   Provide your thoughts:

Preparing Realistic Future Scenarios

As a third and final step in predicting key positions in the future, compare the results obtained from environmental scanning and organizational analysis. Draw an organization chart as decision-makers believe it *should* appear in the future if the organization is to be successful. Write the expected future mission of each organizational function on the chart. (Make several versions of that chart at different future time intervals—at, say, one year, three years, five years, and ten years into the future.) Then add the names of possible leaders—and their successors.

This process is called *preparing realistic future scenarios*. It is based on the process of *scenario analysis*, which has been widely applied to futures research and strategic planning.[6] Use the Activity appearing in Exhibit 9-3 to help decision-makers structure their thinking in preparing realistic scenarios to identify future key positions. While not foolproof or failsafe, this approach is one way to move beyond traditional thinking about SP&M to "lead" the target—what hunters do when they shoot ahead of a moving target.

Three Approaches to Determining Future Work Requirements in Key Positions

Determining future work requirements means predicting possible or probable work activities, duties, and responsibilities in future key positions. Once likely future key positions have been identified, direct attention to predicting work requirements for those positions. Move beyond present- or past-oriented descriptions to assess future work requirements in key positions. To that end, apply the three approaches described below.

1. Conducting Future-Oriented Job and Task Analysis

To conduct future-oriented job and task analysis for key positions,[7] focus attention on summarizing expected future activities, responsibilities, duties, or essential functions. Extend the analysis by examining future tasks linked to those activities, responsibilities, duties, or essential job functions. Write position descriptions as they should exist at a future time if the organization is to be successful in meeting the competitive challenges it faces. In this way, the effects of organizational strategic plans on key positions can be mirrored, and thereby reinforced, in position descriptions and task inventories. By comparing present and future position descriptions, decision-makers should be able to uncover important disparities—and, accordingly, information about desirable developmental opportunities to groom

Exhibit 9-3: An Activity for Preparing Realistic Scenarios to Identify Future Key Positions

---

Directions: The future can seem difficult to envision if predictions about it are left vague. Use this Activity to make predictions more tangible. Using responses to questions appearing in Exhibits 9-1 and 9-2, create a detailed description of the likely future situation of your organization at the end of 5 years from the present. Do that by answering the questions appearing below. When you finish answering the questions, compare what you wrote to what other key decision-makers/strategists have written. Develop an overall scenario that describes the "best-guess situation" of the way the future will appear for the organization.

---

1. What is your "best guess" of how the organization will be functioning in 1 to 5 years, based on environmental scanning or organizational diagnosis? Describe the organization's situation, competition, profitability, and structure:

---

2. What positions do you believe will be key (that is, critically important) in 1 to 5 years? List their job titles below.

---

individuals for advancement. Use the Activity appearing in Exhibit 9-4 to prepare *future-oriented key position descriptions*.

However, future-oriented position descriptions are no panacea. They are prone to the same disadvantages as traditional (present-oriented) position descriptions: (1) a focus on activities, not results; (2) a lack of details about all elements essential to job success, including personal characteristics and attitudes; and (3) a requirement for continual, and time-consuming, revision because they date so rapidly. Additionally, they may be based on inaccurate (or simply wrongheaded) assumptions about the future. However, such disadvantages may be outweighed by their specificity and

Exhibit 9-4: An Activity for Preparing Future-Oriented Key Position Descriptions

Directions: An organization's strategic plans can seem vague to employees—and even to strategists—until they are made job-specific. Use this Activity to help clarify how key positions should change to help the organization realize strategic goals and implement strategic business plans.

In the left column below, list current job activities for each key position. Then, using the results of Exhibits 9-1, 9-2, and 9-3, list how those job activities should change between the present and 1 to 5 years in the future for the job incumbent to function in line with expected environmental trends and organizational changes made to cope with them.

Ask each key job incumbent to complete this activity for his/her position. Then ask strategists to review the results of the activity for each key position in the organization. Use the results as a basis for future-oriented succession planning.

Current Job Activities for Each Key Position	*How Should These Activities Be Carried Out in 1–5 years?*

by helping individuals to envision the future into which they—and their organizations—are headed.

2. Assessing Future Competencies

Competency assessment lends itself to a future orientation better than any other approach.[8] To give a future orientation to competency models, simply direct attention to the future rather than to the present or past. Ask the organization's strategists to review each key position for underlying employee characteristics (including motives, traits, skills, aspects of self-image, social roles, or bodies of knowledge) which should, if assumptions about the future prove correct, simultaneously result in superior performance and actions consistent with organizational strategy. Apply each approach shown in Exhibit 6-2 with an emphasis on future, rather than past or present, competencies. Then use the resulting competency models as a guide to prepare individuals for advancement into key positions.

Alas, however, future competencies may not be identical to present or past competence. Indeed, they may even *conflict* with them. For instance, think about such examples as IBM after downsizing or AT&T after deregulation. In each case, what was required for future success was not what had been historically required—or even desired—by the organization. That created a dilemma. Managers who succeeded under the old conditions were suddenly outmoded and were even unfit to counsel a new generation about what it would take for them to succeed. In these settings, managers had to identify—and cultivate—talent that was quite different from their own if their organizations were to survive. Exemplary future competence, then, represents a moving target, an ideal, a description of what people will probably have to know, do, or feel to perform successfully amid the vague uncertainties of the future.[9]

Future-oriented competency models, like future-oriented position descriptions, suffer from the same strengths and weaknesses as their traditional counterparts. While more rigorous than job analysis, a competency model can be confusing to those who do not clearly understand what it is. Additionally, future-oriented competency models usually require considerable time and expertise to carry out successfully. That may require strategists to devote significant time and resources to it, which they may be reluctant to do.

3. Applying Future-Oriented "Rapid Results Assessment"

This approach to competency identification has very real potential to help decision-makers plan for future work requirements in key positions. Nor does it require substantial expertise, time, or resources to carry out. To use it, simply focus attention on *desirable future competencies*. Apply the steps depicted in Exhibit 9-5. Then use those steps to examine competencies in *each key position* in the organization. Use the results as the basis to plan for individual development and organizational SP&M generally.[10]

"Rapid results assessment" enjoys important advantages: It can be conducted quickly; it enjoys high face validity because it uses experienced job incumbents (or other knowledgeable people) on which to base position-specific information; it permits the personal involvement of key decision-makers, thereby building their ownership in the results; and it can be used to move beyond a focus on mere work activities or tasks to include

Exhibit 9-5: Steps in Conducting Future-Oriented "Rapid Results Assessment"

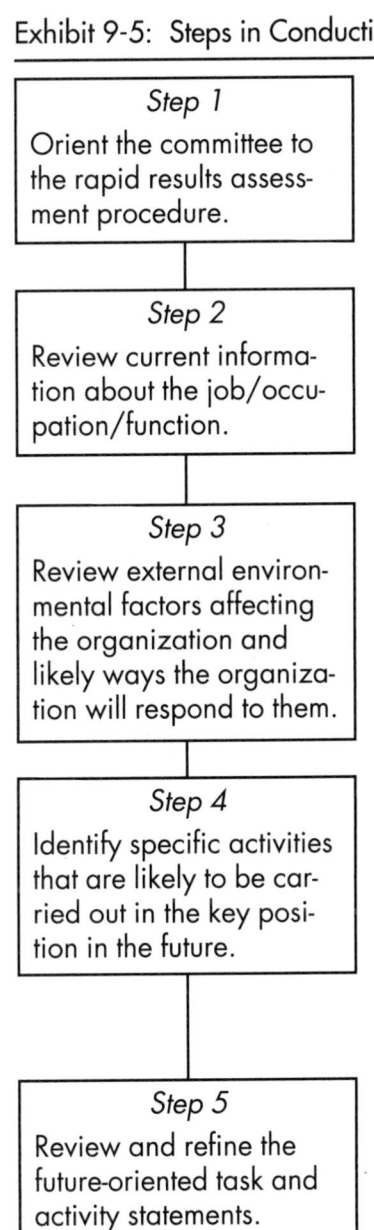

Step 1 Orient the committee to the rapid results assessment procedure.	△ Assemble a group of 5–13 knowledgeable individuals—including job incumbents and their immediate superiors. △ Brief group members on the need to predict changing work requirements.
Step 2 Review current information about the job/occupation/function.	△ Assemble information about one or more specific key jobs/positions in the organization. △ Focus attention in this step on "what job incumbents do now."
Step 3 Review external environmental factors affecting the organization and likely ways the organization will respond to them.	△ Brief group members on trends in the external environment and the organization that may change—or require change—in job duties, activities, responsibilities, tasks, or essential job functions.
Step 4 Identify specific activities that are likely to be carried out in the key position in the future.	△ Ask group members to identify how they believe key positions will be affected by changing external environmental conditions. △ Go around the meeting room and ask each group member to list an activity that he or she envisions will be carried out in the future—continue this process until group members exhaust ideas.
Step 5 Review and refine the future-oriented task and activity statements.	△ Ask group members to review the activities they defined in the previous step, eliminating redundancy and identifying names for general categories.
Step 6 Sequence future-oriented task and activity statements.	△ Ask group members to sequence the future-oriented task and activity statements they identified in the previous step so that they are arranged from easiest to most difficult to learn.

(continues)

Exhibit 9-5: *(continued)*

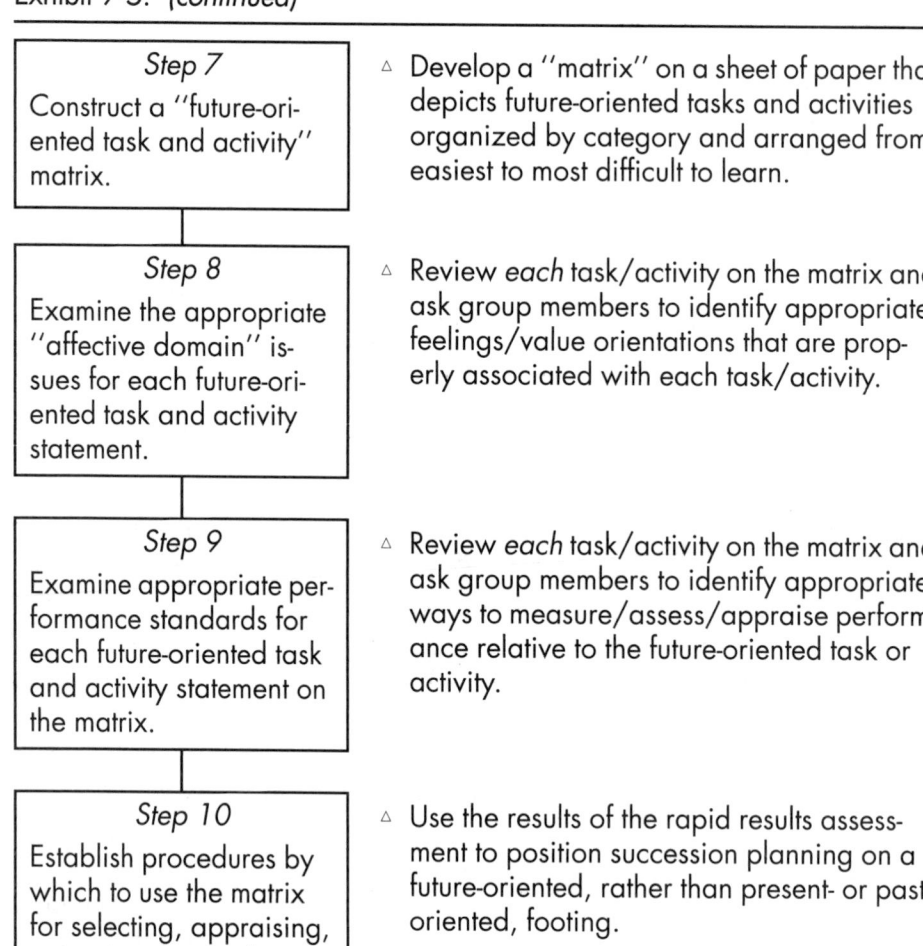

Step 7 Construct a "future-oriented task and activity" matrix.	△ Develop a "matrix" on a sheet of paper that depicts future-oriented tasks and activities organized by category and arranged from easiest to most difficult to learn.
Step 8 Examine the appropriate "affective domain" issues for each future-oriented task and activity statement.	△ Review *each* task/activity on the matrix and ask group members to identify appropriate feelings/value orientations that are properly associated with each task/activity.
Step 9 Examine appropriate performance standards for each future-oriented task and activity statement on the matrix.	△ Review *each* task/activity on the matrix and ask group members to identify appropriate ways to measure/assess/appraise performance relative to the future-oriented task or activity.
Step 10 Establish procedures by which to use the matrix for selecting, appraising, assessing potential, and other important activities.	△ Use the results of the rapid results assessment to position succession planning on a future-oriented, rather than present- or past-oriented, footing.

descriptions of underlying characteristics or work outputs. However, it shares the disadvantages of its traditional counterpart: The results are not as rigorous nor as complete as other competency modeling methods will yield, and the results are heavily dependent on the credibility of the individual panelists. Additionally, as in other future-oriented approaches, it is only as good as the assumptions about the future on which it is based.

Assessing Individual Potential

The centerpiece of most SP&M programs is some means by which to assess individual potential. This effort seeks to determine how to make best use of the organization's existing human resource assets. However, assessing potential should not be confused with appraising performance: Performance appraisal is linked to present job performance; potential assessment is linked to future advancement possibilities. Potential assessment is a critically important activity, if only because as many as one-third of all leadership positions (it has been estimated) would not be filled by present incumbents if decision-makers had it to do over again.[11]

What Is Individual Potential Assessment?

Individual potential assessment is a systematic process of examining individuals' possibilities for job change or movement. It is usually associated with determining whether individuals "have what it takes" to advance to positions of greater management responsibility or positions demanding greater technical knowledge. It should be linked to—and serve as one basis for determining—employee training, education, and development activities, which (collectively) represent a vehicle to help an individual qualify for advancement.[12] It should also be linked to individual career planning activities, which have (unfortunately) been deemphasized in recent years due to widespread downsizing and economic restructuring.

What Is a High-Potential?

The term *high-potential* has more than one possible meaning. High-potentials, who should be identified through the individual potential assessment process, represent the organization's inventory of future leaders. They are usually individuals who are capable of advancing two or more levels beyond their present placement, individuals who are slated for key positions, or those who have not reached a career plateau. (Other definitions are also possible.[13]) It is important to define the term in a way unique to each organization. In fact, each organization may have several definitions.

Distinguishing between Exemplary Performers and High-Potentials

Individuals who are high-potentials are almost always *exemplary performers* who are identified through the performance appraisal process and who exceed minimum job expectations. Exceptional performance in the current job is usually a necessary prerequisite to advancement.[14] However, not all exemplary performers are high-potentials because advancement potential is based on different criteria from present performance.

In any organization or organizational unit, individuals may be classified into four distinct groups based on their performance and their potential. To that end, think of a grid with two axes.[15] (See Exhibit 9-6.) One

Exhibit 9-6: How to Classify Individuals by Performance and Potential

The Performance/Potential Grid

Future Potential

		High	Low
Present Performance	**High**	**Stars** *HR strategy:* △ Keep turnover low. △ Take steps to accelerate their development.	**Workhorses** △ Keep turnover low. △ Keep them motivated and productive where they are.
	Low	**Question Marks** *HR strategy:* △ Convert them to stars. △ Counsel them to accelerate their development.	**Deadwood** △ Convert them to workhorses. △ Terminate them if they cannot be salvaged.

SOURCE: George S. Odiorne, *Strategic Management of Human Resources: A Portfolio Approach* (San Francisco: Jossey-Bass, 1984), p. 305. Adapted with permission of the publisher.

axis represents *present performance* and is divided between *high* and *low* performance; the second axis represents *future potential* and is divided between *high* and *low potential*. The result is a *performance/potential grid* that closely resembles the Boston Consulting Group's widely used portfolio analysis technique for use in strategic planning.

As shown in Exhibit 9-6, *stars* (see the upper left cell of the performance/potential grid) are exemplary individual performers in their present positions. They are also perceived to have high potential for future advancement.[16] A major corporate asset, they are properly regarded as *high-potentials* and are a source of replacements for key positions. An effective HR strategy for stars involves a twofold effort to make the most of their current performance while systematically preparing them for advancement—and even accelerating their development, if possible. Above all, the organization should make every effort to seek to recruit and retain them, keeping their turnover minimal.

Workhorses (see the upper right cell of the performance/potential grid) are exemplary performers in their current jobs who are perceived to have poor future potential.[17] Since they are highly productive where they are, they should remain there. An effective strategy for workhorses is to harness their skills while keeping them motivated and productive. Turnover in their ranks, as with stars, should be kept minimal.

Question marks (see the lower left cell of the performance/potential grid) are poor performers in their present positions who are perceived to have high future potential.[18] The best HR strategy for dealing with them is to focus on improving their present performance, thereby turning them into stars. Their immediate supervisors should be trained to apply appropriate techniques—such as coaching, mentoring, and (when warranted) disciplinary steps—to make them more productive.

Finally, *deadwood* (see the lower right cell of the performance/potential grid) consists of individuals who are neither good performers in their present jobs nor perceived to have future advancement potential.[19] While their ranks may have been dramatically reduced in the 1990s due to downsizing and other reductions in force, their ranks may be swollen in some international subsidiaries where the national culture emphasizes good relationships between bosses and subordinates rather than performance (results).

A twofold HR strategy is most effective with deadwood. First, their immediate organizational superiors should make every effort to help them improve their present performance. If successful, that strategy will convert *deadwood* to *workhorses*. If unsuccessful, that strategy should be followed up by fair and even-handed efforts, consistent with the organization's disciplinary policies and practices, to move them out of the job—or even out of the organization.

Approaches to Assessing Individual Potential

How can the organization identify high-potentials? There are several ways to answer that question, because approaches to assessing individual potential are as diverse as employee performance appraisal—and sometimes resemble each other.

Global Assessment

One way to assess potential is to ask senior executives to furnish the names of individuals in their areas of responsibility who they feel have high potential according to the definition established in the organization. This is called *global assessment*. (See Exhibit 9-7 for a sample Worksheet to be used in making global assessments.)

It is a simple approach, but it is not very effective, for several reasons. First, few senior executives (except those in very small organizations) will know everyone in their areas of responsibility. Second, unless the definition of high-potential is made quite clear, senior executives are likely to

Exhibit 9-7: A Worksheet for Making Global Assessments

Directions: Use this Worksheet to list individuals whom you consider to be "high-potentials" in your organizational area of responsibility. A "high-potential" is an individual who has the capacity to be promoted two or more levels. List the names below, provide their present titles, and the time they have spent in the present positions. Be prepared to discuss, in the future, *why* you believe these individuals have the capacity to be promoted two or more levels. If possible, rank them by their potential—with 1 = highest potential. (Do *not* use current position as a basis for ranking; rather, use your judgment about individual ability.)

Names	*Titles*	*Time in Present Positions*

---

respond to a request for names based on their perceptions. Those perceptions about individuals can be colored too much by recent events (*recency bias*), extremely bad incidents (*the horn effect*), or extremely good incidents (*the halo effect*). Indeed, perceptions can lead to personal favoritism, discrimination, or *pigeonholing* in which individual potential is difficult to change once assessed.

Success Factor Analysis

A second approach to individual potential assessment is based on *success factor analysis*, the process of examining traits or other characteristics perceived to lead to organizational success or advancement. One research study, for instance, revealed that successful women share such characteristics as exemplary educational credentials, a track record of hard work and good performance, supportive mentoring relationships, effective interpersonal skills, and a willingness to take career and work risks.[20]

Success factors may be identified through various means. One way is to ask executives what traits they think will lead to success in the organization. These traits may then be collected in the way depicted in Exhibit 9-8. Executives can be asked to check off what they believe those traits are. Lists completed by numerous executives may be compiled and used as the basis for developing an *individual potential assessment form*, perhaps like the one shown in Exhibit 9-9.

Exhibit 9-8: A Worksheet to Identify Success Factors

Directions: Use this Worksheet to identify success factors. A "success factor" is a past experience or personal characteristic linked to, and correlated with, successful advancement in the organization. Identify success factors by asking individuals who have already achieved success—such as key position incumbents—about their most important developmental experiences and about what they did (or skills they demonstrated) in the midst of those experiences.

Pose the following questions to key position incumbents. Then compile and compare the results. Ask other key position incumbents in the organization to review the results.

---

1. What is the single most difficult experience you encountered in your career? (*Describe the situation below.*)

---

2. What did you *do* in the experience you described in response to question 1? (*Describe, as precisely as you can, what actions you took—and what results you achieved as a result.*)

---

3. Reflect on your answer to question 2. What *personal characteristics* do you feel you exhibited or demonstrated in the action(s) you took? How do you feel they contributed to your present success?

Exhibit 9-9: An Individual Potential Assessment Form

Directions: Individual potential may be assessed through many different approaches. One approach is to ask their immediate organizational superiors to rate employees—particularly those felt to be high-potentials—against various success factors, skills, competencies, values, or abilities that are felt to be correlated with future success.

Ask key job incumbents to rate their subordinates on each of the following generic success factors. (It is better to use success factors specific to the unique organizational culture.) A separate form should be completed on each high-potential. The completed forms may then be used as one source of information about individual strengths/weaknesses.

Ask the raters to place an *x* in the appropriate spot in the right column below the scale and opposite the success factor listed in the left column. Then ask raters to send their completed forms to the HR Department or to the organization's Succession Planning Coordinator. There are no "right" or "wrong" answers in any absolute sense. However, raters may vary in their potential assessments, depending on how they interpret the success factors and the rating scale.

Success Factors	*Needs Improvement* 1 2 3	*Scale Adequate* 4 5 6	*Exceeds Requirements* 7 8 9
Appraising			
Budgeting			
Communicating			
Controlling			
Dealing with Change			
Developing Employees			
Influencing Others			
Making Changes			
Making Decisions			
Managing Projects Effectively			
Organizing			
Planning			
Representing the Organization Effectively			
Staffing the Unit/ Department			

An alternative is to conduct *critical incident interviews* with organizational strategists. This approach is based on critical incident analysis, which has been used in training needs assessment. Critical incidents were first identified for pilots during World War II. They were asked what situations (*incidents*), if ignored, might lead to serious (*critical*) consequences.

If this approach is used, individual interviews should be conducted with strategists with a structured interview guide like the one shown in Exhibit 9-8. The results should then be analyzed and become the basis for establishing success factors. These, in turn, can be used in assessing individual potential and, when appropriate, identifying developmental opportunities.

Approaches to Individual Potential Assessment

There are three basic approaches to individual potential assessment. Each is based on a different philosophy. They are worth reviewing.

Leader-Driven Individual Potential Assessment

The first approach to individual potential assessment might be called *leader-driven*. It is the traditional approach that was probably first used in business. Individual potential is assessed by the organization's strategists— and often solely by key position incumbents for their own subordinates in their immediate areas of responsibility.

The process may be a formal one, in which the organization has established forms for this purpose that are completed periodically on all employees or on a select group of employees (such as those designated as *high-potentials*). Alternatively, the process may be informal: Each function or organizational unit is asked to submit names of individuals who have advancement potential.

This approach is characterized by *secrecy*. Employees have little or no say in the process; indeed they are not always aware that it is being carried out. No effort is made to double-check individual potential assessment results with individual career aspirations or plans to ensure that an appropriate match exists.

An advantage of this approach is that it can be done quickly. Leaders simply fill out forms and return them to the human resources department, the SP&M coordinator, or a designated executive. Employees do not challenge the results because they are unaware of what they are. The organization thus retains strong control over SP&M and its results.

A disadvantage of this approach, however, is that employees have no stake in outcomes they did not help to shape. If the results are ever used in making succession decisions, employees may refuse promotions or transfers that conflict with their perceptions of their own desired work-life balance or their own career goals.

Participative Individual Potential Assessment

A second approach might be called *participative assessment*. Both individuals and their immediate organizational superiors enact important roles in the assessment process. Hence, it is participative. Periodically— such as once a year—employees undergo an individual potential assessment. It may be timed at the halfway point of the annual performance appraisal cycle so that potential assessment is not confused with performance appraisal.

Although there are many ways to carry out the process, one approach involves distributing individual assessment appraisal forms to employees and their immediate organizational superiors. Employees and superiors complete the forms, exchange them, and later meet to discuss the individual's advancement capabilities. As with performance appraisals, the forms for individual potential assessment are usually prepared by the human resources department, distributed from that department, and the results returned to that department for filing in personnel records. (Alternatives to that approach are possible. For instance, completed individual assessment appraisal forms may be retained by the leader of each organizational unit.)

An advantage of this approach is that it allows "reality testing." Individuals learn of possibilities for the future, which may interest them and motivate them; organizational representatives learn more about individual career goals and aspirations, thereby improving the quality of their succession plans. In this way, the assessment process provides an opportunity for mutual candor and information-sharing.

Key to this process is the individual potential assessment interview. It should be carried out in a quiet, supportive setting that is free of interruptions. The employee's immediate organizational superior should set the pace, discussing his or her perceptions about the individual's strengths and weaknesses for advancement—and the realistic possibilities for that advancement. Having an agenda can make an interview of this kind run smoothly.

Another advantage is that employees have a stake in the assessment process. If the organization should have need to make a succession decision, the likelihood is greater that employees will accept offers of promotions or transfers that match their career goals and organizational needs.

A disadvantage of this approach is that it can rarely be done quickly. Leaders and employees must devote time to it if it is to be valuable. Indeed, to gain the full benefits from it, leaders must be trained on effective interviewing skills.

Another disadvantage is that the value of participative assessment is a function of the interpersonal trust existing between leaders and their employees. However, trust is not always present. Nor is complete candor.

Several factors affect trust. Among them are: past dealings between the organization and individual; the perceived candor of the organization's representative; and the match between individual career goals and organizational opportunities.

To cite two examples: Suppose that an employee has personal aspirations that may eventually lead to her departure from the organization. She may be unwilling to share that information for fear of how it might affect her prospects for promotion. Likewise, leaders may be unable to share information about pending changes affecting the organization—such as the sale of a division or the dissolution of a product line—that may also impact career goals or succession plans.

Empowered Individual Potential Assessment

A third approach might be called *empowered individual potential assessment*. Leaders provide guidance and direction for the approach but do not determine the outcomes or make final decisions affecting individual potential. Instead, they just share information and offer coaching suggestions. Individuals remain chiefly responsible for their own self-assessment and their own self-development.

Once a year, employees are encouraged to complete individual potential assessment forms, share them with their immediate organizational superiors, and then schedule meetings to discuss them with their superiors. (Some may even decide to discuss their forms with their mentors.) The form is usually created and supplied by the human resources department. However, it may—or may not—be called an *individual potential assessment form*. Alternative names might include *career planning assessment form*, *individual development planning form*, or even *management career planning form*.

In this approach, the initiative rests entirely with employees. They conduct their own individual assessments; they schedule assessment meetings with their immediate organizational superiors or with mentors in other parts of the organization; they are not required to participate in the assessment process, which remains voluntary. As with other approaches, however, it is usually kept separate from performance appraisals so as not to confuse present performance and future potential. Individual potential assessment becomes a tool to help individuals understand how to qualify for advancement within the framework of the organization's needs and their own career goals.

An advantage of this approach is that, like other empowerment efforts, it can be quite motivating to employees. Further, it discourages a philosophy of entitlement in which employees with a long service record feel that promotions are "owed" to them. Instead, the responsibility for advancement rests squarely on their shoulders, and they are expected to take an active role in setting their own career directions and finding the necessary resources to develop in line with those directions.

Another advantage of this approach is that employees are not given the impression, which is possible with other approaches, that they are guaranteed advancement. Management should state the message, loud and clear, that "we can't guarantee promotions, but we can guarantee that those who have taken the steps to obtain the necessary qualifications for a higher-level position will be given due consideration."

However, the chief disadvantage of this approach is that the organization sacrifices control over employees. Indeed, it may not always be apparent whether replacements exist for each key position. It thus creates a talent pool rather than a position-oriented succession plan. In practical terms, this means that nobody may know at any time if even one person is "ready" to assume important positions in the organization.

Empowered individual potential assessment is likely to remain important, a mainstream approach. One reason is that it matches current thinking about the need to decentralize decision-making and give the control to those who deal with customers or consumers daily. A second reason is that this approach can unleash individual initiative rather than stifle it—thereby motivating people to *want* to qualify for advancement.

Summary

As this chapter has shown, information about future work requirements and individual potential is essential to an effective succession planning and management program. When paired with information about present work requirements and individual job performance, it becomes the basis for preparing Individual Development Plans to narrow the gaps between what individuals already know and do and what they must know and do to qualify for advancement.

Part IV

Closing the "Developmental Gap": Operating and Evaluating a Succession Planning and Management Program

After analyzing work requirements, job performance, and individual potential, the organization is ready to close individual development gaps. At this point, then, the organization is ready to operate a succession planning and management (SP&M) program. To that end, decision-makers should begin by:

- △ Testing bench strength
- △ Formulating internal promotion policy
- △ Preparing individual development plans (IDPs)
- △ Developing successors internally
- △ Assessing alternatives to SP&M, as necessary
- △ Applying online and high-tech approaches to SP&M programs
- △ Evaluating SP&M programs
- △ Taking steps to address predictions about the possible future of SP&M programs

This part treats these and related issues.

Chapter 10
Developing Internal Successors

For a succession planning and management (SP&M) program to be effective, the organization must have some means by which to replace key job incumbents as vacancies occur in their positions. Promotion from within is a time-honored and crucially important, albeit traditional, way to do that.

But, to prepare individuals for promotion, the organization has an obligation to do more than merely identify present and future work requirements and performance. Some way must also be found to clarify—and systematically close—the developmental gap between what possible successors can already do and what they must do to qualify for advancement. *Individual development planning* is the process of clarifying that developmental gap; *internal development* uses planned training, education, development, and other means to close the gap and thereby meet succession needs.

This chapter focuses on determining the organization's collective succession needs, using promotion from within to meet those needs, clarifying individual developmental gaps, and closing those gaps systematically through planned training, education, and development. More specifically, then, this chapter addresses the following questions:

△ What is bench strength, and how can the leaders of an organization test bench strength?
△ Why is internal promotion so important for succession, and when is it—and when is it not—appropriate for meeting SP&M needs?
△ What is an Individual Development Plan (IDP)? How should one be prepared, followed up, and evaluated?
△ What are some important methods of internal development, and when should they be used?

Testing Bench Strength

Once key positions and work requirements have been identified, the organization should test bench strength. That is important because it provides information about the organization's collective succession needs. That information can, in turn, dramatize the importance of taking action to meet SP&M needs.

What Is Bench Strength?

Bench strength is the organization's ability to fill vacancies from within. *Testing bench strength* means determining how well the organization is able to fill vacancies in key positions from within.

Turnover saps bench strength. There are two kinds of turnover. *Unavoidable turnover* is outside the immediate control of the organization. It is the loss of personnel through death, disability, and retirement. It may also include turnover resulting from organizational action—such as layoff, early retirement, buyout, or other means. Although many line managers would like to include promotions and transfers from their areas in the definition of unavoidable turnover, most HR departments do not include internal movements in the definition of unavoidable turnover.

On the other hand, *avoidable turnover* is initiated by employees. It is a loss resulting from resignation as individuals leave the organization, typically moving to positions in other organizations. Although turnover of any kind is costly because the organization must find and train replacements, avoidable turnover is worst because it could be avoided if the organization could find some way to retain the employees.

Avoidable turnover from key positions is particularly distressing, because it creates unnecessary crises. (This is sometimes called *critical turnover.*[1]) One aim of any SP&M program should thus be to find ways to reduce avoidable turnover among key position incumbents—or at least find the means to keep it stable.

Approaches to Testing Bench Strength

To test an organization for bench strength, ask decision-makers how they would replace key positions in their areas of responsibility—or ensure that work requirements will be met through other, more innovative, means. Use any of the means described below.

By Replacement Charting

Prepare an organization chart to show the range of possible replacements for each key position in a work area. (See Exhibits 10-1 and 10-2.) Note how many *holes* can be identified. A *hole* is a position in which no internal replacement can be identified. The lower the percentage of holes relative to key positions, the greater is the organization's bench strength.

Exhibit 10-1: A Sample Replacement Chart Format: Typical Succession Planning and Management Inventory for the Organization

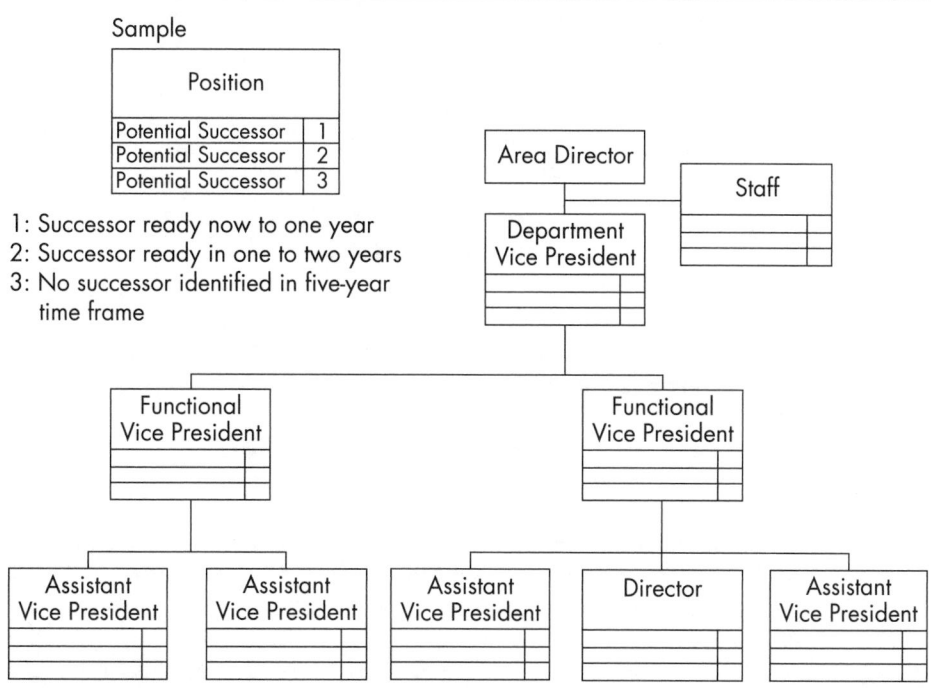

Sample

1: Successor ready now to one year
2: Successor ready in one to two years
3: No successor identified in five-year time frame

SOURCE: Norman H. Carter, "Guaranteeing Management's Future through Succession Planning," *Journal of Information Systems Management* (Summer 1986) p. 19. Used by permission of the *Journal of Information Systems Management.*

By Questioning

Ask senior executives who will replace key position incumbents in their areas in the event of a vacancy. Note how many holes by function can be identified. Track the holes. The lower the percentage of holes to key positions, the greater is the organization's bench strength.

By Evidence

Using the results of an analysis of personnel records over the last few years, find out which departures created the worst problems for the organization. Note the number of such problems relative to total departures (turnover). The higher the percentage, the weaker the bench strength.

By Combination

Use a combination of the methods identified above to assess bench strength. Note the percentage of holes. Feed that information back to decision-makers to dramatize the value and importance of the SP&M program.

Exhibit 10-2: Succession Planning and Management Inventory by Position

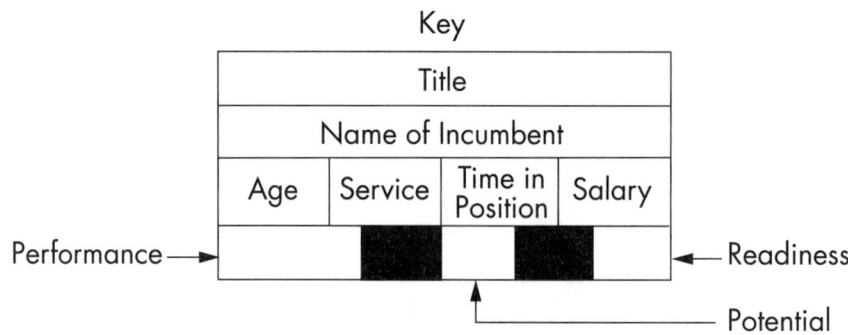

Performance Rating   Definition
X   New—in position less than three months. Not evaluated.
1   Unsatisfactory results and performance.
2   Marginal—does not meet requirements of position (with learning
        discounted). Attitude and/or initiative not acceptable.
        Remedial action indicated.
3   Satisfactory—generally meets job requirements but room for improvement.
        If in a major learning phase, considerable room for improvement.
4   Above average—surpasses overall job requirements but lacks strength in
        some areas.
5   Superior—some elements of performance may rate as exceptional, but
        overall performance falls below an exceptional rating.
6   Exceptional—general all-around excellence in quality/quantity of work,
        initiative, self-development, new ideas, and attitude. Rapid learner.

Potential
A   Outstanding—can advance two levels above present position.
B   Considerable—can advance at least one level above present position
        and/or assume substantial added responsibility at present level.
C   Some—can assume added responsibilities at present level.
D   Limited—at or near capacity in present position.
E   Key capacity in current position—vital technical knowledge precludes
        movement.
X   New—in position less than three months. Not evaluated.

Readiness
R/O   Qualified to move now.
R1   Within one to two years.
R2   Within two to four years.
N/A   Current level appropriate.

Source: Norman H. Carter, "Guaranteeing Management's Future through Succession Planning," *Journal of Information Systems Management* (Summer 1986), 20. Used by permission of the *Journal of Information Systems Management*.

Formulating Internal Promotion Policy

The centerpiece of a systematic SP&M program is a written policy favoring internal promotion. Lacking such a policy, organizations may have difficulty keeping ambitious high-potentials and exemplary performers who seek advancement. If they grow discouraged, they can contribute to a devastating increase in avoidable, and critical, turnover. It is thus essential for the organization to make all reasonable efforts to retain them. One way to do that is to place the organization "on the record" as favoring promotion from within. Not only does a promotion-from-within policy motivate employees by showing that their efforts can pay off through promotion, but promotion from within also saves the organization money in recruiting, selecting, and training a newcomer.[2]

Essential Components of an Internal Promotion Policy

To be effective, an internal promotion policy should:

△ Unequivocally state the organization's commitment to promoting employees from within whenever possible and whenever they are qualified to meet the work requirements of new positions
△ Define internal promotion
△ Explain the business reasons for that policy
△ Explain the legitimate conditions under which that policy can be waived and an external candidate can be selected

Since an internal promotion policy will (naturally) build employee expectations that most promotions will be made from within, decision-makers should anticipate challenges—legal and otherwise—to every promotion decision that is made. For that reason, the policy should be reviewed by HR professionals, operating managers, and legal professionals before it is implemented or widely communicated. In any case, reviewing the policy before adoption is more likely to build consistent understanding—and ownership—of it.

When Are Internal Promotions Appropriate—and Inappropriate—for Meeting Succession Planning and Management Needs?

Internal promotion is appropriate to meet a vacancy in a key position when a qualified replacement from the organization is:

△ "Ready" to assume the duties of the key position by demonstrated mastery of at least 80 percent of the position requirements and progress toward meeting or exceeding the remaining 20 percent of the position requirements

△ "Willing" to accept the position, expressing a desire to do the work
△ "Able" to accept the position by having his or her own replacement prepared in a reasonably short time span and by being ready to assume the duties of a key position

But promotion from within is not appropriate for meeting SP&M needs when any of these conditions cannot be met. Alternatives to internal promotions are thus appropriate when a qualified internal candidate cannot be found after a reasonable search, when possible candidates refuse to accept a position, or when possible candidates cannot be freed up from their present duties in a reasonable time.

The Importance of Job Posting

Job posting is an internal method of notifying and recruiting employees for new positions in the organization. To begin such a program, the organization should establish a policy that position opening notices will be "posted" in prominent locations—such as next to building entrances and exits, near cafeteria entrances, on bulletin boards, near restrooms, or on-line. A typical job posting notice contains information about the position that is open—such as its title, pay grade, organizational location, and desirable starting date. Employees from all areas of the organization are encouraged to apply, and selection decisions are typically made on the basis of the applicant who brings the best qualifications to the job. (In some organizations, however, seniority may be an overriding factor in making a selection decision. Additionally, posting may be restricted to include only some, but not all, job categories or functions in the organization.)

In many cases, positions are posted internally while also advertised externally. In that way, both internal and external applicants are attracted. The organization can thus seek the most qualified applicant, whether or not that person is presently employed by the organization.

The major benefit of job posting is that it gives individuals a say in their career directions. Further, it permits the organization to consider applicants from outside the immediate work area, from which successors for key positions may frequently be selected.[3] It also reduces the chance of *employee hoarding,* in which an employee's manager blocks promotions or transfers of high-potential or exemplary performers so they will remain forever trapped, though very productive, in the manager's work area.[4]

The major drawback to job posting has more to do with the management of such programs than with the posting concept itself. If employees are allowed to jump to new jobs merely to realize small wage increases, posting can be costly and demoralizing—especially to those responsible for training "mercenary job hoppers." Hence, to be used effectively as a tool in SP&M, job posting should be done for all jobs. However, careful restrictions should be placed on the process to ensure that employees remain in their positions for a period sufficient to recoup training costs.

Preparing Individual Development Plans

Testing bench strength should clarify the organization's collective SP&M needs. However, it does not indicate what individuals should do to qualify for advancement to key positions. That is the reason for preparing Individual Development Plans.

What Is an Individual Development Plan?

An *Individual Development Plan* (IDP) results from a comparison of individual strengths and weaknesses on the current job and individual potential for advancement to possible key positions in the future. Preparing an IDP is a process of planning activities that will narrow the gap between what individuals can already do and what they should do to meet future work requirements in one or more key positions.

An IDP is a hybrid between a learning contract, a performance contract, and a career planning form. A *learning contract* is an agreement to learn. Contract learning has enjoyed a long and venerable history.[5] It is particularly well suited to participative, learning organizations that seek to balance individual career needs and interests with organizational strategy and work requirements. A *performance contract* is an agreement to achieve an identifiable, measurable level of performance.[6] Sometimes tied to performance appraisal, it is directed toward future performance improvement rather than past performance. Finally, a *career planning form* is a tool for helping individuals identify their career goals and establish effective strategies for realizing them in the future. A career planning form is typically linked to an organizational career planning program, which can reinforce and support SP&M.

An IDP goes a step beyond performance appraisal for the individual's present job and potential assessment of the individual's capability for future advancement to other, often key, positions in the organization. It results in a detailed plan to furnish individuals with what they need to know or do to qualify for advancement into their next positions.

Developing an IDP usually requires a systematic comparison of the individual's present abilities (as indicated by competency requirements, work activities appearing on job descriptions, and current performance as measured by performance appraisals) and future capabilities (as revealed through individual potential assessment). The IDP should narrow the gap between them, providing a clearcut plan by which to prepare the individual for future advancement.

How Are Individual Development Plans Prepared?

Preparing an IDP shares strong similarities to preparing a learning contract. Take ten key steps when preparing individual development plans. (Exhibit 10-3 depicts these steps in a simple model.)

Step One: Selecting Possible Key Positions for Which to Prepare the Individual

Begin by targeting a family of key positions in the organization for the individual. In most cases, this should be done only after a significant dialog has taken place between the individual and an organizational representative. As Deegan notes, "it is important that the individual understand the illustrative nature of the position you select as the targeted one and focus not on that specific job but on the family of jobs represented by it. Otherwise there may be disappointment if that job is not offered even though a future offer might actually meet the person's needs better as well as those of the firm."[7] Of course, if it is anticipated that the individual will be prepared for a specific key position that will soon become vacant, then planning should be focused on that position after discussion with the individual.

Step Two: Considering the Likely Time during Which the Individual Must Be Prepared

Time affects what kind of—and how many—developmental activities can be carried out. When individuals are slated for rapid advancement, there is little or no time for preparation. Hence, those developmental activities that are selected should be absolutely critical to effective job performance. There is thus a need to *prioritize* developmental activities. That should be done, of course, even when time is ample. The key issue in this step, then, amounts to this: How much time is available for development?

Step Three: Diagnosing Learning Needs

Exactly what is the difference between the individual's present knowledge and skills and the work requirements of key positions for which the

Exhibit 10-3: A Simplified Model of Steps in Preparing Individual Development Plans (IDPs)

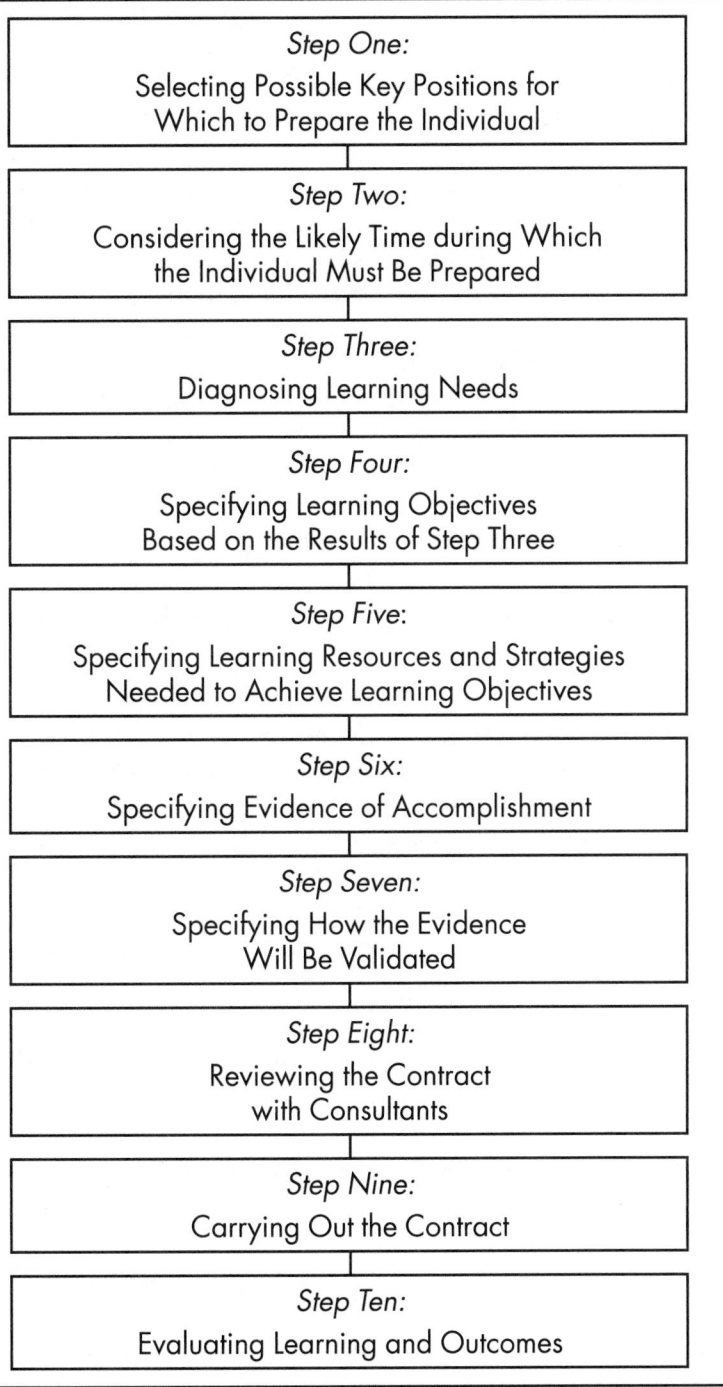

Step One:
Selecting Possible Key Positions for
Which to Prepare the Individual

Step Two:
Considering the Likely Time during Which
the Individual Must Be Prepared

Step Three:
Diagnosing Learning Needs

Step Four:
Specifying Learning Objectives
Based on the Results of Step Three

Step Five:
Specifying Learning Resources and Strategies
Needed to Achieve Learning Objectives

Step Six:
Specifying Evidence of Accomplishment

Step Seven:
Specifying How the Evidence
Will Be Validated

Step Eight:
Reviewing the Contract
with Consultants

Step Nine:
Carrying Out the Contract

Step Ten:
Evaluating Learning and Outcomes

individual is to be prepared? The answer to that question clarifies the developmental gap.

One way to determine this difference is to compare the individual's present work requirements and performance to those required in a targeted key position. (You might think of that as akin to conducting a performance appraisal to which the individual aspires or for which he or she is being groomed.) As a simple example, it may involve comparing how well an employee could perform his or her immediate supervisor's job.

Another way to determine this difference is to ask the key position incumbent to review the individual's present work requirements and performance against the requirements of the incumbent's position and to recommend planned developmental activities to narrow the gap between what the employee already knows and can do and what he or she should know or do to perform in the place of the key position incumbent.

When diagnosing learning needs, be aware that the quality of the results depends on the quality of the diagnosis. Shortcuts are not conducive to useful outcomes. While busy executives might prefer to short-circuit this process, that will usually prove to be counterproductive.

Step Four: Specifying Learning Objectives Based on the Results of Step Three

Learning objectives are the outcomes or results that are sought from planned developmental activities. Needs represent deficiencies or problems to be solved; objectives, on the other hand, represent desired solutions. Each need should be linked to one—or more—learning objectives to ensure that each "problem" will be "solved."

Learning objectives should always be stated in measurable terms. As Robert F. Mager has noted,[8] all learning objectives should have three components:

- △ *Resources*. What equipment, tools, information, or other resources must be provided for the learner to demonstrate the necessary knowledge, skills, or abilities?
- △ *Criteria*. How will achievement of learning objectives be measured? What minimum performance standards must be achieved for the individual to demonstrate competence?
- △ *Conditions*. Under what conditions must the learner perform?

Use the Worksheet appearing in Exhibit 10-4 to prepare learning objectives based on individual developmental needs.

Exhibit 10-4: A Worksheet for Preparing Learning Objectives Based on Individual Development Needs

Directions: Use this Worksheet to help you prepare specific, measurable learning objectives to guide the process of meeting individual development needs.

In the left column below, indicate activities, responsibilities, duties, tasks, or essential job functions to which the individual needs exposure in order to qualify for advancement. Then, in the right column below, draft specific and measurable learning objectives to describe what individuals should be able to know, do, or feel upon completion of a planned development/learning experience tied to those activities, responsibilities, duties, tasks, or essential job functions. When you finish drafting the objectives, double-check them to ensure that you have listed (1) resources, such as information, equipment, or tools that are necessary for demonstrating the objective; (2) measurable criteria by which to assess how well the learning objective was achieved.

Indicate Activities, Responsibilities, Duties, Tasks, or Essential Job Functions to Which the Individual Needs Exposure in Order to Qualify for Advancement	*Specific and Measurable Learning Objectives*

Step Five: Specifying Learning Resources and Strategies Needed to Achieve the Learning Objectives

Learning strategies are the means by which learning objectives are to be achieved. There are many strategies by which to achieve learning objectives. Appropriate learning strategies depend on the learning objectives that are to be met. They answer this question: What planned learning activities will help narrow the gap between what individuals already know and what they must know to meet key position requirements in the future?

Learning resources are what must be provided to achieve the learning objectives. Resources might include people, money, time, expertise, equipment, or information. People resources could include trainers, coaches, mentors, or sponsors. Money resources could include funding for participation in on-the-job or off-the-job developmental experiences. Time resources could include released time from work to participate in planned training, education, or developmental activities. Expertise could include access to knowledgeable people or information sources. Equipment could include access, for developmental purposes, to specialized machines or tools. (Use the Worksheet appearing in Exhibit 10-5 to identify the resources necessary to develop individuals for key positions for which they have been targeted.)

Step Six: Specifying Evidence of Accomplishment

How can the organization track accomplishment of learning objectives? Answer that question by providing clear, measurable learning objectives and by providing regular feedback about the learner's progress to the learner and those interested in the learner's development. If possible, use short, informal "project appraisals" or more formalized, written "developmental appraisals" to document individual progress, provide evidence of accomplishment, and give the individual specific feedback that can lead to future performance improvement.

Step Seven: Specifying How the Evidence Will Be Validated

Be clear about the means by which achievement of learning objectives will be validated. Will a knowledgeable expert, such as a key position incumbent, review the results? Will the learner be asked to complete an oral interview to demonstrate results? Will learners' performance on developmental projects be reviewed by those with whom they work? These questions must be answered separately for *each* learning objective and for *each* learning project or assignment on which the learners are to work to qualify for advancement.

Exhibit 10-5: A Worksheet for Identifying the Resources Necessary to Support Developmental Experiences

Directions: Use this Worksheet to help you identify the resources necessary to support planned learning/developmental experiences.

In the left column below, indicate learning objectives and the planned learning/developmental experiences that will be used in helping an individual qualify for promotion. Then, in the right column below, indicate specifically what resources—such as information, money, trainers, equipment, time, and so forth—will be needed to allow the individual to meet each learning objective and participate in each planned learning/developmental experience.

Learning Objectives and Planned Learning/Development Experiences Intended to Help an Individual Qualify for Advancement	*What Specific Resources Will Be Needed to Achieve each Objective and Participate in each Planned Learning/Development Experiences*

Step Eight: Reviewing the Contract with Consultants

Before the Individual Development Plan is approved, it should be reviewed by knowledgeable experts. In this context, *experts* and *consultants* are meant to have broad meanings. For instance, experts and consultants might include any—or all—of the following:

△ Members of SP&M committees
△ Friends
△ Spouses
△ Immediate organizational superiors
△ The learners' peers
△ The learners' subordinates
△ Academic experts
△ Recognized authorities in other organizations

Depending on the organization, the individual, and the key position for which the individual is being prepared, other experts or consultants might prove useful. For instance, individuals may wish to identify their own mentors and ask for their advice while negotiating an IDP. In unionized settings, union members may also wish to include union representatives.

Ask the experts to provide information on which they are qualified to comment. For instance, from their perspective, does an IDP appear to have identified the right learning needs, established the right learning objectives, identified the most appropriate learning strategies and resources, and established the best means by which to evaluate results? Is it practical and capable of being completed in the time allowed? What suggested changes, if any, do the "experts" recommend—and why?

Step Nine: Carrying Out the Contract

I have found that the implementation of IDPs is the Achilles' heel of many otherwise exemplary SP&M programs. While well conceived, many IDPs are not well executed. Hence, some means must be established to ensure accountability—and monitor results during the IDP's time span. That can be done by planning quarterly IDP review meetings with representatives from each major area of the organization so they can report on the progress made in their areas. Alternatively, an SP&M coordinator can pay visits to individual managers to review the progress made on IDPs in their areas of responsibility. The effect of these actions is to draw attention to the plans—and to maintain an impetus for action.

Step Ten: Evaluating Learning and Outcomes

Be sure that results (learning outcomes) are measured against intentions (learning objectives and needs).

There are several ways to do that. One way is to establish periodic developmental assessments, much like project-oriented performance appraisals. If this approach is used, develop a simple feedback form to provide documentation of learners' progress on each developmental experience. They can then be reviewed upon completion of learning objectives or at agreed-upon intervals during the developmental experiences.

A second way is to provide a checklist on the IDP form to indicate whether learning objectives have been achieved. That is a simpler, albeit less ambitious and rigorous, approach than periodic developmental assessments. However, it does have the advantage of being a time-efficient approach that makes it more likely to be used by busy decision-makers. A sample Individual Development Plan (IDP) is shown in Exhibit 10-6 on page 230.

Developing Successors Internally

Internal development is a general term that refers to those developmental activities sponsored by the organization that are intended to help an individual qualify for advancement by closing the gap between present work requirements/performance and future work requirements/potential. Indeed, it is the means by which individual potential is realized as the future unfolds in the present.

There are many approaches to internal development. Many ways have been devised to develop individuals in their present positions,[9] and as many as 300 ways have been devised to develop individuals.[10] My 1999 survey identified common approaches to internal development. The survey results are summarized in Exhibit 10-7, and each strategy is briefly summarized in Exhibit 10-8.

Other strategies may also be used. These include:

1. *Who-based strategies*. These learning strategies focus on pairing up high-potentials with individuals who have special talents—or management styles—worthy of emulation. Example: matching up a high-potential with a participative manager or those possessing special abilities in start-ups, turnarounds, or shutdown efforts.

2. *What-based strategies*. These learning strategies focus on giving high-potentials exposure to specific types of experiences—such as projects, task forces, committees, jobs, or assignments that require the individ-

Exhibit 10-6: A Sample Individual Development Plan

Directions: Use this Individual Development Plan to help an individual qualify for advancement. The individual's immediate organizational superior should complete the form and then discuss it with the individual. If the individual feels that modifications to it should be made, then the reasons for that should be discussed.

Employee's Name _____ Job Title _____

Department _____ Time in Position _____

Appraiser's Name _____ Job Title _____

Department _____ Time in Position _____

Today's Date _____ Plan Covering _____ to _____
            mo./day/yr.   mo./day/yr.   mo./day/yr.

1. For what key position should this individual be prepared? Over what time span?

2. What are the individual's career plans/objectives?

3. What learning objectives should guide the individual's development? (*Note to appraiser: Be sure to systematically compare the individual's current job description to a current job description for the targeted position[s] and list the identifiable gap below.*)

4. By what methods/strategies may the objectives be met? (*Indicate a specific learning plan below, indicating learning objectives, strategies by which to achieve the objectives, deadlines for achieving each result, and a checklist indicating whether the learning objective was achieved.*) Add paper if necessary.

			Verified?	
Learning		*Deadlines/*	*Yes*	*No*
Objectives	*Strategies*	*Benchmark Dates*	( )	( )

---

5. How can the relative success of each learning objective be measured?

Learning	
Objectives	*Evaluation Approach*

---

ual to master or demonstrate analytical skills, leadership skills, or skills in starting up an operation, shutting down an operation, converting a manual to an automated process, or another project of a specific kind. Additionally, service on interteam, interdepartmental, or interdivisional committees can give the individual visibility and exposure to new people and new functions.

3. *When-based strategies.* These learning strategies focus on giving high-potentials exposure to time pressure. Examples: meeting a nearly impossible deadline or beating a wily competitor to market.

4. *Where-based strategies.* These learning strategies focus on giving high-potentials exposure to special locations or cultures. Examples: sending high-potentials on international job rotations or assignments to give them exposure to the business in another culture or else send them to another domestic site for a special project. Like any job rotation or temporary assignment, international assignments should be preceded by a well-prepared plan that clarifies what the individual is to do and learn—and why that is worth doing or learning. This approach will shape expectations and thereby exert a powerful influence on what people learn as well as on how they perform.

5. *Why-based strategies.* These learning strategies focus on giving high-potentials exposure to mission-driven change efforts that are, in turn, learning experiences. Examples: asking high-potentials to pioneer start-up efforts or to visit competitors or "best-in-class" organizations to find out "why they do what they do."

(Text continues on page 237.)

Exhibit 10-7: Methods of Grooming Individuals for Advancement*

There are many ways by which to implement succession plans, since individuals may be "groomed" in different ways. Review the list of possible methods by which to groom individuals in column 1 below. Then, in column 2, check ( ) yes or no to indicate whether your organization is using it and, in column 3, circle the code indicating how effective you feel that method is in developing people to assume future responsibilities. In column 3, use the following scale: 1 = Not at all effective; 2 = Not very effective; 3 = Somewhat effective; 4 = Effective; 5 = Very effective.

	Column 1	Column 2			Column 3				
	Possible Methods by Which to "Groom" Individuals	Is Your Organization Using This Method to Develop People?			How Effective Do You Feel This Method Is for Developing People to Assume Future Job Responsibilities?				
		Y/N	Freq.	%	Mean	SD	Mode	Median	Response
A	Off-the-job degree programs sponsored by colleges/ universities	Yes No	9 3	75.00 25.00	3.67	0.99	4	4	40%
B	On-site degree programs at colleges/universities	Yes No	3 9	25.00 75.00	3.25	0.97	5	3	40%
C	Off-the-job seminars sponsored by vendors	Yes No	8 4	66.67 33.33	3.17	0.94	4	3	40%
D	Off-the-job public seminars sponsored by universities	Yes No	12 0	100 0.00	3.75	0.62	5	4	40%

E	In-house classroom courses tailor-made for management-level employees	Yes No	9 3	75.00 25.00	3.75	1.14	4	4	40%
F	In-house classroom courses purchased from outside sources and modified for in-house use	Yes No	7 5	58.33 41.67	3.42	1.31	3,4,5	3.5	40%
G	Unplanned on-the-job training	Yes No	10 2	83.33 16.67	3.83	1.27	5	4	40%
H	Planned-on-the-job training	Yes No	10 2	83.33 16.67	4.50	0.79	5	5	40%
I	Unplanned mentoring programs	Yes No	4 8	33.33 66.67	3.17	1.47	3,5	3	40%
J	Planned mentoring programs	Yes No	3 9	25.00 75.00	4.08	1.08	5	4.5	40%
K	Unplanned job rotation programs	Yes No	6 6	50.00 50.00	3.58	0.10	4	3	40%
L	Planned job rotation programs	Yes No	4 8	33.33 66.67	4.42	0.67	5	4.5	40%

*SOURCE: William J. Rothwell, *Results of a Survey on Succession Planning and Management Practices,* unpublished survey results (University Park, Pa.: The Pennsylvania State University, 2000).

Exhibit 10-8: Key Strategies for Internal Development

Strategy	How to Use It	Appropriate and Inappropriate Uses
1. Off-the-job degree programs sponsored by colleges/universities	△ Clarify job-related courses tied to work requirements of key positions. △ Compare individual skills to work requirements. △ Identify courses related to individual needs. △ Tie job requirements to degree/course requirements, if possible.	△ *Appropriate:* —For meeting specialized individual needs that are not widely enough shared to warrant on-site training △ *Inappropriate:* —For meeting highly specialized needs unique to one employer
2. On-site degree programs sponsored by colleges/universities	△ Same basic procedure as listed in #1 above.	△ *Appropriate:* —When funding and time are available —When several people share similar needs —When in-house expertise is not available △ *Inappropriate:* —When conditions listed above cannot be met —For meeting highly specialized needs
3. Off-the-job public seminars sponsored by vendors	△ Compare work requirements to the instructional objectives indicated by information about the off-the-job seminar.	△ *Appropriate:* —When needs are limited to a few people —When in-house expertise does not match the vendor's △ *Inappropriate:* —For meeting needs unique to one employer

4. Off-the-job public seminars sponsored by universities

△ Same as #3 above.

△ *Appropriate:*
—Same as #3 above
△ *Inappropriate:*
—Same as #3 above

5. In-house classroom courses tailor-made for employees

△ Define specific instructional objectives that are directly related to work requirements in key positions.
△ Use the courses to achieve instructional objectives for many individuals.

△ *Appropriate:*
—When adequate resources exist
—When in-house expertise is unavailable
—When needs can be met in time
△ *Inappropriate:*
—For meeting requirements unique to one organization
—For meeting objectives requiring lengthy and experiential learning

6. In-house classroom courses purchased from outside sources and modified for in-house use

△ Identify a learning need shared by more than one person.
△ Find published training material from commercial publishers and modify for in-house use.
△ Deliver to groups.

△ *Appropriate:*
—When several people share a common learning need
—When expertise exists to modify materials developed outside the organization
—When appropriate training materials can be located

7. Unplanned on-the-job training

△ Match up a high-potential employee with an exemplary performer in a key position.
△ Permit long-term observation of the exemplar by the high-potential.

△ *Appropriate:*
—When time, money, and staffing are not of primary importance
△ *Inappropriate:*
—For efficiently and effectively preparing high-potentials to be successors for key job incumbents

(continues)

Exhibit 10-8: *(continued)*

Strategy	How to Use It	Appropriate and Inappropriate Uses
8. Planned on-the-job training	△ Develop a detailed training plan allowing a "tell, show, do, follow-up approach" to instruction.	△ *Appropriate:* —When key job incumbent is an exemplar —When time and safety considerations permit one-on-one instruction △ *Inappropriate:* —When the conditions listed above cannot be met
9. Unplanned mentoring programs	△ Make people aware of what mentoring is. △ Help individuals understand how they can establish mentoring relationships and realize the chief benefits from them. △ Encourage key job incumbents and exemplars to serve as mentors.	△ *Appropriate:* —For establishing the basis for mentoring without obligating the organization to oversee it —For encouraging individual autonomy △ *Inappropriate:* —For encouraging diversity and building relationships across "unlike" individual —For transferring specific skills
10. Planned mentoring programs	△ Match up individuals who may establish useful mentor-protégé relationships. △ Provide training to mentors on effective mentoring skills and to protégés on the best ways to take advantage of mentoring relationships.	△ *Appropriate:* —For building top-level ownership and familiarity with high-potentials —For pairing up "unlike individuals" on occasion △ *Inappropriate:* —For building specific skills

11. Unplanned job rotation programs	△ Arrange to move individuals into positions that will give them knowledge, skills, or abilities they will need in the future, preferably (but not necessarily) geared to advancement. △ Track individual progress.	△ *Appropriate:* —When sufficient staffing exists —When individual movement will not create a significant productivity loss to the organization △ *Inappropriate:* —When the conditions listed above cannot be met
12. Planned job rotation programs	△ Develop a specific Learning Contract (or IDP) that clarifies the learning objectives to be achieved by the rotation. △ Ensure that the work activities in which the individual gains experience are directly related to future work requirements. △ Monitor work progress through periodic feedback to the individual and through performance appraisal geared to the rotation and related to future potential.	△ *Appropriate:* —When there is sufficient time and staffing to permit the rotation to be effective △ *Inappropriate:* —When time and staffing will not permit planned learning

6. *How-based strategies.* These learning strategies focus on furnishing high-potentials with in-depth, "how-to" knowledge of different aspects of the business in which they are otherwise weak. Examples might include lengthy job assignments, task force assignments, or job rotations that expose a high-potential to another area of the business with which he or she is unfamiliar.

Summary

Promotion from within is an important way to implement succession plans. To that end, the organization should test bench strength, establish an unequivocal internal promotion policy to ensure internal promotion when appropriate, prepare Individual Development Plans (IDPs) to close the gap between what individuals presently do and what they must do to qualify for promotion, and use internal development when appropriate to realize the learning objectives established on IDPs.

But internal promotion and internal development are not the only means by which succession planning and management needs can be met. Alternative means, which usually fall outside the realm of succession planning and management, are treated in the next chapter. In these days of business process reengineering and process improvement, those involved in succession planning and management should have some awareness of approaches to meeting work requirements other than traditional succession methods relying on job movements.

Chapter 11

Assessing Alternatives to Internal Development

The traditional approach is to prepare successors for key positions internally. Some descriptions of succession planning and management (SP&M) treat it as nothing more than a form of replacement planning. In this process, several key assumptions are usually made: (1) Key positions will be replaced whenever a vacancy occurs; (2) Employees already working in the organization—and often within the function—will be the prime source of replacements; and (3) A key measure of effectiveness is the percentage of key positions that can be filled from within, with minimal delay and uproar, whenever a vacancy occurs. Some organizations add a fourth: the relative racial and sexual diversity of replacements should be enhanced so that protected labor groups are well represented among the qualified replacements for key positions prepared internally.

A systematic approach to SP&M has major advantages, of course. First, it makes succession predictable. Each time a vacancy in a key position occurs, people know precisely what to do—find a replacement. Second, since a high percentage of successors are assumed to be employed by the organization, investments in employee development can be justified to minimize losses in productivity and turnover.

However, when SP&M is treated in this way it can occasionally become a mindless exercise in "filling in the blank name on the organization chart." Concern about that should be sufficient to lead strategists to explore innovative alternatives to the traditional replacement-from-within mentality. This chapter focuses on those alternatives—and on when they should be used instead of the traditional approach to SP&M.

Assessing Alternatives

"The natural response to a problem," writes James L. Adams in *Conceptual Blockbusting*, "seems to be to try to get rid of it by finding an answer—often taking the first answer that occurs and pursuing it because of one's reluctance to spend the time and mental effort needed to conjure up a richer storehouse of alternatives from which to choose. This hit-and-run approach to problem-solving begets all sorts of oddities. . . ."[1]

Succession planning and management can fall victim to the same natural response to which Adams refers: Whenever a vacancy occurs, the organization is confronted with a problem. The "natural response" is to find an immediate replacement. There may also be a tendency to "clone the incumbent"—that is, find someone who resembles the present position incumbent in order to minimize the need to make adjustments to a new person.

But replacement is not always appropriate. Consider a replacement unnecessary when any one of the questions listed below can be answered "yes." (Review the flowchart appearing in Exhibit 11-1 as a simplified aid in helping with this decision process.)

Question One: Is the Key Position No Longer Necessary?

A replacement is not necessary when a key position is no longer worth doing. In that situation, a "key" position is no longer "key." Decision-makers can simply choose not to fill the key position when a vacancy occurs. Of course, if this question is answered "no," then a replacement may still have to be found.

Question Two: Can a Key Position Be Rendered Unnecessary by Finding New Ways to Achieve Comparable Results?

A replacement may not be necessary if key work outcomes can be achieved in new ways. In this sense, then, SP&M can be affected by *business process reengineering*, defined by best-selling authors Michael Hammer and James Champy as "the fundamental rethinking and radical redesign of business processes to achieve dramatic improvements in critical, contemporary measures of performance, such as cost, quality, service, and speed."[2] If the organization can reengineer work processes and thereby eliminate positions that were once "key" to an "old" process, then replacing a key job incumbent will be unnecessary. In short, key positions may be reengineered out of existence.

To that end, try applying the model suggested by Rummler and Brache to process improvement:[3]

1. Identify the critical business issue or process that is to be reexamined.
2. Select critical processes related to the issue or subprocesses.
3. Select a leader and members for a process improvement team.

(Text continues on page 247.)

Exhibit 11-1: Deciding When Replacing a Key Job Incumbent Is Unnecessary: A Flowchart

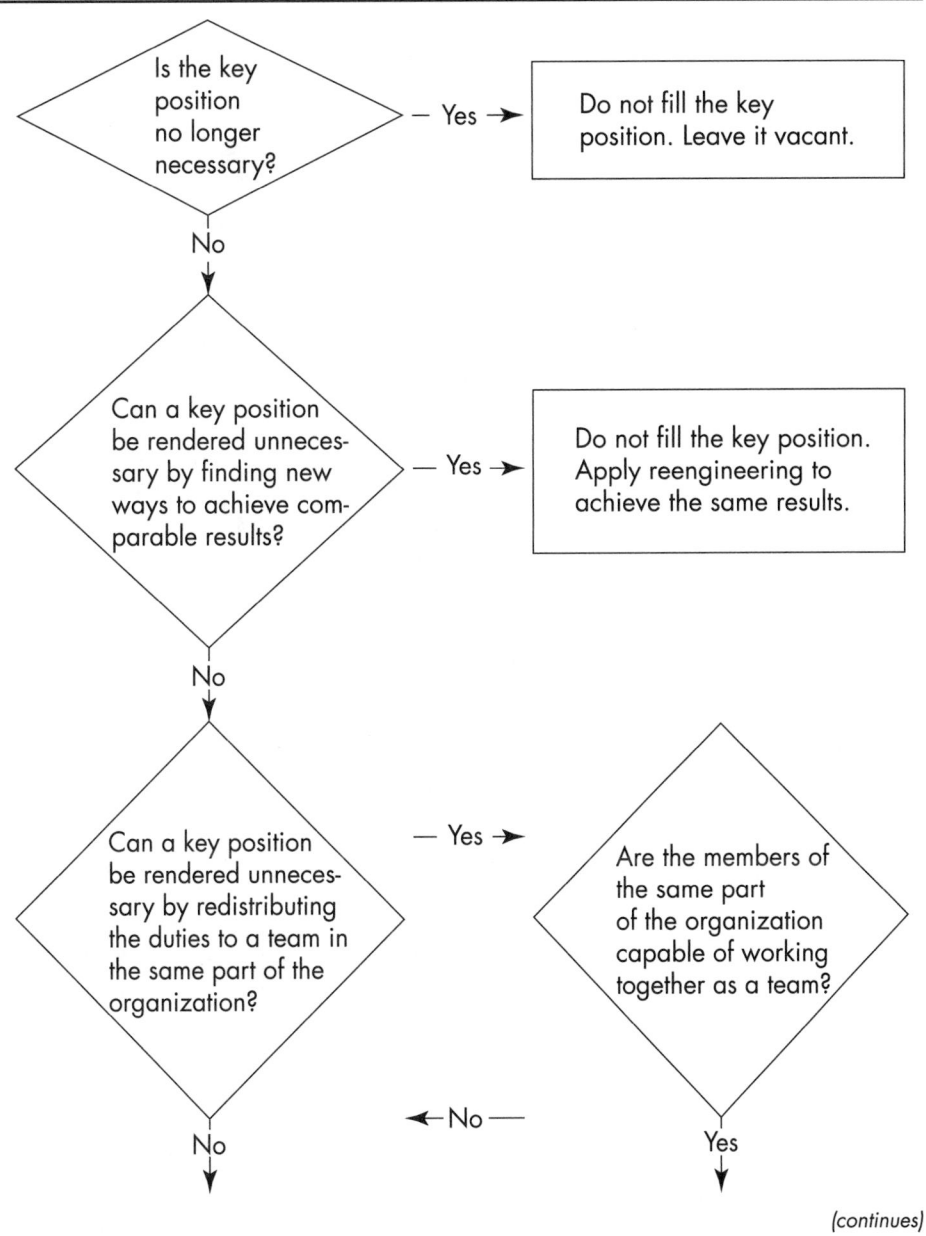

(continues)

Exhibit 11-1: *(continued)*

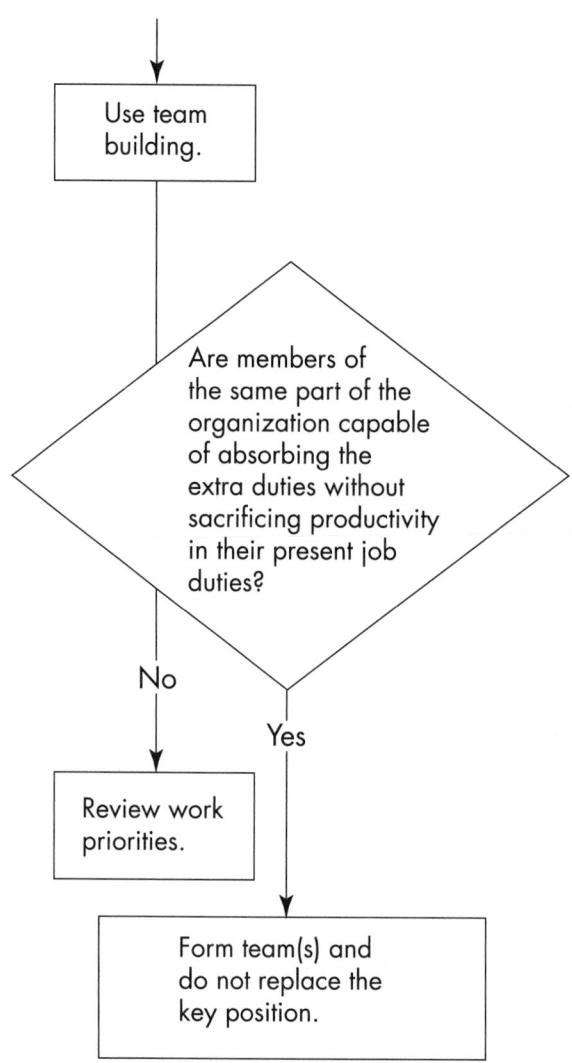

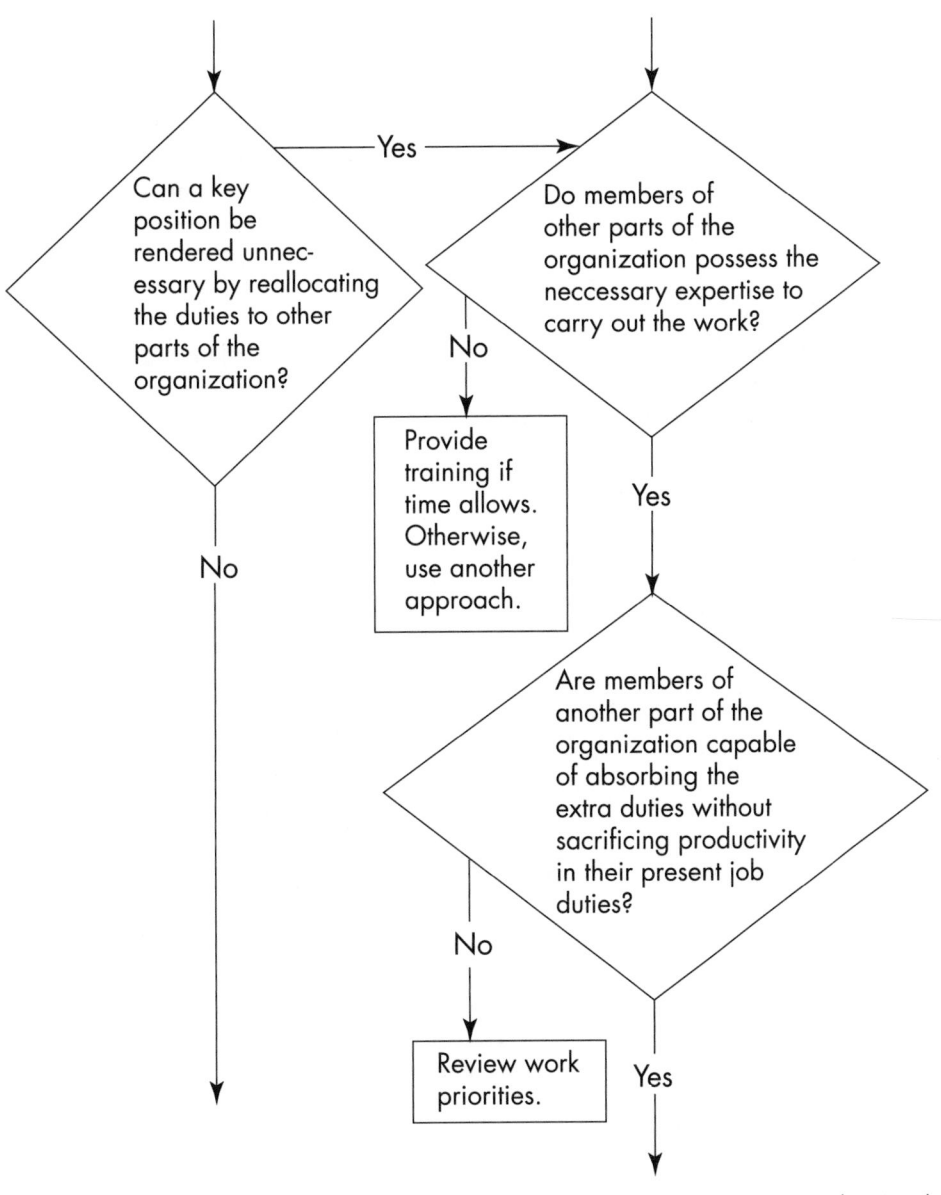

(continues)

Exhibit 11-1: *(continued)*

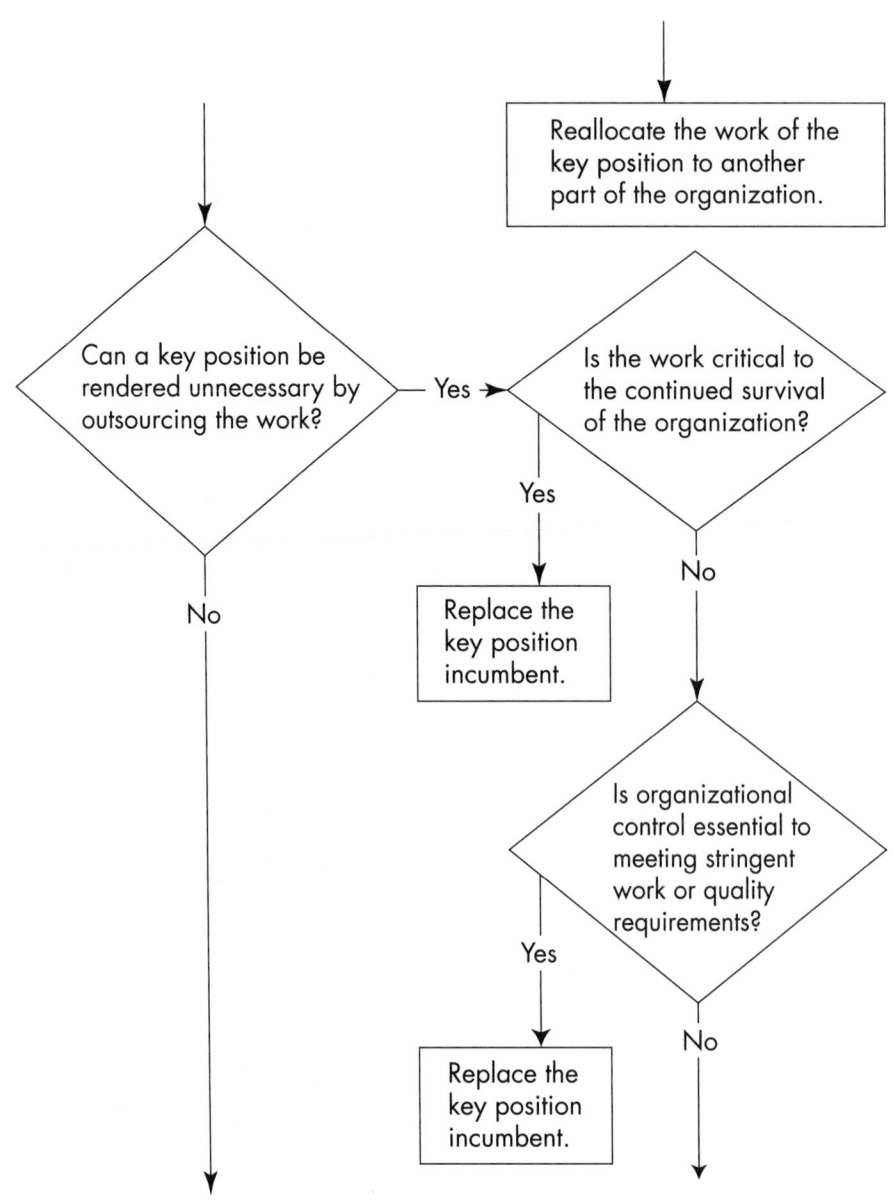

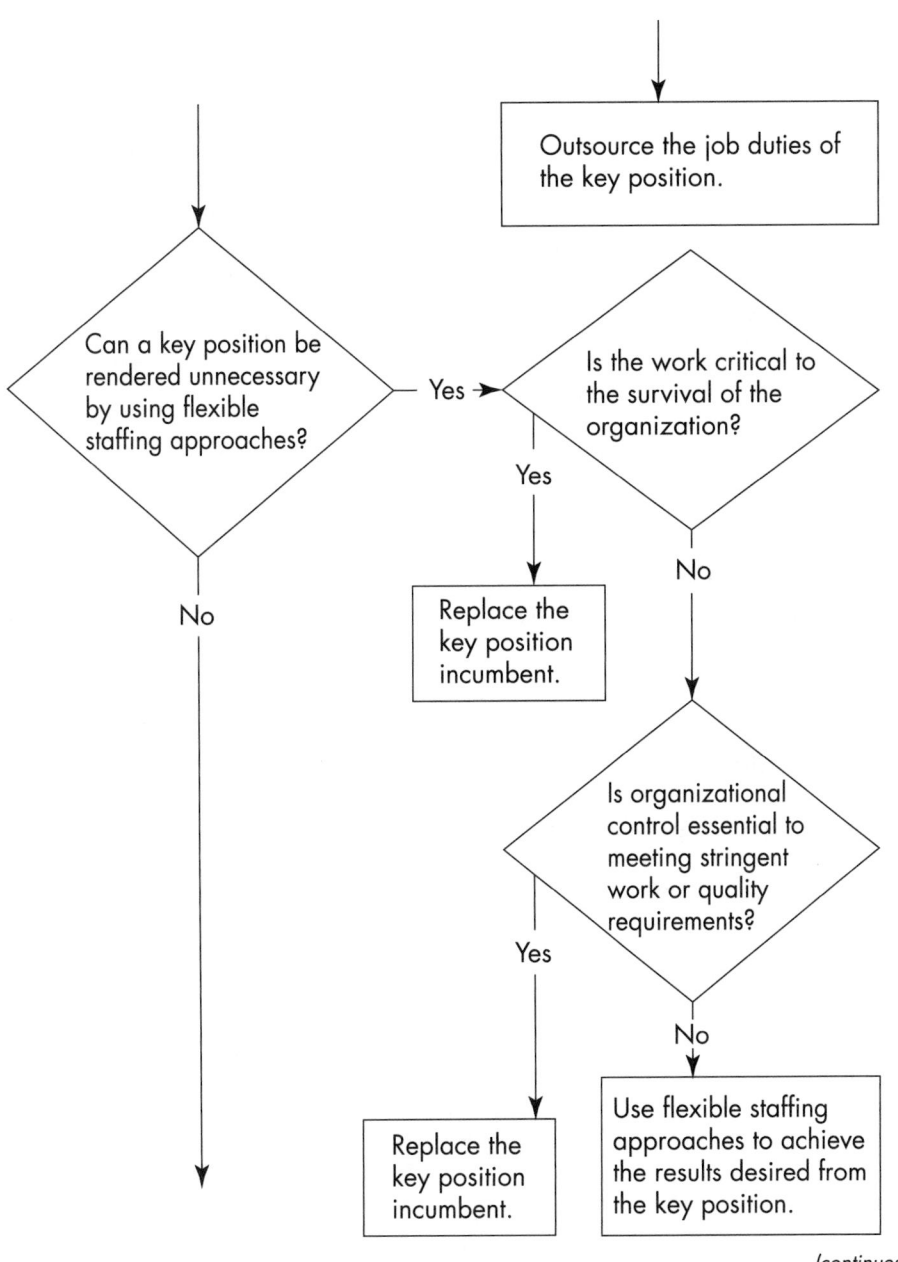

(continues)

Exhibit 11-1: *(continued)*

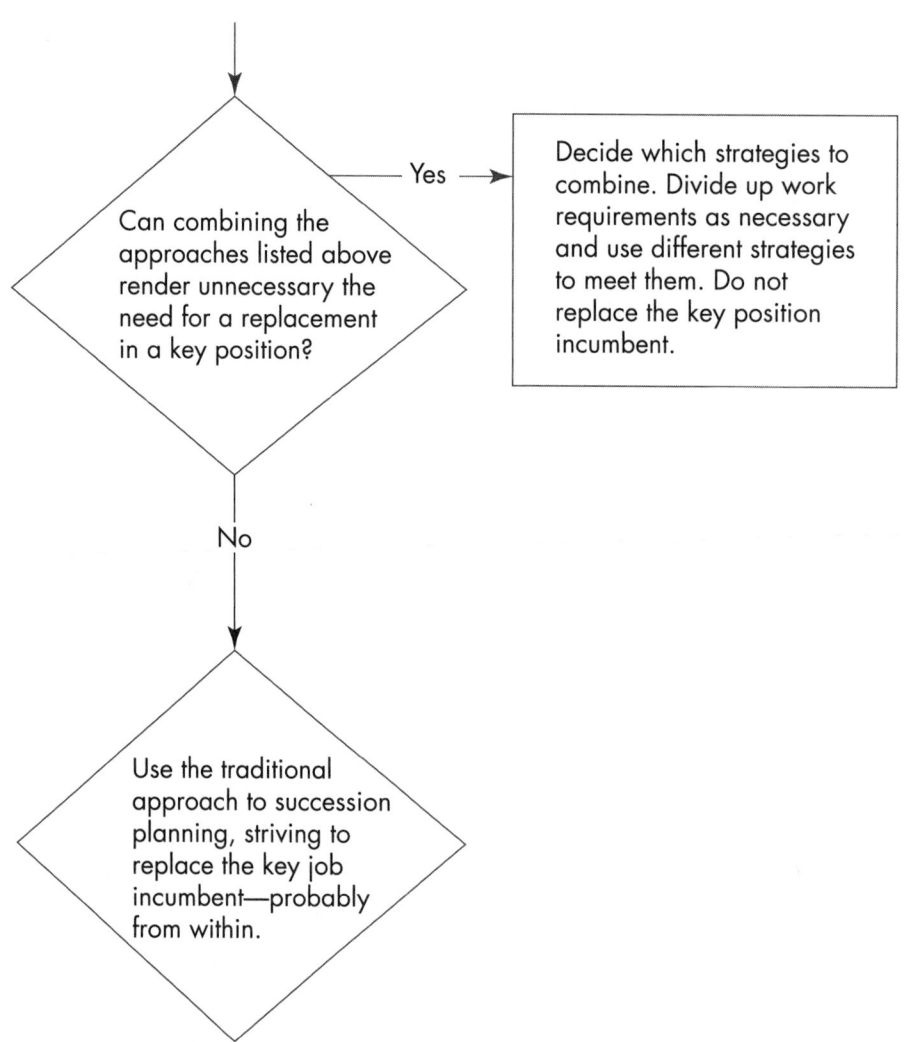

4. Train the team on process improvement methods.
5. Develop "is" maps to show the relationship between where and how work flows into a system, how it is transformed through work methods, and where it goes when the products or services are provided to the "customers."
6. Find "disconnects," which are missing, redundant, or illogical factors that could affect the critical business issue or the process.
7. Analyze the disconnects.
8. Develop a "should" map to present a more efficient or effective method of handling the work.
9. Establish measures or standards for what is desired.
10. Recommend changes.
11. Implement the changes.

In essence, the same steps described above can be used to determine whether there are ways to "engineer a key position out of existence." If there is, then no successor will be needed. (However, the work process may be broken up and reallocated, necessitating new skills and abilities for those who absorb the new duties.)

Question Three: Can a Key Position Be Rendered Unnecessary by Redistributing the Duties to a Team in the Same Part of the Organization?

If the answer is "yes," then it should be possible to achieve the same work results by placing responsibility in a team of workers from the same function or work unit.

However, two caveats should be considered. First, if the workers have never functioned as a team, then they will probably require team-building and training on team skills to work as a cohesive group. Second, if prospective team members are already working at—or beyond—their individual capacities, then loading additional duties on a team will not be successful.

Question Four: Can a Key Position Be Rendered Unnecessary by Reallocating the Duties to Other Parts of the Organization?

Can the results achieved by a key position incumbent be reallocated to other parts of the organization? In short, is it possible to avoid filling a key position by reorganizing, moving the work responsibility to another function or organizational unit? If the answer is "yes," then replacing a key job incumbent may prove to be unnecessary.

But, as in redistributing work to a team in the same part of the organization, assess whether the inheritors of key position duties are trained adequately to perform the work and can do them without sacrificing productivity in their present jobs. If both conditions can be met, consider moving responsibilities to another part of the organization to avoid replacing a key job incumbent.

Question Five: Can a Key Position Be Rendered Unnecessary by Outsourcing the Work?

Can the same results achieved by a key position be moved outside the organization and conducted by a contractor? If the answer is "yes," then replacing a key job incumbent may be unnecessary. The same results may be achieved more cost-effectively than by replacing a key job incumbent.

Pay particular attention to two key issues when answering the question—*criticality* and *control*. If the work is critical to the continued survival of the organization, then outsourcing it may be unwise because that may vest too much influence in an individual or group having little or no stake in the organization's continued survival. If the work must meet stringent, specialized requirements for which few external sources can be found, then outsourcing may also prove to be unwise because controlling the activities of an external contractor may become as time-consuming as performing the work in-house.

Question Six: Can a Key Position Be Rendered Unnecessary by Using Flexible Staffing Approaches?

Can the same results achieved by a key position be met through flexible staffing approaches other than outsourcing—such as the use of permanent part-time or temporary part-time staff, rotating employees, or internships? If the answer is "yes," then replacing a key job incumbent may be unnecessary.

However, as in outsourcing, pay attention to *criticality* and *control*. If the work is critical to the continued survival of the organization, then using innovative staffing approaches may prove to be unwise because it will place too much influence over the organization's survival in an individual or group having little or no stake in the organization's continued existence. If the work must meet stringent, specialized requirements that require an extended time span for mastery, then innovative staffing may prove to be impractical because part-time talent may not be able to achieve or maintain mastery.

Question Seven: Can Combining the Approaches Listed Above Obviate the Need for a Replacement in a Key Position?

Finally, can the need to replace a key job incumbent be avoided by relying on a combination of the approaches listed above? In other words, is it possible to split apart the key results or outcomes desired from the key position and handle them separately—through reengineering, team-based management, organizational redesign, or other means? If that question can be answered "yes," then it should be possible to ensure that the organization achieves the same results as those provided by the key job incumbent—but without the need for a replacement.

Use the Worksheet appearing in Exhibit 11-2 to decide when it is possible to answer "yes" to any one—or all—of the questions listed above.

Deciding What to Do

There is no foolproof way to integrate SP&M with alternatives to replacement from within. The important point is to make sure that alternatives to simple replacement are considered. Often, that responsibility will rest with HR generalists, HRD specialists, SP coordinators, and even CEOs or others who bear major responsibility for succession planning and management. A good strategy is to raise the issue at two different—and opportune—times: (1) during review meetings to identify successors; and (2) on the occasions when a vacancy occurs in a key position and permission is sought to fill it.

During the review process, ask operating managers how they plan to meet replacement needs. At that time, raise the alternatives—and ask them to consider other possibilities as well. Be sure that only key positions are being considered in succession planning and management efforts in order to focus attention on areas of critical need.

When a vacancy occurs—or is about to occur—in a key position, raise the issue again. Ask operating managers what alternatives to simple replacement they have considered. Briefly review some of them to ensure that succession is driven by work requirements and not by custom, resistance to change, or other issues that may be needlessly costly or inefficient.

Summary

This chapter has reviewed alternatives to traditional replacement from within. Alternatives may be used when any one or all of the following seven questions may be answered "yes":

1. Is the key position no longer necessary?
2. Can a key position be rendered unnecessary by finding new ways to achieve comparable results?

(Text continues on page 252.)

Exhibit 11-2: A Worksheet for Identifying Alternatives to the Traditional Approach to Succession Planning and Management

Directions: Use this Worksheet to help you identify alternatives to the traditional approach to succession planning—that is, promoting from within the organization and within the function.

In the first space below, identify by title the key position which you are examining. Then answer the questions about it appearing in the left column of the second space below. Write your responses in the right column, making notes about ways by which you can use alternatives to the traditional approach to succession planning. When you finish, share your responses with others in the organization for their thoughts—and, if possible, to compare their comments to yours. Add paper if necessary.

There are no "right" or "wrong" answers to this Activity; rather, the aim is to provide you with an aid to creative ways by which to meet succession planning needs.

Space One: What is the key position? (Provide a job title:)

Questions about the key position	*Question Responses (Describe ideas to avoid simple replacement from within)*
Is the key position no longer necessary?	
Can a key position be rendered unnecessary by finding new ways to achieve comparable results?	

Questions about the key position	*Question Responses (Describe ideas to avoid simple replacement from within)*
Can a key position be rendered unnecessary by redistributing the duties to a team in the same part of the organization?	
Can a key position be rendered unnecessary by reallocating the duties to other parts of the organization?	
Can a key position be rendered unnecessary by outsourcing the work?	
Can a key position be rendered unnecessary by using flexible staffing approaches?	
Can combining the approaches listed above eliminate the need for a replacement in a key position?	

3. Can a key position be rendered unnecessary by redistributing the duties to a team in the same part of the organization?
4. Can a key position be rendered unnecessary by reallocating the duties to other parts of the organization?
5. Can a key position be rendered unnecessary by outsourcing the work?
6. Can a key position be rendered unnecessary by using flexible staffing approaches?
7. Can combining the approaches listed above obviate the need for a replacement in a key position?

Pose these questions during review meetings to identify successors and on the occasions when a vacancy occurs in a key position. Be sure that key positions are filled only when absolutely necessary to achieve essential work requirements.

Chapter 12

Applying Online and High-Tech Approaches to Succession Planning and Management Programs*

The Internet and the World Wide Web have profoundly influenced the world. That fact is as true for succession planning and management (SP&M) practices as for anything else. Many organizations are in a competitive race to enter e-commerce, or to consolidate the competitive edge they are already acquiring from it.

Online and high-tech approaches have also had a dramatic impact on succession planning and management practices. This chapter focuses attention on four key questions: (1) How are online and high-tech methods defined? (2) In what areas of succession planning and management can online and high-tech methods be applied? (3) How are online and high-tech applications used? and (4) What specialized competencies are required by succession planning coordinators to use these applications?

How Are Online and High-Tech Methods Defined?

An *online method* relies on the Internet, a company or organizational intranet, an extranet, or the World Wide Web. Examples of online methods range from traditional print-based electronic mail to Web-based multimedia productions that integrate print, sound effects, music, animation, still graphics, and video.

A *high-tech method* is anything other than an online method that substitutes technology for face-to-face interpersonal interaction. Examples of high-tech methods include videoconferencing or audioteleconferencing.

*Note: The Web sites and software packages described in this chapter are current at the time this book went to press. However, they may change over time. Descriptions of Web sites and software packages in this chapter are not meant to be endorsements.

One way to conceptualize online and high-tech methods is to think of them as existing on one continuum ranging from simple to complex and on a second continuum ranging from noninteractive to fully interactive, as depicted in Exhibit 12-1. *Simple methods* are usually easy to design and inexpensive to use. *Complex methods* are usually difficult to design and are often expensive to design and use. *Noninteractive methods* do not involve people in real time, while *interactive methods* require people to participate actively. These distinctions are important when planning and budgeting the use of online and high-tech methods. The most complex or interactive methods often necessitate special skills in the design process and are more expensive and time-consuming to plan and use.

In What Areas of Succession Planning and Management Can Online and High-Tech Methods Be Applied?

To state the issue simply, online and high-tech methods can be applied to almost any area of an SP&M program. Such methods may be used in: (1) formulating SP&M program policy, procedures, and action plans; (2) assessing present work requirements; (3) evaluating current employee performance; (4) determining future work requirements; (5) assessing potential; (6) closing developmental gaps; (7) maintaining talent inventories; and (8) evaluating the program. Of course, online and high-tech methods can also be used for communicating about a succession program

Exhibit 12-1: Continua of Online and High-Tech Approaches

	Simple	*Complex*
Noninteractive	△ Electronic mail △ Web-based documents △ Audiotape-based training or instructions △ Videotape-based training or instructions	△ Online help with forms △ Policies, procedures, instructions, forms, or instruments distributed by disk or CD-ROM
Interactive	△ Print surveys sent electronically △ Print surveys completed over the Web △ PC-based audioteleconference △ PC-based videoteleconference	△ Groupware △ Interactive television △ Multimedia training material △ Virtual reality applications

and providing training and skill building or even real-time coaching. They substitute virtual interaction for face-to-face interaction. Of course, the maddening thing about them is that they date so quickly. Almost nothing today changes as fast as technological innovations.

How Are Online and High-Tech Applications Used?

To understand how to use online and high-tech applications in SP&M programs, you can use a hierarchy of applications. Such a hierarchy is presented in Exhibit 12-2. The subsections below first describe the hierarchy and then provide specific descriptions about ways to apply online and high-tech methods to each important component of an SP&M program.

A Hierarchy of Applications

Researching secondary information is the first, and lowest, level of the hierarchy of online and high-tech applications for SP&M. You can use the Web—or your organization's Human Resource Information Systems (HRIS)—to collect and analyze information that is readily available. Use secondary information of this kind to look for articles, books, or websites about best practices and research on succession issues. Surf the Web, using search engines or metasearch engines (see a full list of metasearch engines at http://www.searchiq.com/directory/multi.htm), around key words or phrases linked to succession planning. Conduct analyses of your organization's workforce about such important issues as the ages of your workers at various levels (executive, managerial, professional, and technical) and their projected retirement ages, their racial or gender composition at various levels, performance ratings, turnover rates, absenteeism, and other information of use in planning for succession. Try to use this information to answer such questions as these:

- △ How many people exist at each level of the organization and in each important occupational or hierarchical grouping?
- △ When are those people expected to retire?
- △ What percentage of those people fall into protected labor classes?
- △ What is the turnover rate by level?
- △ What is the critical turnover rate by level?
- △ How well are people performing?
- △ How many potential candidates for succession exist at each level, and how many potential candidates may be needed to exist to support the organization's expected growth?

Exhibit 12-2: A Hierarchy of Online and High-Tech Applications for Succession Planning and Management

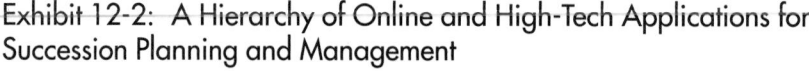

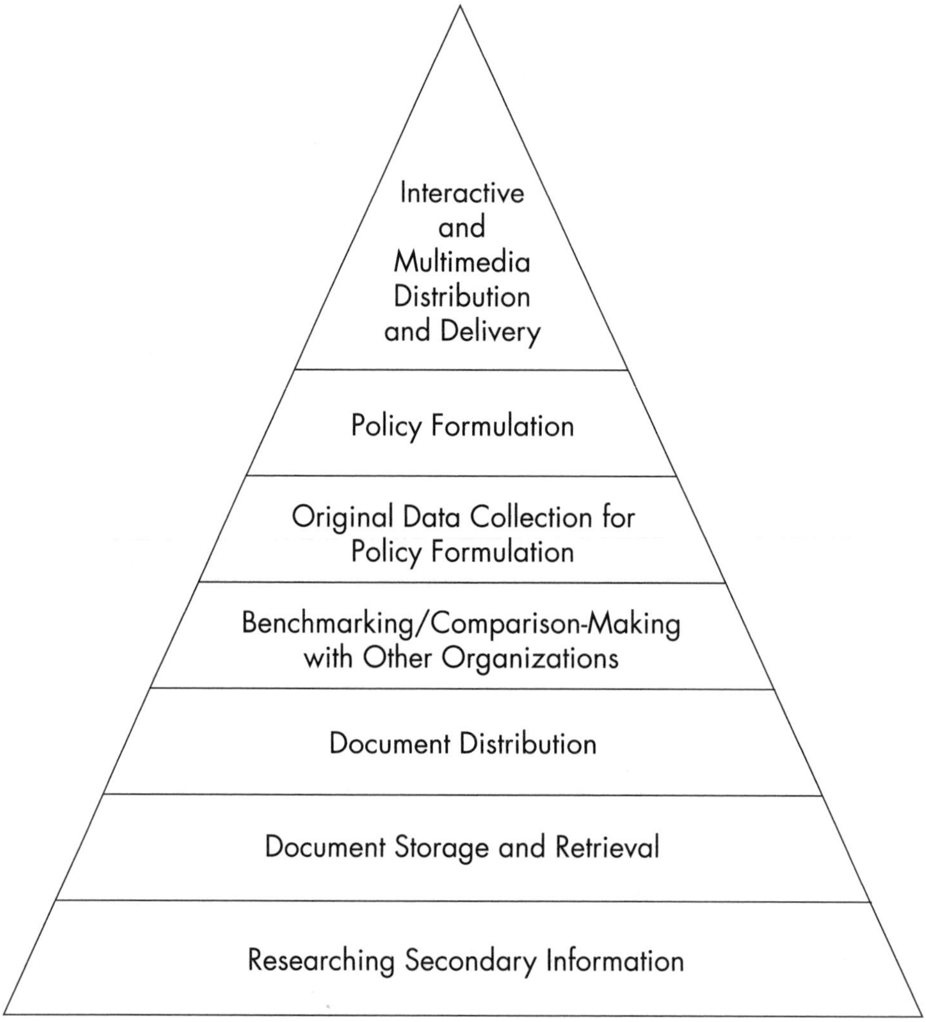

Interactive
and
Multimedia
Distribution
and Delivery

Policy Formulation

Original Data Collection for
Policy Formulation

Benchmarking/Comparison-Making
with Other Organizations

Document Distribution

Document Storage and Retrieval

Researching Secondary Information

In each case, these questions involve analysis of existing information. This is the lowest level of the hierarchy of applications, and it is also the easiest to use—provided that the necessary records exist and can be manipulated in ways permitting analysis.

Document storage and retrieval is the second level of the hierarchy. Online methods are often useful for storing and retrieving such documents important to SP&M as job descriptions, performance appraisal forms, potential assessments, and replacement charts. As organizations move toward realizing the promise of the paperless office, document storage and retrieval becomes more important. *Document imaging* permits hard copy to be scanned and kept electronically.

Document distribution is the third level of the hierarchy. This level adds interactivity and permits SP&M coordinators to place documents online. For instance, company websites can be used so that users can download documents such as job descriptions, job analysis questionnaires or interview guides, competency models, performance appraisal forms, individual potential assessment forms, individual development plans, and even training that can prepare people for advancement. Additionally, users may even complete the forms directly online and send them for analysis to SP&M coordinators so that transactions are paperless. Data can then be analyzed directly online. (That also improves data security.)

Benchmarking is the fourth level of the hierarchy. While the third level permits document distribution and analysis within an organization, benchmarking permits information sharing among organizations. For instance, a succession planning coordinator in one organization can send electronic questionnaires—or even sample documents, such as succession planning policies—to consultants, college professors, or SP&M coordinators in other organizations. That permits easy comparisons and discussions of important issues across organizations.

Original data collection for policy formulation is the fifth level of the hierarchy. Using online survey software, for instance, SP&M coordinators can poll managers, workers, and other stakeholders about emerging problems that affect succession planning. For instance, an attitude survey could be conducted periodically online to gather information about employee job satisfaction (which can affect turnover rates), attitudes about existing succession practices, and other relevant issues. This information is valuable in formulating new policies or revising existing policies.

Policy formulation is the sixth level of the hierarchy. Decision-makers can use *groupware*, software that links individuals virtually for decision-making in real time, to formulate new policies on issues affecting SP&M. For instance, during policy formulation, decision-makers can work together on virtual teams to establish a new or revised succession policy, devise a competency model, prepare a job description, plan training to close developmental gaps, carry out potential assessment or performance appraisal, or offer confidential advice on a difficult succession issue.

Interactive and multimedia distribution and delivery is the seventh and highest level of the hierarchy. This is usually the most complex, and often the most expensive, to create. It includes multimedia training prepared and delivered over the Web or over a company intranet. It also includes CD-ROM-based training designed to build competencies to prepare people for advancement and other high-tech methods, such as desktop video, that can link decision-makers in discussions about individual development or about SP&M policy issues.

Use the Worksheet appearing in Exhibit 12-3 to brainstorm when and how to use online and high-tech methods according to the hierarchy of applications described in this section.

Formulating Succession Planning and Management Program Policy, Procedures, and Action Plans

Recall from earlier in this book that an important starting point for any SP&M program is a policy to guide the program as well as procedures and action plans to implement the program. Lacking those, decision-makers will probably not share the same views about what results are to be achieved, how they are to be achieved, or even why the program exists. The process of formulating SP&M program policy, procedures, and action plans is important because the process is key to gaining stakeholder ownership and understanding.

Online and high-tech methods can be helpful in formulating policy, procedures, and action plans. It is not always necessary, of course, to formulate policies in face-to-face meetings. Some (and on occasion all) of the work can be done online, and some work can be done by virtual teams when decision-makers are geographically scattered.

Groupware can bring stakeholders together to make a decision in real time. (For an example of groupware that can be downloaded for free, see http://teamwave.com/.) Some people can be in the United States; some can be in Europe; some can be in South America; some can be in Australia; and some can be in Asia. But they all assemble online at the same time and focus attention around discussing, and reaching conclusions about, key issues.

High-tech methods can also be used. Conference calls are probably the simplest of these methods. Users discuss succession policies, procedures, and action plans over the phone. To hold down costs, such calls can be made over personal computers by using software such as netphone™ (see http://www.sonoma-systems.com/news/netphone.htm.)

With the advent of small and inexpensive video cameras that can be attached to the top of personal computers or even to laptops and the easy availability of software to link those cameras (such as Microsoft's Netmeeting™, available for download at http://www.microsoft.com/windows/netmeeting/), decision-makers can meet from their desktops from almost anywhere. Netmeeting permits real-time video and audio conferencing, graphics collaboration through a whiteboard feature, text conversations through a chat feature, an Internet directory for reaching others, a file transfer feature to permit document swapping in real time, program sharing, and many other features. In short, Netmeeting provides most of the advantages of a face-to-face meeting and some that cannot be obtained in such a meeting.

Experienced videoconferencing users, however, have learned that it is advisable to test the equipment and software before the scheduled meeting time to make sure that it works. They have also learned that a meeting agenda should be sent out beforehand with short questions intended to keep the meeting focused. Meetings should be kept short, since participants find that watching compressed video can be tedious. The number of callers should be kept to a minimum, since multiple sites can be difficult to manage in videoconferencing.

What are some tips to make these meetings most effective? Here are a few:

△ Make sure the time schedules are clear, especially when callers are located in different time zones.

△ Open all meetings with introductions so that everyone knows who is there, why they are there, and what they can contribute.

△ Keep the structure of the meeting simple. If difficult decisions are to be made, provide material in advance and ask people to review it before the meeting.

△ Send out, by e-mail, sample policies, procedures, and action plans governing succession planning and invite participants to focus their attention on them. Sample documents tend to focus attention faster.

△ Schedule follow-up discussions to resolve differences of opinion rather than trying to iron them out in a videoconference.

△ Make sure everyone has contact information for everyone else, such as e-mail addresses, so that they can discuss important issues of interest among themselves later.

Assessing Present Work Requirements

Assessing present work requirements is a second important component of any effective SP&M program. People cannot prepare for the future if they do not know what is expected of them at present.

Traditionally, assessing present work requirements has been handled in several ways. One way is for the supervisor to write a job description. Another way is for a specialist in the human resources department to interview one or more job incumbents and their supervisors, draft a job description, and then ask for a review by those interviewed.

Online and high-tech approaches have added new dimensions to this process. It is now possible to send worksheets or questionnaires for pre-

Exhibit 12-3: A Worksheet for Brainstorming When and How to Use Online and High-Tech Methods

Directions: Use this Worksheet to help you brainstorm when and how to use various online and high-tech methods in your organization's SP&M program. For each area of SP&M listed in the left column below, jot down ideas under the appropriate headers in the right column on ways that your organization may appropriately and effectively use the online and high-tech approaches described. Add paper if necessary.

Area of Succession Planning and Management	Notes on When and How to Use Online and High-Tech Approaches						
	Researching secondary information	Document storage and retrieval	Document distribution	Benchmarking	Original data collection for policy formulation	Policy formulation	Interactive and multimedia distribution and delivery
1 Formulating SP&M policy							
2 Assessing present work requirements							
3 Evaluating current employee performance							

4	Determining future work requirements							
5	Assessing potential							
6	Closing developmental gaps							
7	Maintaining talent inventories							
8	Evaluating the program							
9	Others (List below)							

paring job descriptions as attached documents from one location. Supervisors or HR specialists can then draft a job description, send it around electronically for supervisors or HR specialists and job incumbents to review and modify, make corrections, and reach agreement virtually. Alternatively, audioconferences or videoconferences can be substituted for face-to-face meetings.

Additionally, many resources now exist to help the harried HR specialist or supervisor write job descriptions. For instance, supervisors or HR specialists can invest in software such as Descriptions Now!™ (see http://www.gneil.com/item.html?s=5040&i=21&pos=2&sessionid=S9nac7q 435), which provides draft language for job descriptions and helps the user draft newspaper advertisements to recruit applicants. As an alternative, supervisors or HR specialists can find thousands of free job descriptions on the Web as a starting point for discussion and for ideas in preparing them. As just one example, visit http://www.stepfour.com/jobs/ to find 12,741 job descriptions from the *Dictionary of Occupational Titles* arranged in alphabetical order. Real-time training on the Web is also available to help supervisors or workers learn how to write job descriptions. (See http://www.siu.edu/~humres/doitright/descrip.html).

The important point to remember in using these methods is that no online substitute exists for reaching agreement among supervisors, incumbents, and HR specialists on what are the current work requirements, why they are necessary for success in the job, and how they can be met. In other words, online and high-tech approaches should be used as supplements, not as substitutes, for traditional job analysis and other approaches to assessing present work requirements.

Evaluating Current Employee Performance

A third important component of any effective succession planning program is some means of evaluating current employee performance. As noted earlier in the book, people are rarely considered for promotion—or any other advancement opportunity for that matter—if they are not performing well in their current jobs. Of course, a good performance appraisal system should measure individual performance as it relates to work requirements, standards, performance targets or expectations, or behavioral indicators tied to job competencies.

Traditionally, the process of evaluating current employee performance has been handled with paper forms that are completed and then followed up on by means of face-to-face interviews between workers and their immediate supervisors. Often, the human resources department is responsible for establishing the process by which individual performance is appraised. The information gathered in this process is, in turn, used in making wage or salary determinations, identifying training or individual development needs, and planning for future improvement.

Online and high-tech approaches have added new dimensions to this process. It is now possible to solicit, through e-mail or websites, opinions of other people about an individual's performance. For instance, a performance appraisal form may be sent for input to (among others) an individual's organizational superiors, peers, subordinates, customers, company suppliers, and company distributors.

Additionally, software resources now exist that can help supervisors write performance appraisals. For instance, supervisors or HR specialists can invest in software such as Performance Now!™ (see http://www.gneil.com/item.html?s=5040&i=20&pos=8&sessionid=S9nac7q-435) that supplies draft language for employee performance appraisals and can offer legal advice about what is and is not advisable to put in writing on appraisal forms. Free resources can also be found on the Web to support the formulation of policies on employee performance appraisal (such as, for instance, sample policies at http://ukcc.uky.edu/~hrinfo/hrp/hrp061.txt, http://www.tempe.gov/hradmin/docs/Perf_Appr_Inst.htm, and http://www.infosys.ilstu.edu/ohr/PAexempt.html); complete appraisal systems for a fee (see http://www.performance-appraisal.com/manual/download.htm); and sample forms (see http://fcn.state.fl.us/dms/hrm/forms/forms.html and http://ohioline.ag.ohio-state.edu/hrm-fact/0007.html).

Using online and high-tech methods with employee performance appraisal can be beneficial. However, SP&M coordinators should always remember that every useful performance appraisal system comes at a price. This means that, while online aids can be helpful and can offer valuable support, no substitute exists for the laborious process of establishing and measuring the unique performance requirements of one organization.

Determining Future Work Requirements

Forecasting or planning for future work requirements is a fourth important component of any effective SP&M program. After all, it is no more likely that work requirements will remain static than it is that the organization itself will remain static. Organizational needs change, and so do work requirements. It is therefore important to engage stakeholders and decision-makers in planning for the expected changes that may occur in the organization and in its work requirements. That is essential if individuals are to be prepared to meet those requirements in the future.

Few organizations regularly and systematically forecast future work requirements. However, the need to do that is growing. It is simply not possible to prepare people if future work requirements remain unknown.

Online and high-tech approaches have, however, provided new approaches to job forecasting, scenario planning, and future-oriented competency modeling. *Job forecasting* estimates future job requirements. It may address such questions as these:

- △ What will be the future purpose of the job? How will that be different from the job's present purpose?
- △ What are the expected work duties or responsibilities of the job in the future, and how are they expected to change?
- △ What knowledge, skills, or attitudes are needed by individuals in the future to quality for those jobs?
- △ How important will be the various duties or responsibilities of those jobs, and which ones will be considered most critical to success in the future?

Answering such questions is the process of job forecasting.

Scenario planning identifies possible alternative futures. Instead of assuming that jobs or work will change in one way, as job forecasting does, scenario planning offers probabilities. Scenarios resemble written stories about the future. They help people plan by giving them clear descriptions of what the future may look like, or different pictures of various futures. Groupware, described in an earlier section, can be useful as an online approach to conducting job scenario planning. It is thus possible to prepare different versions of job descriptions for the future and then use those to stimulate planning among job incumbents and their immediate organizational supervisors.

Another way to carry out scenario planning is to rely on software or websites that make it relatively easier than it might otherwise be. One resource for conducting scenario planning is the website of the Global Business Network (found at http://www.gbn.org/public/help/map.htm). This website offers member services for conducting scenario planning. While the key emphasis in most scenario planning is business planning and financial analysis, it is possible to find help in doing job scenario planning.

Future-oriented competency modeling projects the future competencies required by departments or job groups. Its focus, unlike traditional competency modeling, is on what will set exemplary performers apart from fully successful performers in the future. It is therefore future-oriented and is sometimes based on trends.

Many resources exist to help SP&M coordinators conduct future-oriented competency modeling. For instance, you can find a list of competencies needed in businesses in the future by consulting http://cithr.cit.cornell.edu/FutComp.html, or a compelling article about organizational core competencies of the future at http://www.bah.de/viewpoints/insights/cmt_core_comp.html. You can also purchase software for competency modeling, such as The Competence Expert™ (described at http://www.kravetz.com/compexpert.html) or the Competency Coach for Windows™ (described at http://www.coopercomm.com/ccchfact.htm) One other source is Kenneth Carlton Cooper's *Effective Competency Modeling & Reporting* (AMACOM, 2000), which includes a working model on CD-ROM of Competency Coach for Windows.

Assessing Potential

A fifth important component of any effective succession planning program is some means by which to assess individual potential for the future. What is the individual's potential for advancement to higher levels of responsibility, or to higher levels of technical expertise in his or her specialization? That is the question answered by this component.

One approach that is increasingly used for potential assessment is full-circle, multi-rater feedback. Described in an earlier chapter, this involves assessing an individual's potential based on the perceptions of those surrounding him or her in the organization. It is important to remember, however, that potential assessment should be conducted in the context of work requirements. In other words, an individual should not just be appraised for his or her current abilities. Instead, he or she should be assessed for meeting future job requirements or future competencies.

Both PC-usable software and Web-based full-circle, multi-rater assessment instruments are widely available. To find many of them, it is only necessary to type "360 assessment" into a search engine on the Web. But a word of caution is again in order: Most full-circle, multi-rater assessment instruments have been based on competency models from other organizations. That means they are not necessarily useful, applicable, or even appropriate in all corporate cultures. To be most effective, a company-specific competency model must be prepared for every department or every job category (such as supervisor, manager, and executive). Potential assessment is only useful when done in this way. Indeed, rating individual potential on competencies that are not company-specific can lead to major mistakes and miscalculations. Hence, while online and high-tech approaches can be useful, they should be used appropriately to measure individual potential within a unique corporate culture.

Closing Developmental Gaps

Closing developmental gaps is a sixth important component of any effective SP&M program. This component leads to an action plan to help individuals narrow the gap between what they can do now and what they need to do to advance in the future. Individual development planning is the process by which this is accomplished.

Although few software packages exist to support the individual development planning process—in fact, I could find none at all after an extensive search on the Web—many resources can be found on the Web to assist with the process. For instance, sample forms can be found at http://www.johnco.cc.ks.us/acad/sd/sdidp.htm, http://www.grc.nasa.gov/WWW/OHR/next6.htm, and http://www.hr.lanl.gov/CareerDevelopment/IDPs.htm. Sample policies guiding the use of an Individual Development Planning form can also be found at http://www.lerc.nasa.gov/WWW/ODT/idp.htm and http://ohr.gsfc.nasa.gov/DevGuide/idp.htm, and a sample training plan about individual development planning can be found at http://wtw.doleta.gov/ohrw2w/volume1/v1md11.htm.

Maintaining Talent Inventories

A seventh important component of any effective SP&M program is some means by which to maintain talent or skill inventories. How can the organization keep track of the knowledge, skills, and competencies of existing staff? That is the question answered by talent or skill inventories. Organizations possessing no means by which to inventory talent will have a difficult time locating qualified people in the organization when vacancies occur in key positions. Every organization should have some way to inventory its talent.

Succession planning and management inventories may take two forms—*manual* or *automated*. A *manual system* relies on paper files. It consists of individual personnel files or specialized records, assembled especially for SP&M, that take the form of a succession planning and management notebook or Rolodex file. These files contain information relevant to making succession decisions, such as:

- △ Descriptions of individual position duties or competencies (for instance, a current position description)
- △ Individual employee performance appraisals
- △ Statements of individual career goals or career plans
- △ Summaries of individual qualifications (for instance, educational and training records)
- △ Summaries of individual skills (for instance, a personal skill inventory that details previous work experience and languages known)[1]

Of course, other information may also be added, such as individual potential assessment forms and replacement planning charts.

A manual inventory will suffice for a small organization having neither specialized expertise available to oversee SP&M activities nor resources available for automated systems. A chief advantage is that most of the information is filed in personnel files anyway, so no monumental effort is necessary to compile information on individual employees. However, a manual inventory can lead to difficulties in handling, storing, cross-referencing, and maintaining security over numerous (and sometimes lengthy) forms. Even in a small organization, these disadvantages can present formidable problems.

Even small organizations, however, can now gain access to relatively inexpensive PC-based software that places much information at a manager's (or HR specialist's) fingertips. One example is People Manager™ (see http://www.gneil.com/item.html?s=5040&i=878&pos=5&sessionid=S9nac7q-43 5). A second is PeopleTrak™ (see http://www.gneil.com/item.html?s=5040&i=695&pos=7&sessionid=S9nac7q-43 5). A third is !Trak-IT HR™ (see http://www.gneil.com/item.html?s=5040&i=591&pos=17&sessionid=S9nac7q-4 35). Each software package permits some limited talent inventorying which can be useful even in small businesses.

Automated inventories used in SP&M take any one of three typical forms: (1) simple word processing files; (2) tailored SP&M software; or (3) SP&M software integrated with other personnel records.

Simple word processing files are the next step beyond paper files. Special forms (*templates*) are created for SP&M using a popular word processing program, such as Microsoft Word. Blank forms are placed on disk or CD-ROM. Managers are asked to complete the forms on disk and return them, physically or electronically, to a central location. This approach reduces paper flow and makes handling, storing, and security easier to manage than is possible with paper records. Unfortunately, SP&M information that is inventoried in this manner will usually be troublesome to cross-reference.

Tailored SP&M software is becoming more common. Much of it is now Web-based or suitable for Web applications. Succession planning and management coordinators should review several such packages before purchasing one.

The chief advantage of this software is that it is designed specifically for SP&M. Indeed, it can give decision-makers good ideas about desirable features to change, add to, or subtract from the SP&M program. Handling, storing, cross-referencing, and maintaining security over much information is greatly simplified. While software prices were relatively high even a few years ago, they are now affordable to most organizations employing fifty or more people.

The only major disadvantage of this software is that it can present temptations to modify organization needs to satisfy software demands. In other words, software may not provide sufficient flexibility to tailor SP&M

forms and procedures to meet the unique needs of one organization. That can be a major drawback. For this reason, SP&M software should be carefully reviewed, in cooperation with the vendor, prior to purchase. Of course, it may be possible for the vendor to modify the software to meet organizational needs at a modest cost.

Succession planning and management software may also be integrated with other personnel systems. In this case—and some large organizations attempt to keep all data in one place, usually in a mainframe system, in an effort to economize the problems inherent in multiple-source data entry and manipulation—SP&M information is included with payroll, training, and other records. Unfortunately, such software is usually of limited value for SP&M applications. To be tailored to a large organization's uses, such software may have to undergo lengthy and large-scale programming projects. A typical—and major—problem with such mainframe HRIS programs is that they provide insufficient storage space for *detailed, individualized* recordkeeping tailored to unique organizational procedures. When that is the case, it may be easier to use a personal-computer-based system—or else mount a massive, expensive, and probably quickly dated programming effort to modify a mainframe program.

Evaluating the Program

An eighth and final important component of any effective SP&M program is some means by which to evaluate the SP&M program and each of its components. This ensures that continuous program improvement can be made. At this writing, however, no online software currently exists that is specifically tailored to evaluating SP&M programs. Thus SP&M coordinators must prepare their own online and high-tech approaches if they wish to use them for evaluating their programs.

Of course, it should be relatively simple to prepare online questionnaires or other surveys to gather information about the relative value of SP&M programs. Typical evaluation issues that should be addressed will be discussed in the next chapter. Using online methods, however, may increase the speed and ease of response and facilitate data analysis.

Other Applications

There are other online and high-tech applications for SP&M. For instance, you can use software to prepare replacement charts. Best known, and perhaps least expensive, for doing that is probably OrgPlus™ (see http://www.gneil.com/item.html?s=5041&i=601&pos=6&sessionid=S9nac7q 435).

Software can also be purchased to facilitate preparation of forms for succession planning (such as Formtool™, described at http://www.cdrom shop.com/cdshop/desc/p.730526347135.html) or online training support to build competencies. Many so-called e-learning sites exist on the Web, and they can be tied to the competencies that individuals need to build to qualify for advancement opportunities.

What Specialized Competencies Are Required by Succession Planning and Management Coordinators to Use These Applications?

The specialized competencies required by SP&M program coordinators to use online and high-tech applications in their programs will, of course, vary by the medium or media that they use and their applications. It is not advisable to try to be all things to all people, so it is best to target specific applications of potential value to the organization and spend only the time necessary to master those.

Succession planning and management coordinators can apply online and high-tech methods in essentially three ways. First, they can try to learn it on their own. The competency requirements to do that can be the most daunting. It means mastery of the subject matter—such as, for instance, performance appraisal—and the technical issues associated with the application. As a simple example, putting the company's performance appraisal system on the Web might mean that technical knowledge is required of HTML and JAVA languages. Likewise, preparing Web-based training may require knowledge of the subject matter, instructional design, and the programming languages necessary to place it on the Web.

Second, contractual assistance could be hired to provide help with all or part of the project. That would permit the SP&M coordinator to concentrate on the subject matter and on managing the project. Hence, necessary competencies would focus around the subject area and project management. Technical issues would be handled by a contractor.

Third, the SP&M coordinator could create a team whose members collectively possess the competencies necessary to perform the work. In this case, the coordinator would at least require subject matter competence, project management competence, and facilitation competence to help team members work together. The coordinator may be able to choose team members from within the organization who possess the requisite technical knowledge of the media or medium.

Some competencies are shared no matter which of the three approaches is chosen. First, patience is an essential competency to work with any online or high-tech application. (It is never as easy as it appears to be.)

Second, knowledge of the organization's corporate culture and politics is also important. The SP&M coordinator must understand how decisions are made in the organization and be able to work through that process to achieve the desired results. Third and finally, the SP&M coordinator must be able to excite enthusiasm among other people for the project. Without these competencies, it will be difficult to make any application successful.

Summary

As this chapter has pointed out, online and high-tech approaches are having an important impact on succession planning and management practices. This chapter focused attention on four key questions: (1) How are online and high-tech methods defined? (2) In what areas of succession planning and management can online and high-tech methods be applied? (3) How are online and high-tech applications used? and (4) What specialized competencies are required by succession planning and management coordinators to use these applications?

The next chapter focuses on the important issue of evaluating succession planning and management programs. As decision-makers devote more time and other resources to succession issues, they naturally wonder if their efforts are paying off. For that reason, evaluation is becoming more important in succession planning and management.

Chapter 13
Evaluating Succession Planning and Management Programs

After a succession planning and management (SP&M) program has been implemented, top managers will eventually ask, "Is this effort worth what it costs? How well is it working? Is it meeting the organization's needs?"

Simple answers to these questions will prove to be elusive because an SP&M program will affect many people—and will usually have to satisfy conflicting goals, interests, and priorities. But the questions do underscore the need to establish some way to evaluate the program. This chapter, then, will explore three simple questions: (1) What is evaluation? (2) What should be evaluated in SP&M? and (3) How should an SP&M program be evaluated?

What Is Evaluation?

Evaluation means *placing value or determining worth*.[1] It is a process of determining how much value is being added to an activity by a program. It is through evaluation that the need for program improvements is identified and such improvements are eventually made. Evaluation is typically carried out by an evaluator or team of evaluators against a backdrop of client expectations about the program and the need for information on which to make sound decisions.

Interest in Evaluation

The evaluation of human resource programs has been a popular topic of numerous books, articles, and professional presentations.[2] Treatments of it have tended to focus on such bottom-line issues as cost/benefit analysis and return on investment,[3] which should not be surprising in view of the perception of HR practitioners that these issues are of chief interest to top managers. Training has figured most prominently in this literature—probably because it continues to enjoy the dubious reputation of being the first HR program to be slashed when an organization falls on hard times.

On the other hand, writers on evaluation have tended to pay far less attention to SP&M than to training. One reason could be that systematic SP&M is less common in organizations than training is. A second reason could be that evaluations of SP&M are informally made on a case-by-case basis whenever a vacancy occurs in a key position: if a successor is "ready, willing, and able" when needed, the SP&M program is given the credit; otherwise, it is blamed. While the value of SP&M should (of course) be judged on more than that basis alone, the reality is often far different.

Key Questions Governing Evaluation

To be performed effectively, evaluation for SP&M should focus on several key questions:

1. *Who* will use the results?
2. *How* will the results be used?
3. *What* do the program's clients expect from it?
4. *Who* is carrying out the evaluation?

The first question seeks to identify the audience. The second question seeks to clarify what decisions will be made based on evaluation results. The third question grounds evaluation in client expectations and program objectives. Finally, the fourth question provides clues about appropriate evaluation techniques based on the expertise of the chosen evaluator(s).

What Should Be Evaluated?

Some years ago, Donald Kirkpatrick developed a four-level hierarchy of training evaluation that may be usefully modified to help conceptualize what should be evaluated in SP&M.[4]

Kirkpatrick's Hierarchy of Training Evaluation

The four levels of Kirkpatrick's training evaluation hierarchy are *reaction, learning, behavior,* and *organizational outcomes* or *results*. Reaction forms the base of the hierarchy and is easiest to measure. It examines customer satisfaction—that is, how much did participants like what they learned? Learning, the second level on the hierarchy, has to do with immediate change. In other words, how well did participants master the information or skills they were supposed to learn in training? The third level of the hierarchy, behavior, has to do with on-the-job application. How much change occurred on the job as a result of learner participation in training? The highest level of Kirkpatrick's hierarchy, the fourth and final one, is organizational outcomes or results. It is also the most difficult to measure. How much influence did the results or effects of training have on the organization?

Modifying Kirkpatrick's Hierarchy of Training Evaluation for Succession Planning and Management

Use Kirkpatrick's Hierarchy of Training Evaluation to provide a conceptual basis for evaluating an SP&M program. (Examine the Hierarchy of Succession Planning and Management Evaluation depicted in Exhibit 13-1.)

Make the first level *customer satisfaction*, which corresponds to Kirkpatrick's *reaction* level. Pose the following questions:

△ How satisfied with the SP&M program are its chief customers?
△ How satisfied are its customers with *each* program component—such as job descriptions, competency models, performance appraisal processes, individual potential assessment processes, individual development forms, and individual development activities?
△ How well does SP&M match up to individual career plans? How do employees perceive SP&M?

Make the second level *program progress*, which is meant to correspond to Kirkpatrick's *learning* level. Pose the following questions:

△ How well is each part of the SP&M program working compared to stated program objectives?
△ How well are individuals progressing through their developmental experiences in preparation for future advancement into key positions?

Make the third level *effective placements*, which is meant to correspond to Kirkpatrick's *behavior* level. Pose these questions:

△ What percentage of vacancies in key positions is the organization able to fill internally?
△ How quickly is the organization able to fill vacancies in key positions?

Exhibit 13-1: The Hierarchy of Succession Planning and Management Evaluation

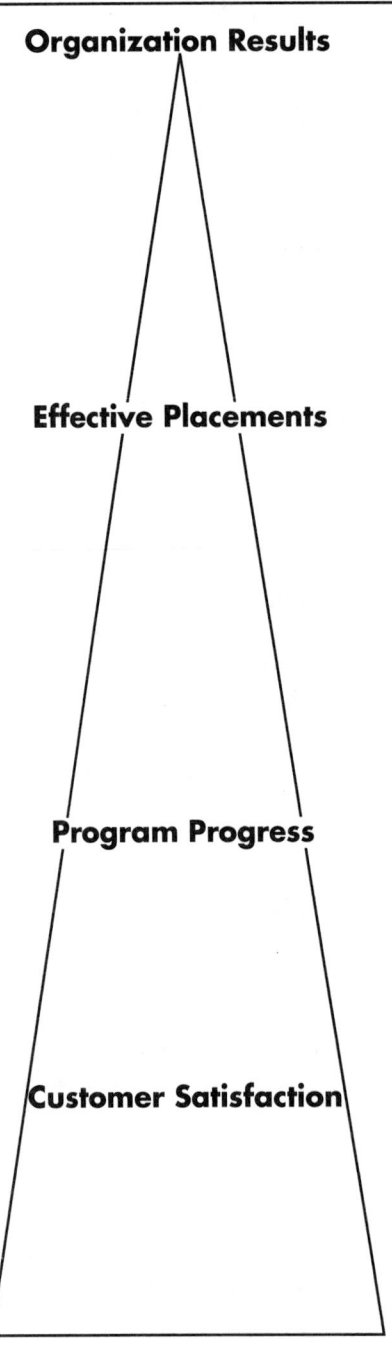

Organization Results

Effective Placements

Program Progress

Customer Satisfaction

△ How is succession planning contributing to documentable organization results?

△ What organizational successes and failures, if any, can be attributed solely to succession planning?

△ What percentages of vacancies in key positions is the organization able to fill internally?

△ How quickly is the organization able to fill vacancies in key positions?

△ What percentage of vacancies in key positions is the organization able to fill successfully (without avoidable turnover in the first two years in the position)?

△ How quickly are internal replacements for key positions able to perform at the level required for the organization?

△ What savings, if any, can be demonstrated from *not* filling key positions for which alternative, and more innovative, approaches were used to maintain equivalent results?

△ How well is each part of the succession planning program working compared to its stated objectives?

△ How well are individuals progressing through their developmental experiences in preparation for future advancement into key positions?

△ How satisfied with the succession planning program are its chief customers?

△ How satisfied are targeted clients with each program component?

△ How well does succession planning match up to individual career plans?

△ What percentage of vacancies in key positions is the organization able to fill successfully (that is, without avoidable turnover in the first two years in the position)?

△ How quickly are internal replacements for key positions able to perform at the level required for the organization?

△ What savings, if any, can be demonstrated from *not* filling key positions for which alternative, and more innovative, approaches were used to achieve results?

Make the fourth level *organizational results*, which is meant to correspond to Kirkpatrick's *outcomes* or *results*. Direct attention to the impact of SP&M on the organization's ability to compete effectively—which is (admittedly) difficult to do. Consider the following questions:

△ How is SP&M contributing, if at all, to documentable organizational results?

△ What successes or failures in organizational strategic plans, if any, can be attributed to SP&M?

Use the Guidelines appearing in Exhibit 13-2 and the Worksheet appearing in Exhibit 13-3 to consider ways to evaluate SP&M in an organization on each level of the Hierarchy.

How Should Evaluation Be Conducted?

Evaluation may be conducted *anecdotally, periodically,* or *programmatically*.

Anecdotal Evaluation

Anecdotal evaluation is akin to using testimonials in evaluating training.[5] It examines the operation of the SP&M program on a case-by-case basis. As vacancies occur in key positions, someone—often the SP&M coordinator—documents in *incident reports* how they are filled. (See Exhibit 13-4 for an example of an incident report.) The incident reports are eventually brought to the organization's SP&M committee for review and discussion. They provide a solid foundation for troubleshooting problems in SP&M that the organization is confronting. They can then be used as a basis for planning to handle similar problems in the future.

Anecdotal evaluation dramatizes especially good and bad practices. This draws attention to them and provides an impetus for change, a chief advantage of the anecdotal approach.

(Text continues on page 280.)

Exhibit 13-2: Guidelines for Evaluating the Succession Planning and Management Program

Type/Level	Purpose	Strengths	Weaknesses
Customer Satisfaction	To measure client feelings about the program and its results	△ Easy to measure. △ Provides immediate feedback on program activities and components.	△ Subjective. △ Provides no objective measurement of program results.
Program Progress	To measure results of each component of the succession planning program	△ Provides objective data on the effectiveness of the succession planning program.	△ Requires skill in program evaluation. △ Provides no measurement of skills of benefit to the organization.
Effective Placements	To measure the results of the succession decisions made	△ Provides objective data on impact to the job situation.	△ Requires first-rate employee performance appraisal system.
Organizational Results	To measure impact of the succession planning program on the organization	△ Provides objective data for cost-benefit analysis and organizational support.	△ Requires high level of evaluation design skills; requires collection of data over a period of time. △ Requires knowledge of the organization's strategy and goals.

Type/Level	Examples	Guidelines for Development
Customer Satisfaction	△ "Happiness reports." △ Informal interviews with "clients" at all levels. △ Group discussion in succession planning meetings.	△ Design a survey form that can be easily tabulated. △ Ask questions to provide information about what you need to know: attitudes about each component of the succession planning program. △ Allow for anonymity and allow the respondents the opportunity to provide additional comments.
Program Progress	△ Examine individual movements through the organization.	△ Design an instrument that will provide quantitative data. △ Include "pre" and "post" level of skill/knowledge in design. △ Tie evaluation items directly to program objectives.
Effective Placements	△ Performance checklists. △ Performance appraisals. △ Critical incident analysis. △ Self-appraisal.	△ Base measurement instrument on systematic analysis of key positions. △ Consider the use of a variety of persons to conduct the evaluation.
Organizational Results	△ Organizational analysis. △ Speed of replacement. △ Cost of replacements. △ Cost of nonreplacements. △ Turnover.	△ Involve all necessary levels of the organization. △ Gain commitment to allow access to organization indices and records. △ Use organization business plans and mission statements to compare organizational needs and program results.

Exhibit 13-3: A Worksheet for Identifying Appropriate Ways to Evaluate Succession Planning and Management in an Organization

Directions: Use this Worksheet to help you identify appropriate ways to evaluate the SP&M program in your organization.

In column 1 below, indicate the various stakeholder groups (such as top managers, key position incumbents, line managers, and the SP&M coordinator) who will be primarily interested in evaluation results on SP&M in your organization. Then, in column 2, indicate what *levels* of evaluation—customer satisfaction, program progress, effective placements, and organizational results—will probably be of prime interest to each stakeholder group. Then, in column 3, indicate *how* evaluation of SP&M may be carried out in your organization.

Column 1	*Column 2*	*Column 3*
Stakeholder groups for evaluation	What levels of evaluation will probably be of prime interest to each group?	How should evaluation of the SP&M program be carried out in your organization?

Exhibit 13-4: A Sample "Incident Report" for Succession Planning and Management

Directions: The purpose of this "incident report" is to track successor/replacement experiences in your organization.

Answer the questions appearing in the spaces below. Be as truthful as possible because the collective results of many incident reports will be used to identify program improvement initiatives for the succession planning program.

Fill out this report for each position filled from within. (This report should be completed *in addition to* any personnel requisitions/justification forms that you are to complete.) Submit the completed form to (*name*) at (*organizational address*) within 3 weeks after filling the vacancy.

Name of Departing Employee _____ Job Title _____

Department _____ Time in Position _____

Reason for Leaving (*if known*)_____

Name of Replacing Employee _____ Job Title _____

Department _____ Work Unit/Team _____

Time in Position _____ Today's Date _____

1. Describe how this position is being replaced (internally/externally)

_____

2. Was there an identifiable "successor" who had been prepared to assume this position previously? If so, briefly explain who and how the individual was being prepared; if not, briefly explain reasons for not preparing a successor.

_____

3. Who was selected for the position, and why was he/she selected?

_____

4. If an individual other than an identifiable successor was chosen for the position, explain why.

_____ Approval _____

Management Employee _____ Title _____
                        (Signature)

On the other hand, anecdotal evaluation suffers from a lack of research rigor. It is not necessarily representative of typical SP&M practices in the organization. (Indeed, it focuses on "special cases," "horror stories," and "war stories.") It may thus draw attention to unique, even minor, problems with SP&M in the organization.

Periodic Evaluation

Periodic evaluation examines components of the SP&M at different times, focusing attention on program operations at present or in the recent past. Rather than evaluate critical incidents (as anecdotal evaluation does) or all program components (as programmatic evaluation does), periodic evaluation examines isolated program components. For instance, the SP&M coordinator may direct attention to:

- The program mission statement
- Program objectives, policy, and philosophy
- Methods of determining work requirements for key positions
- Employee performance appraisal
- Employee potential assessment
- Individual development planning
- Individual development activities

Periodic evaluation may be conducted during regular SP&M meetings and/or in SP&M committee meetings. Alternatively, the organization's decision-makers may wish to establish a task force, create a subcommittee of the SP&M committee, or even involve a committee of the board of directors in this evaluation process.

A chief advantage of periodic evaluation is that it provides occasional, formal monitoring of the SP&M program. That process can build involvement, and thus ownership, of key stakeholders while simultaneously surfacing important problems in the operation of the SP&M program.

A chief disadvantage of periodic evaluation is that it makes the improvement of SP&M an incremental rather than a continuous effort. Problems may be left to fester for too long before they are targeted for investigation.

Programmatic Evaluation

Programmatic evaluation examines the SP&M program comprehensively against its stated mission, objectives, and activities. It is an in-depth program review and resembles the *Human Resources Audit* that may be conducted of all HR activities.[6]

Programmatic evaluation is usually carried out by a formally appointed committee or by an external consultant. The SP&M coordinator is usually a member of a committee. Representatives of key line management areas—and the CEO or members of the corporate board of directors—may also be members.

Examine the steps in Exhibit 13-5 and the checksheet in Exhibit 13-6 as starting points for conducting a program evaluation of SP&M in an organization. (Compare Exhibit 13-6 to the survey responses appearing in Exhibit 2-1 as a means of comparing your organization's SP&M program to others.)

Summary

This chapter addressed three simple questions: (1) What is evaluation? (2) What should be evaluated in succession planning and management? and (3) How should a succession planning and management program be evaluated?

Evaluation was defined as the process of placing value or determining worth. It is through evaluation that the need for improvements is identified and such improvements are eventually made to the succession planning and management program. Evaluation should focus on several key questions: (1) *Who* will use the results? (2) *How* will the results be used? (3) *What* do the program's clients expect from it? and (4) *Who* is carrying out the evaluation?

Focus the evaluation of succession planning and management on four levels, comparable to those devised by Donald Kirkpatrick to describe training evaluation. Those four levels are: *customer satisfaction, program progress, effective placements*, and *organizational results*.

Conduct evaluation *anecdotally, periodically,* or *programmatically*. Anecdotal evaluation is akin to using testimonials in evaluating training. Periodic evaluation examines isolated components of the succession planning and management program at different times, focusing attention on program operations at present or in the recent past. Programmatic evaluation examines the succession planning and management program comprehensively against its stated mission, objectives, and activities.

Exhibit 13-5: Steps for Completing a Program Evaluation of a Succession
Planning and Management Program

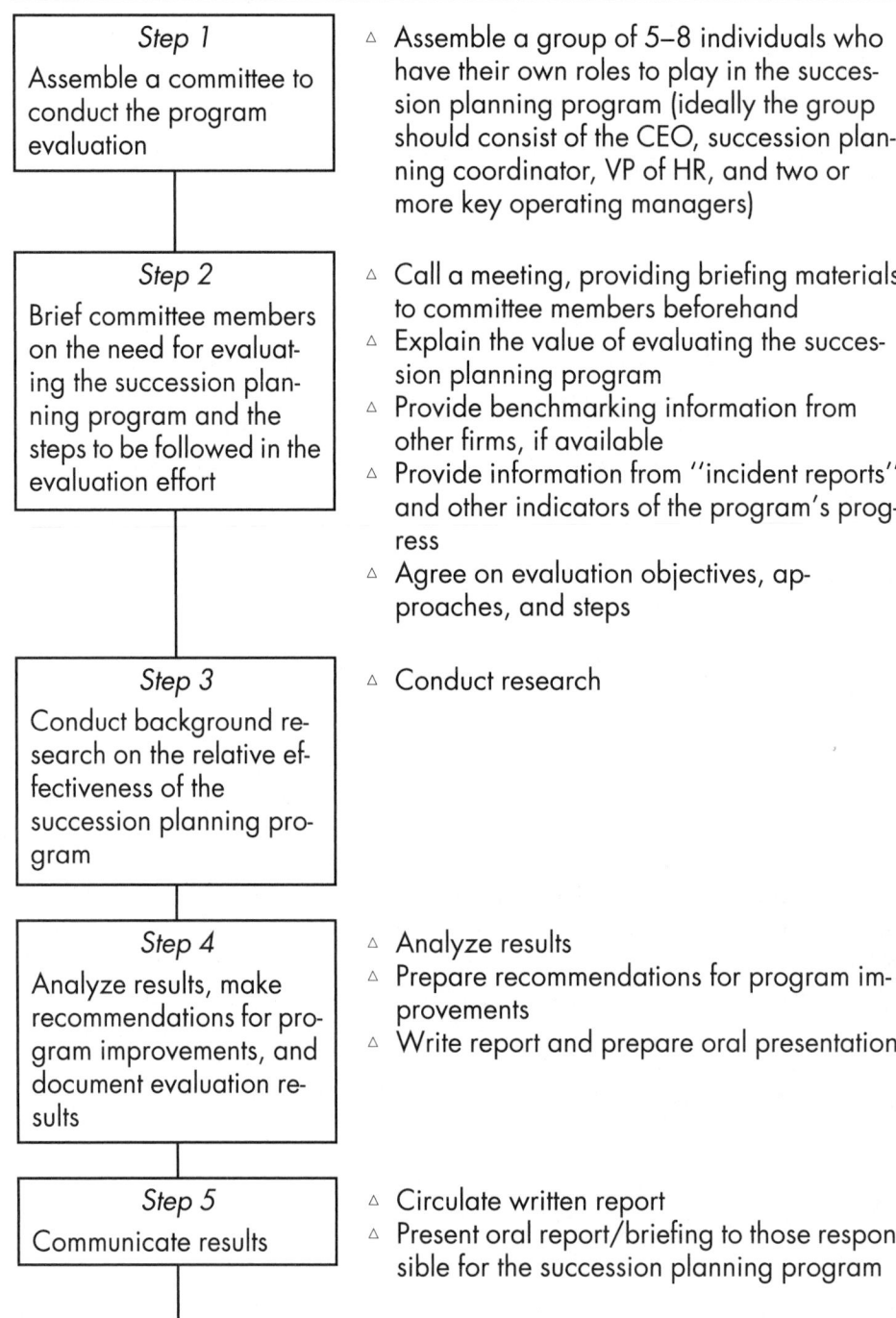

Step 1	
Assemble a committee to conduct the program evaluation	△ Assemble a group of 5–8 individuals who have their own roles to play in the succession planning program (ideally the group should consist of the CEO, succession planning coordinator, VP of HR, and two or more key operating managers)

Step 2	
Brief committee members on the need for evaluating the succession planning program and the steps to be followed in the evaluation effort	△ Call a meeting, providing briefing materials to committee members beforehand △ Explain the value of evaluating the succession planning program △ Provide benchmarking information from other firms, if available △ Provide information from "incident reports" and other indicators of the program's progress △ Agree on evaluation objectives, approaches, and steps

Step 3	
Conduct background research on the relative effectiveness of the succession planning program	△ Conduct research

Step 4	
Analyze results, make recommendations for program improvements, and document evaluation results	△ Analyze results △ Prepare recommendations for program improvements △ Write report and prepare oral presentation

Step 5	
Communicate results	△ Circulate written report △ Present oral report/briefing to those responsible for the succession planning program

Step 6
Identify specific actions for improvement

△ Ask those with responsibility for succession planning, such as key operating managers, to establish improvement objectives

Step 7
Take continuing action for program improvement

△ Take continuing action for improvement through training, briefings, and other means

Exhibit 13-6: A Checksheet for Conducting a Program Evaluation for the Succession Planning and Management Program

Directions: Use this checksheet as a starting point for deciding what to evaluate in your organization's succession planning program. Ask members of a program evaluation committee to complete the following checksheet, compare notes, and then use the results as the basis for recommending improvements to the succession planning program. Add, delete, or modify characteristics in the left column as appropriate.

Characteristics of Effective Programs	*Does your organization's succession planning program have this characteristic?*		*How important do you believe this characteristic to be for an effective succession planning program?*				
For the succession planning program, has your organization:	YES (√)	NO (√)	*Not Important* 1	2	3	4	*Very Important* 5
1. Tied the succession planning program to organizational strategic plans?	( )	( )	1	2	3	4	5
2. Tied the succession planning program to individual career plans?	( )	( )	1	2	3	4	5
3. Tied the succession planning program to training programs?	( )	( )	1	2	3	4	5
4. Prepared a written program purpose statement?	( )	( )	1	2	3	4	5
5. Prepared written program goals to indicate what results the succession planning program should achieve?	( )	( )	1	2	3	4	5
6. Established *measurable* objectives for program operation (such as number of positions replaced per year)?	( )	( )	1	2	3	4	5
7. Identified what groups are to be served by the program, in priority order?	( )	( )	1	2	3	4	5

8. Established a written policy statement to guide the program?	( )	( )	1	2	3	4	5
9. Articulated a written philosophy about the program?	( )	( )	1	2	3	4	5
10. Established a program action plan?	( )	( )	1	2	3	4	5
11. Established a schedule of program events based on the action plan?	( )	( )	1	2	3	4	5
12. Fixed responsibility for organizational oversight of the program?	( )	( )	1	2	3	4	5
13. Fixed responsibility of each participant in the program?	( )	( )	1	2	3	4	5
14. Established incentives/rewards for identified successors in the succession planning program?	( )	( )	1	2	3	4	5
15. Established incentives/rewards for managers with identified successors?	( )	( )	1	2	3	4	5
16. Developed a means to budget for a succession planning program?	( )	( )	1	2	3	4	5
17. Devised a means to keep records for individuals who are designated as successors?	( )	( )	1	2	3	4	5
18. Created workshops to train management employees about the succession planning program?	( )	( )	1	2	3	4	5
19. Created workshops to train individuals about career planning?	( )	( )	1	2	3	4	5
20. Established a means to clarify *present position responsibilities?*	( )	( )	1	2	3	4	5

(continues)

Exhibit 13-6: (continued)

Characteristics of Effective Programs	Does your organization's succession planning program have this characteristic?		How important do you believe this characteristic to be for an effective succession planning program?				
For the succession planning program, has your organization:	YES (√)	NO (√)	Not Important 1	2	3	Very Important 4	5
21. Established a means to clarify *future position responsibilities?*	( )	( )	1	2	3	4	5
22. Established a means to appraise individual performance?	( )	( )	1	2	3	4	5
23. Established a means to compare individual skills to the requirements of a future position (potential assessment)?	( )	( )	1	2	3	4	5
24. Established a way to review organizational talent at least annually?	( )	( )	1	2	3	4	5
25. Established a way to forecast future talent needs?	( )	( )	1	2	3	4	5
26. Established a way to plan for meeting succession planning needs through individual development plans?	( )	( )	1	2	3	4	5
27. Established a means to track development activities to prepare successors for eventual advancement?	( )	( )	1	2	3	4	5
28. Established a means to evaluate the results of the succession planning program?	( )	( )	1	2	3	4	5

Chapter 14

Predictions for the Future of Succession Planning and Management

No organization is immune to changing external environmental conditions. However, *what* external conditions affect an organization will vary—depending on such variables as the organization's industry, size, and relative market dominance. Moreover, *how* those conditions affect an organization will depend on the ways in which its leaders and workers choose to address them. These principles hold as true for succession planning and management (SP&M) programs as for strategic planning.

In this final chapter, I will gaze into the crystal ball and offer eight predictions for the future of SP&M that stem, in whole or in part, from changing external environmental conditions. I predict that SP&M will:

△ Prompt efforts by decision-makers to find flexible strategies to address future organizational talent needs.

△ Lead to integrated retention policies and procedures that are intended to identify high-potential talent earlier, retain that talent, and preserve older high-potential workers.

△ Have a global impact.

△ Be influenced increasingly by real-time technological innovations.

△ Become an issue in government agencies, academic institutions, and nonprofit enterprises in a way never before seen. Businesses will not be the only organizations interested in succession issues.

△ Lead to increasing organizational openness about possible successors.

△ Increasingly be integrated with career development issues.

△ Be heavily influenced in the future by concerns about work/family balance and spirituality issues.

Before you read about these predictions, use the Worksheet appearing in Exhibit 14-1 to structure your thinking (and that of decision-makers in your organization) about them.

Exhibit 14-1: A Worksheet to Structure Your Thinking about Predictions for Succession Planning and Management in the Future

Directions: Use this Worksheet to structure your thinking about possible predictions that may influence SP&M programs in the future. For each prediction listed in Column 1 below, indicate in Column 2 whether you believe that the prediction is true. Then describe under Column 3 what you believe the prediction means in your organization and under Column 4 how much impact that prediction will have in your organization. Finally, under Column 5, offer suggestions about what your organization should *do* about the prediction. There are no "right" or "wrong" approaches to addressing these predictions. Instead, use this Worksheet to do some brainstorming about predictions affecting SP&M in your organization in the future. Add paper if necessary.

Column 1 What is the prediction?		Column 2 Do you believe the prediction is true?		Column 3 What does the prediction mean in your organization?	Column 4 How much impact will that prediction have in your organization?	Column 5 What actions should your organization take to address the prediction?
Succession planning and management will:		Yes ☒	No ☒			
1	Prompt efforts by decision-makers to find a flexible range of strategies to address organizational talent needs.	☐	☐			
2	Lead to integrated retention policies and procedures that seek the early identification of high-potential talent, efforts to retain that talent, and efforts to retain older high-potential workers.	☐	☐			

3	Have a global impact.	☐	☐			
4	Be influenced increasingly by real-time technological innovations.	☐	☐			
5	Become an issue in government, academic institutions, and nonprofit organizations in a way never before seen.	☐	☐			
6	Lead to increasing organizational openness about possible successors.	☐	☐			
7	Increasingly seek to integrate effectively succession issues with career development issues.	☐	☐			
8	Be heavily influenced by concerns about work/family balance and spirituality.	☐	☐			

Prediction 1: Decision-Makers Will Seek Flexible Strategies to Address Future Organizational Talent Needs

In the future, decision-makers will not view succession issues as one problem requiring only one solution. Instead, they will seek a range of strategies to address future organizational talent needs that will include, but will go beyond, SP&M programs. In other words, succession problems will be solved using many possible solutions. The choice of a solution will be made on a case-by-case basis but with a strategic view that seeks an integration of approaches.

Think about it for a minute. In how many ways can an organization's talent needs be met through approaches other than an SP&M program that is designed to build in-house bench strength over time? Consider at least fifteen possible alternative approaches. Each approach should be considered at the time decision-makers plan for succession needs. Decision-makers should begin by clarifying *what* talent needs they require, *why* their organization experiences that need, and *how* the need might be met.

The first alternative approach to SP&M is to hire from the outside. In fact, this is probably the most obvious way to meet a talent need other than through internal promotion or development. It is sometimes chosen before internal replacements are considered. A key advantage of this approach is that it prevents inbreeding, since newcomers often bring with them fresh solutions to old organizational problems. A key disadvantage of this approach is that the cycle time required to fill a vacancy can be agonizingly long—and there is no guarantee that someone chosen from outside the organization will successfully adapt to its unique corporate culture.

A second approach is to reorganize. Take just one example: If the vice president of human resources retires, dies, or leaves the organization, the CEO may choose to meet the need by assigning the HR function to another manager. That is just one example of how to solve a talent need by reorganizing. The same approach can be used with meeting talent needs in other key positions. Of course, this approach only works if someone who can assume the added responsibility is available—and has sufficient interest, motivation, and ability to do it.

A third approach is to outsource the work. Instead of trying to find a suitable candidate to meet key needs from inside or outside the organization, the organization can seek an external partner to meet that need. If this approach is chosen, the challenge is to find a suitable outsourcing partner. That cannot always be done, but it is one option. A disadvantage is that this approach should only be used with activities that are not directly related to the organization's core competence, the key strategic strength that sets an organization apart from competitors. It is, after all, unwise to outsource the essence of what makes an organization competitive, since that path can lead to bankruptcy or to a takeover.

A fourth approach is to insource the work. If this approach is used, decision-makers seek to find synergy between two functions. Of course, this assumes that some excess capacity—that is, people or resources—exists somewhere else in the organization. Suppose, for instance, that a vacancy for a key position exists in one industrial plant. That need could be met by insourcing the work to another plant operated by the same company. An external partner is not sought. Instead, the function is performed internally. This approach differs from reorganization because the insourcing partner does not permanently assume the duties of the new function but performs them only temporarily.

A fifth approach is to hire, on contract, a temporary replacement for a key position. The work is performed for a time by the temp. Some firms specialize in supplying such temporary help—even for positions such as CEO with which temps have not been historically associated.

A sixth approach is to bring in a consultant to help. While similar to using a temp, this approach differs in that a consultant is usually not on site every day to perform the work, as temps generally are. The consultant, in short, performs the work on a project-to-project basis and may even telecommute. This can reduce costs but may also diminish the impact of the key position and the function on the organization.

A seventh approach is to transfer someone from another part of the organization, temporarily or permanently, to meet a succession need. Of course, it is usually assumed that an individual who is transferred meets at least the basic entry-level requirements for the job. Internal transfers, however, have the disadvantage of touching off a *domino effect* (sometimes called a *musical chairs effect*), in which the movement of one person can prompt movements by many others.

An eighth approach is to acquire another organization that possesses the needed talent. In the past, mergers, acquisitions, purchases, and takeovers were sought to realize savings resulting from economies of scale, a desire for higher executive salaries resulting from correlations between senior executive pay and organizational size, and the pursuit of improved integration with such key groups as suppliers, distributors, and even competitors.

In the future, however, CEOs will regard mergers, acquisitions, purchases, and takeovers as one means to address talent shortages.[1] Organizations with well-known core competencies will become acquisition targets for other firms that are cash rich but are experiencing talent shortages. Instead of struggling to fill one vacancy at a time, organizations will look for other firms to absorb outright to achieve a massive infusion of new talent.

The ninth approach is to reduce or eliminate the work completely. In other words, the work performed by an otherwise critically important function or position could be reduced or eliminated to solve a succession problem. As one way to do that, the CEO can choose to spin off or sell the business or function so that a succession problem no longer exists.

A tenth approach is to delegate the work of a high-potential up in the organization. This is, of course, a form of reorganization. But instead of giving responsibility to another manager when the organization experiences the need through loss of talent, the work is absorbed by the immediate organizational superior.

An eleventh approach is to delegate the work down in the organization. Like the tenth approach, it is another form of reorganization. The work of a high-potential employee is absorbed by one or more of his or her subordinates without promotion. A variation of this approach is to form a team and delegate the work of the departing key job incumbent to that group of people.

A twelfth approach is to form a strategic alliance with another organization to meet succession needs. This usually means that a short-term partnership is arranged between two organizations. While strategic alliances have often been formed in product manufacturing, they could also be formed to shore up succession needs. However, this approach is potentially useful on a short-term basis only, since few organizations want to lose high-potential talent forever.

A thirteenth approach is to trade needed talent, temporarily or permanently, with other organizations. Similar to a strategic alliance, this approach differs only in that it tends to be shorter-term. Some organizations provide "loaned executives," for instance, to build the competencies of their high-potentials. However, this approach is potentially useful on a short-term basis only, since (as in the case of a strategic alliance) few organizations want to lose their high-potentials for extended time spans.

A fourteenth approach is to recruit globally rather than domestically, targeting individuals with needed talent outside the borders of the United States. This approach is especially useful for multinational corporations. They may be able to trade talent from one part of the world to others and thereby treat succession issues on a global chessboard.

A fifteenth approach is to hire back needed managers or other talent after they have departed from the organization. As the U.S. population ages, this approach is already being used by many organizations. Perhaps best known of these is Deloitte's Senior Leaders Program, which is being launched to preserve the knowledge and experience of talent after the traditional retirement age.[2]

Use the Worksheet appearing in Exhibit 14-2 to structure your thinking about ways to meet succession needs based on the approaches described above. Whenever a talent need exists in your organization—such as upon the pending retirement of a key manager or the unexpected loss of an incumbent in a key position—use the Worksheet to contemplate possibilities for meeting the need. Also use the Worksheet to think about integrating the strategies so that your organization is not solely dependent on one of them.

Prediction 2: Decision-Makers Will Seek Integrated Retention Policies and Procedures

Employers in the United States are faced with a genuine problem in finding and keeping talent. At the time this book goes to press, employment levels are at a record high. No longer can employers assume that they can find talent whenever they need it. They are in competition with many other employers—and this competition is especially intense for high-potential workers with proven track records.

To address this problem, employers should formulate and implement policies and procedures designed to identify high-potential talent earlier, retain that talent, and find ways to retain older, high-potential workers. Employers will thus need to take such steps as these:

△ Develop early tracking systems to find new hires having special promise. That can be done with potential assessments performed within the first few months of employment.

△ Track the reasons for "quits" generally and the reasons for the departure of high-potential talent specifically. That may require revamped exit interview procedures to capture information about why people (and especially high-potentials) leave, where they go, and what they believe could have prompted them to stay.

△ Use attitude surveys on a continuing basis to predict turnover and measure job satisfaction. That can be done simply by asking workers on a survey whether they plan to quit within the next year and then supplying questions about chief sources of dissatisfaction. These can be cross-tabulated, and the results can provide useful information for improving retention and making accurate predictions of turnover.

△ Track voluntary turnover and critical turnover *by department* and examine increases in each department closely for trends or patterns. Then act to address problems in these hot spots.

△ Provide incentives for people to remain with the organization. (Do

Exhibit 14-2: A Worksheet to Structure Your Thinking about Alternative Approaches to Meeting Succession Needs

Directions: Use this Worksheet to structure your thinking about alternative approaches to meet succession needs. First, describe the succession need in the space below and indicate how important it is to the organization, why it is important, and when action needs to be taken to meet the need. Then, rate possible alternatives to internal succession. Then rate each alternative approach, using the following scale:

1 = Not at all effective.
2 = It may be somewhat useful.
3 = It will be useful.
4 = It will be very useful.

What is the succession need? (*Describe the need. Then answer these questions: (1) How important is this succession need to the organization? (2) Why is it important? (3) When does action need to be taken to meet the need?*)

Approach How well can the succession need be met by:	Rating of the Approach				Notes
	Not at all effective.	It may be somewhat useful.	It will be useful.	It will be very useful.	
1 Hiring from the outside?	1	2	3	4	
2 Reorganizing?	1	2	3	4	
3 Outsourcing the work?	1	2	3	4	
4 Insourcing the work?	1	2	3	4	
5 Hiring a temporary replace- ment on contract?	1	2	3	4	

6	Bringing in a consultant to help?	1	2	3	4	
7	Transferring someone from another part of the organization, temporarily or permanently, to meet the succession need?	1	2	3	4	
8	Acquiring another organization that possesses the needed talent?	1	2	3	4	
9	Reducing or eliminating the work completely?	1	2	3	4	
10	Delegating the work up in the organization?	1	2	3	4	
11	Delegating the work down in the organization?	1	2	3	4	
12	Forming a strategic alliance with another organization to meet the need?	1	2	3	4	
13	Trading needed talent, temporarily or permanently, with other organizations?	1	2	3	4	

(continues)

Exhibit 14-2: *(continued)*

	Approach *How well can the succession need be met by:*	Rating of the Approach				Notes
		Not at all effective.	*It may be somewhat useful.*	*It will be useful.*	*It will be very useful.*	
14	Recruiting globally rather than domestically, targeting individuals with needed talent outside the borders of the United States?	1	2	3	4	
15	Hiring back needed managers or other talent after they have departed from the organization?	1	2	3	4	
16	What other alternative approaches can you think of, and how effective are they? *(List them below.)*	1	2	3	4	

not assume that all incentives are financial.) Find out what people need to encourage them to remain with the employer.

By taking these and similar actions, employers can devise an integrated retention strategy to reduce turnover and thereby improve retention.

Prediction 3: Succession Planning and Management Issues Will Have a Global Impact

Succession issues have emerged as front-burner topics in the United States because of the well-known demographic trend that points toward growing numbers of people reaching traditional retirement ages in future years. (See Exhibit 14-3 for the projected U.S. population breakdown in the year 2025.) Indeed, the age category between fifty-five and sixty-four is expected to *increase* by 54 percent between 1996 and 2006.[3] At the same time, there will be a *decrease* of 8.8 percent in the number of people expected to enter the workforce between the traditional entry-level ages of twenty-five and thirty-four.[4]

What is not so well known is that population trends elsewhere in the world also point toward growing numbers of older people. For instance, consider Exhibits 14-4, 14-5, and 14-6. These exhibits depict the projected population breakdown in China, the United Kingdom, and France (respectively) in the year 2025. Note the numbers of people in the traditional postretirement categories in each nation and compare them. Recent policy

Exhibit 14-3: Age Distribution of the U.S. Population in 2025

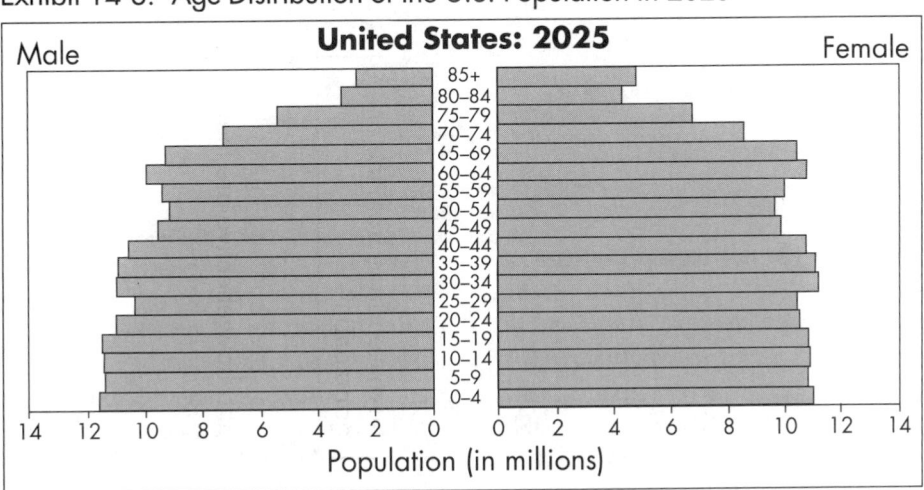

SOURCE: U.S. Census Bureau (2000). Population pyramid summary for the U.S. http://www.census.gov/egi-bin/ipc/idbpyrs..pl?cty=IN&out=s&ymax=250

Exhibit 14-4: Age Distribution of the Chinese Population in 2025

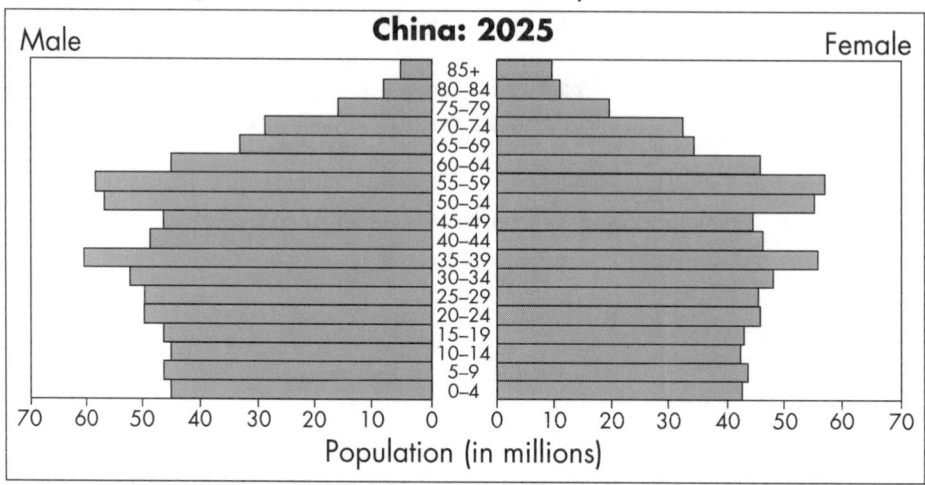

SOURCE: U.S. Census Bureau (2000). Population pyramid summary for China. http://www.census.gov/egi-bin/ipc/idbpyrs..pl?cty = IN&out = s&ymax = 250

Exhibit 14-5: Age Distribution of the Population in the United Kingdom in 2025

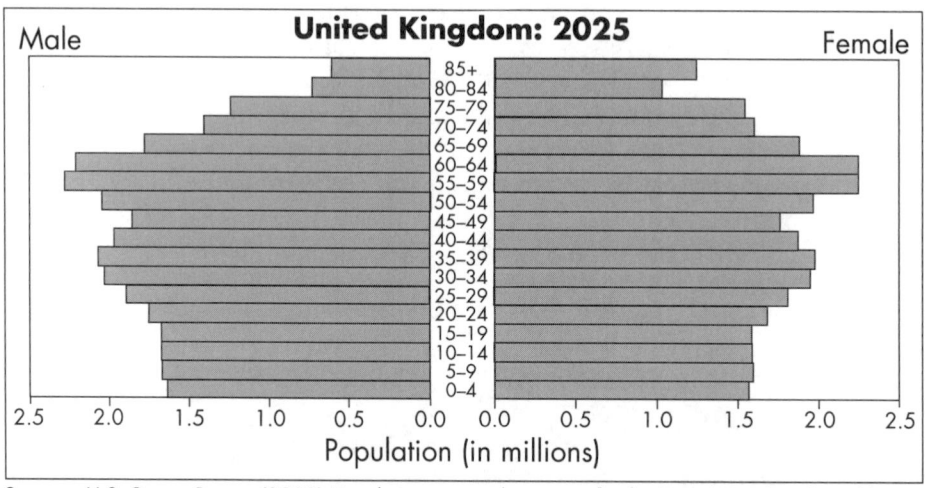

SOURCE: U.S. Census Bureau (2000). Population pyramid summary for the United Kingdom. http://www.census.gov/egi-bin/ipc/idbpyrs..pl?cty = IN&out = s&ymax = 250

changes (such as the "one child per couple" policy in China) and population trends point toward growth in the number of elder citizens in many important economies around the globe. As more elderly people exist around the world, succession issues will emerge as issues of global concern.

Based on these demographic projections, I predict that SP&M issues will emerge as a challenge to many nations by the year 2025. It is likely that

Exhibit 14-6: Age Distribution of the French Population in 2025

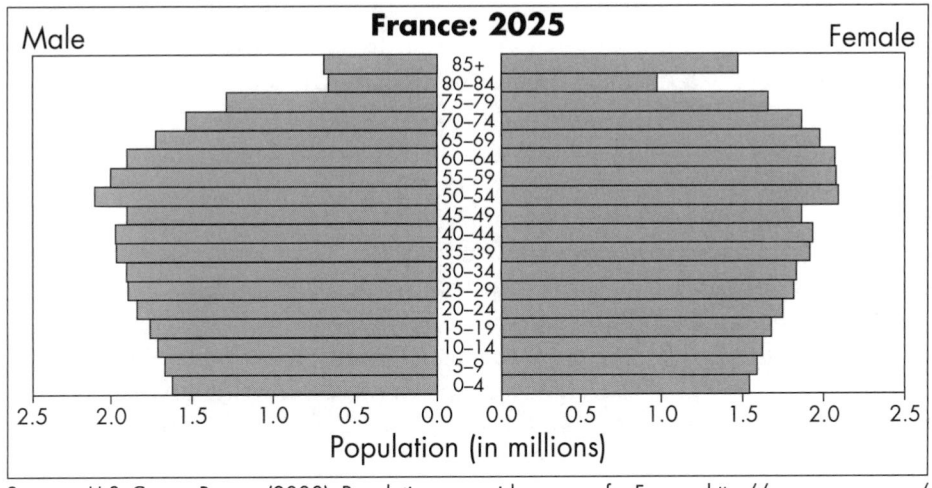

SOURCE: U.S. Census Bureau (2000). Population pyramid summary for France. http://www.census.gov/ egi-bin/ipc/idbpyrs..pl?cty = IN&out = s&ymax = 250

many organizations, both large and small, will need to devote attention to succession issues in a way they have not traditionally done. Also influenced will be national policies encouraging the employment of older citizens. Expect that many nations will begin to focus concerns on older workers— and institute policies to encourage people to retire at older ages than has traditionally been the case. Older workers will represent an important political group in many nations as well, exerting influence directly or indirectly on government policy-makers.

Although managers in the United States are often tempted to think in terms of domestic talent only, the fact remains that SP&M issues have a global impact and may therefore require global solutions. At one time many companies relied heavily on expatriate labor forces to meet succession needs globally. In other words, when they needed specialized skills not available in the developing world, they would simply export talent from the developed world. But this strategy is less frequently used as decision-makers pursue *localization strategies* designed to identify and accelerate the development of high-potential local talent.

A localization strategy has many advantages. One advantage is that it builds the bench strength across a total corporation, serving as a rising tide to lift all boats. In other words, the corporation builds bench strength everywhere rather than relying on exported talent. A second advantage is that local talent faces no problems in adapting to local cultures in the way that expatriates do. A third advantage is that local talent is not resented, as expatriates often are, for the higher wages and better benefit packages they receive. A fourth advantage is that a localization strategy provides political and public relations advantages to the organizations adopting it, since they are seen as building the local economy rather than merely exploiting it.

In the future, localization efforts will increase. Government policy-makers may even require it. Additionally, forward-thinking corporations will begin to find ways to hitchhike on the talent they have internationally by using online and other virtual methods to encourage "sharing," "tele-commuting," "videocommuting," "concurrent work" (prepared in one nation but used in another), and "idea generation" across borders. These developments have profound implications for SP&M, too, since they can build competencies at the same time that work is performed.

The challenge for SP&M program coordinators will be to find ways to transfer so-called *soft skills technologies*—such as management and HR practices—across cultures. That may require special programs to encour-age information-sharing and skill building across cultures, through either online or face-to-face approaches.

Prediction 4: Succession Issues Will Be Influenced by Real-Time Technological Innovations

As Chapter 12 showed, technological innovation is already exerting a major influence on succession issues. This trend will continue. Right now, many organizations are already using online methods for recruitment. In the future, online methods will be increasingly used in real time to con-duct competency modeling, potential assessment, performance appraisal, individual development planning, and individual coaching.

The challenge for SP&M program coordinators will be to find and apply these approaches. One major goal, of course, is to slash cycle time for filling key positions and sourcing talent. Another major goal is to lower geographical barriers, making it possible to access—and develop—talent anywhere and at any time.

Prediction 5: Succession Planning and Management Will Emerge as an Issue in Government Agencies, Academic Institutions, and Nonprofit Enterprises

Traditionally, sectors of the economy other than business have been slow to adopt effective SP&M practices. Government agencies, academic institu-tions, and nonprofit enterprises have not typically attempted to identify replacements for key positions and have often relied on a talent-pool approach, which is more consistent with the laws, rules, regulations, political realities, and organizational cultures found in these economic sectors. Additionally, government agencies and academic institutions in particular have found systematic succession approaches difficult to use because of institutional policies or Civil Service regulations that require competitive searches, job posting, and preferences based on factors other than individual performance. Efforts to groom individuals in these settings have sometimes been prohibited rather than encouraged. One result has been that long lead times often exist between the appearance of a vacancy and the appointment of a successor.

However, as a direct result of increasing turnover, increasing retirement rates, lagging salary and performance bonuses, and a booming private-sector economy that makes the (relative) security of government service and academic appointments less appealing than they once were, I predict that government agencies and academic institutions will be forced to adopt more systematic succession practices. It is no longer effective to follow the business-as-usual approach of "calling for the list" of qualified individuals who have taken Civil Service exams, or "conducting a national search" for each academic appointment by simply placing one advertisement in the *Chronicle of Higher Education*. The reason? There are few, if any, candidates on the Civil Service "list"—and few, if any, applicants sending in material to *Chronicle* advertisements for academic positions. This problem is particularly acute at senior levels in government and in educational institutions where people do not want or need to move.

It is important to understand that these problems take different shapes in government, educational institutions, and nonprofit organizations. Hence, they require different solution strategies. Within each economic sector, differences also exist. In government, human resource practices have not been the same among local, state, and federal agencies. In academic institutions, human resource practices have differed among government-supported and privately-funded colleges and universities. In nonprofit enterprises, unlike in government agencies and in academic institutions, the intrinsic satisfaction of the work has also been a major attractor of talent that has mediated the need to pay competitive salaries or provide competitive benefits.

However, the challenges across these three economic sectors do share similarities. Indeed, the key challenge is to find better ways to recruit, retain, motivate, and cultivate talent for the future without sacrificing existing Civil Service laws and rules and without sacrificing merit-based employment in favor of questionable practices such as political patronage, nepotism, or unlawful discrimination. There are no simple answers, and each institution will need to form a task force and focus attention on the need to improve succession within the framework of existing organizational policies and procedures and governmental laws, rules, and regulations. The challenge for SP&M program coordinators will be to find ways to adapt the approaches recommended in this book to the unique settings of government agencies, academic institutions, and nonprofit enterprises.

Prediction 6: Succession Planning and Management Will Lead to an Increasing Policy of Organizational Openness

Many organizations still do not share information about successors with the prospective successors or replacements for key positions. Some executives worry that such openness might lead to problems—such as "greenmail" or the "crown prince dilemma." *Greenmail* occurs when designated successors attract lucrative offers from other employers and then leverage them to achieve counteroffers from their current employers. This is called greenmail because it is akin to blackmail. The *crown prince dilemma* occurs when designated successors believe they are guaranteed advancement, rest on their laurels, and let their performance decline.

Despite these potential problems, however, I predict that organizations will be forced to become more open about naming future successors. If they do not, they risk losing their high-potentials to other employers that are more open to making promises and more forthcoming in offering attractive employment packages.

Prediction 7: Succession Planning and Management Will Increasingly Be Integrated with Career Development

Career planning and management programs are usually planned by individuals. They are thus planned from the bottom up. Succession planning and management programs are usually planned by senior executives and are thus planned from the top down. As described elsewhere in the book, the two work together and should be integrated.

In the future, decision-makers in organizations will recognize how important it is to have both. Their synergistic power together is greater than the sum of their individual parts. For that reason, organizations will revive company-sponsored career planning and management programs so that they will empower individuals to take greater responsibility to prepare themselves for the future. This also serves a useful purpose as a double-check on, and verification of, replacement and succession plans.

The challenge for SP&M program coordinators will be to find ways to integrate career and succession programs. Exhibit 14-7 lists some important characteristics of career planning and management programs. Exhibit 14-8 provides an assessment sheet for you to structure your thinking about ways to integrate career planning and management programs with SP&M programs.

Prediction 8: Succession Planning and Management Will Be Heavily Influenced by Concerns about Work/Family Balance and Spirituality

A booming economy has led many managers to devote more time to their work. In fact, the average number of working hours per week of managers has been on the rise. The same may well be true of other groups. That, in turn, has prompted many people to question their priorities. There is more to life than work, and they know it. Some seek more time with their families or others in their lives. Some seek religion or a deeper feeling about the meaning of life. These desires to balance work and life or achieve a greater sense of spirituality are major drivers for change.

I predict that these will become growing issues of importance to organizational decision-makers. They will find that high-potentials refuse additional responsibility if that requires too much personal sacrifice. That would include job assignments that prompt upheavals in their personal lives.

The challenge for SP&M program coordinators will be to find ways to help high-potentials balance their work responsibilities and their personal lives. This may require organizations to use time off as an incentive or to give people time away from work when they desire it so they can balance work and personal life or pursue a deeper understanding of their spirituality.

Summary

This chapter has offered eight predictions about succession planning and management. In the future, succession planning and management will: (1) prompt efforts by decision-makers to find flexible strategies to address future organizational talent needs; (2) lead to integrated retention policies and procedures that are intended to identify high-potential talent earlier, retain that talent, and preserve older high-potential workers; (3) have a global impact; (4) be influenced increasingly by real-time technological innovations; (5) become an issue in government agencies, academic insti-

(Text continues on page 308.)

Exhibit 14-7: Important Characteristics of Career Planning and Management Programs

Directions: Use this Worksheet to rate your organization on how well it addresses important issues in career planning and management. For each characteristic of an effective career planning and management program listed in the left column below, rate how well you believe your organization rates on that characteristic in the right column. Use the following scale:

1 = Not at all effective
2 = Somewhat ineffective
3 = Somewhat effective
4 = Effective

Characteristic of a Career Planning and Management Program *The career planning and management program is:*	*Rating*			
	Not at all effective *1*	*Somewhat ineffective* *2*	*Somewhat effective* *3*	*Effective* *4*
1 Focused on meeting specific business needs or issues of the organization	1	2	3	4
2 Targeted on specific groups in the organization	1	2	3	4
3 Responsive to the organization's unique corporate culture and "ways of doing things"	1	2	3	4
4 Organized around a unified model that can be easily and readily explained to such stakeholders as managers and workers	1	2	3	4
5 Based on a comprehensive approach that goes well beyond a "one-shot" approach to addressing career planning in the organization	1	2	3	4

6	Involves, and thereby commands the ownership of, all key stakeholder groups (such as executives, managers, HR specialists, and workers)	1	2	3	4
7	Well publicized to stakeholders	1	2	3	4
8	Evaluated both on how well it helps individuals achieve their goals and the organization achieve its goals	1	2	3	4
Score		*Add up the numbers in the column above and place the sum in the box below:*			

Interpretation of the Score

Score 1–8	Your organization does not have a career planning and management program—or, if your organization does possess such a program, it is regarded as singularly ineffective. Grade it as an F.
Score 9–16	Your organization possesses a career planning and management program, but it is not regarded as effective or useful; only as somewhat so. Grade it as a C.
Score 17–24	Your organization's career planning and management program is regarded as generally effective. Grade it a B.
Score 25+	Your organization's career planning and management program is regarded as highly successful and effective. Grade it an A.

Exhibit 14-8: An Assessment Sheet for Integrating Career Planning and Management Programs with Succession Planning and Management Programs

Directions: Use this Worksheet to assess how well your organization's career planning and management program is integrated with your SP&M program. For each characteristic of effective career and succession programs listed in the left column below, rate how well you believe your organization has integrated them in the right columns. Use the following scale:

1 = Not at all integrated
2 = Somewhat integrated—but not enough
3 = Well integrated
4 = Very well integrated

Characteristics of Effective Career and Succession Programs *Both the career planning and management program and the SP&M program:*	*Rating*			
	Not at all integrated 1	*Somewhat integrated —but not enough* 2	*Well integrated* 3	*Very well integrated* 4
1 Are focused on meeting specific business needs	1	2	3	4
2 Are guided by program objectives that have been compared and inte-grated	1	2	3	4
3 Use work requirements or competencies as com-mon denominators	1	2	3	4
4 Identify gaps between what people know or can do now and what they need to know	1	2	3	4
5 Clarify what career goals are sought by indi-viduals	1	2	3	4

6	Can, and often do, use full-circle, multi-rater assessments	1	2	3	4
7	Rely on individual development plans to narrow individual developmental gaps	1	2	3	4
8	Are evaluated	1	2	3	4
Score		*Add up the numbers in the column above and place the sum in the box below:*			

Interpretation of the Score

Score 1–8	Your organization has not integrated career planning and management with SP&M.
Score 9–16	Your organization has somewhat integrated career planning and management with SP&M. However, they are not perceived as sufficiently integrated.
Score 17–24	Your organization has effectively integrated career planning and management with SP&M.
Score 25+	Your organization has succeeded in achieving a very good integration between career planning and management with SP&M.

tutions, and nonprofit enterprises in a way never before seen; (6) lead to increasing organizational openness about possible successors; (7) increasingly be integrated with career development issues; and (8) be heavily influenced in the future by concerns about work/family balance and spirituality.

Notes

Preface

1. Warren Bennis and Burt Nanus, *Leaders: The Strategies for Taking Charge* (New York: Harper and Row, 1985), p. 2.
2. Bradley Agle, "Understanding Research on Values in Business," *Business & Society* (September 1999), 326–387.
3. Charlene Marmer Solomon, "The Loyalty Factor," *Personnel Journal* (September 1992), 52–62.
4. Shari Caudron, "The Looming Leadership Crisis," *Workforce* (September 1999), 72–79.
5. Arthur Deegan, *Succession Planning: Key to Corporate Excellence* (New York: Wiley-Interscience, 1986), p. 5.
6. As quoted in Harper W. Moulton and Arthur A. Fickel, *Executive Development: Preparing for the 21st Century* (New York: Oxford University Press, 1993), p. 29.
7. E. Zajac, "CEO Selection, Succession, Compensation and Firm Performance: A Theoretical Integration and Empirical Analysis," *Strategic Management Journal* 11:3 (1990), 228.
8. R. Sahl, "Succession Planning Drives Plant Turnaround," *Personnel Journal* 71:9 (1992), 67–70.
9. "Long-Term Business Success Can Hinge on Succession Planning," *Training Directors' Forum Newsletter* 5:4 (1989), 1.
10. Dirk Dreux, "Succession Planning and Exit Strategies," *CPA Journal* 69:9 (1999), 30–35; Oliver Esman, "Succession Planning in Small and Medium-Sized Companies," *HR Horizons* 103 (1991), 15–19; Barton C. Francis, "Family Business Succession Planning," *Journal of Accountancy* 176:2 (1993), 49–51; John O'Connell, "Triple–Tax Threat in Succession Planning," *National Underwriter* 102:40 (1998), 11, 19; T. Roger Peay and W. Gibb Dyer, Jr., "Power Orientations of Entrepreneurs and Succession Planning," *Journal of Small Business Management* 27:1 (1989), 47–52; Michael J. Sales, "Succession Planning in the Family Business," *Small Business Reports* 15:2 (1990), 31–40.

Chapter 1

1. Henry Fayol, *Administration Industrielle et Generale* (Paris: Société de l'Industrie Minerale, 1916).
2. Norman H. Carter, "Guaranteeing Management's Future Through Succession Planning," *Journal of Information Systems Management* 3:3 (1986), 13–14.
3. Michael Leibman, "Succession Management: The Next Generation of Succession Planning," *Human Resource Planning* 19:3 (1996), 16–29.
4. Richard Hansen and Richard H. Wexler, "Effective Succession Planning," *Employment Relations Today* 15:1 (1989), 19.
5. See Chris Argyris and Donald Schön, *Organizational Learning: A Theory of Action Perspective* (Reading, Mass.: Addison-Wesley, 1978); Peter Senge, *The Fifth Discipline: The Art and Practice of the Learning Organization* (New York: Doubleday/Currency, 1990).
6. Walter R. Mahler and Stephen J. Drotter, *The Succession Planning Handbook for the Chief Executive* (Midland Park, N.J.: Mahler Publishing Co., 1986), p. 1.
7. "Long-Term Business Success Can Hinge on Succession Planning," *Training Directors' Forum Newsletter* 5:4 (1989), 1.
8. Wilbur Moore, *The Conduct of the Corporation* (New York: Random House, 1962), p. 109.
9. Rosabeth Moss Kanter, *The Men and Women of the Corporation* (New York: Basic Books, 1977), p. 48.
10. Norman H. Carter, "Guaranteeing Management's Future Through Succession Planning," *Journal of Information Systems Management* 3:3 (1986), 13–14.
11. Peter Capelli, "A Market-Driven Approach to Retaining Talent," *Harvard Business Review* 78:1 (2000), 103–111; Joanne Cole, "De-Stressing the Workplace," *HRFocus* 76:10 (1999), 1, 10–11; Robert Leo, "Career Counseling Works for Employers Too," *HRFocus* 76:9 (1999), 6.
12. Thomas Gilmore, *Making a Leadership Change: How Organizations and Leaders Can Handle Leadership Transitions Successfully* (San Francisco: Jossey-Bass, 1988), p. 19.
13. William J. Rothwell and H. C. Kazanas, *Human Resource Development: A Strategic Approach*, rev. ed. (Amherst, Mass.: HRD Press, 1994), p. 48.
14. Lynda Gratton and Michel Syrett, "Heirs Apparent: Succession Strategies for the Future," *Personnel Management* 22:1 (1990), 34.
15. A. Walker, "The Newest Job in Personnel: Human Resource Data Administrator," *Personnel Journal* 61:12 (1982), 5.

16. William J. Rothwell and H. C. Kazanas, *Planning and Managing Human Resources: Strategic Planning for Personnel Management*, rev. ed. (Amherst, Mass.: HRD Press, 1994).

17. Andrew O. Manzini and John D. Gridley, *Integrating Human Resources and Strategic Business Planning* (New York: AMACOM, 1986), p. 3.

18. Patricia McLagan, *The Models* (Alexandria, Va.: The American Society for Training and Development, 1989), p. 7.

19. Rothwell and Kazanas, *Human Resource Development*, p. 16.

20. Meg Kerr, *Succession Planning in America's Corporations* (Palatine, Ill.: Anthony J. Fresina and Associates and Executive Knowledgeworks, 1987).

21. "The Numbers Game," *Time*, 142:21(1993), 14–15.

22. Ann Morrison, *The New Leaders: Guidelines on Leadership Diversity in America* (San Francisco: Jossey-Bass, 1992), p. 1.

23. Ibid., p. 7.

24. Gilmore, *Making a Leadership Change*, p. 10.

25. Arthur Sherman, George Bohlander, and Herbert Chruden, *Managing Human Resources*, 8th ed. (Cincinnati: South-Western Publishing Co., 1988), p. 226.

26. Warren Boroson and Linda Burgess, "Survivors' Syndrome," *Across the Board* (1992), 29:11 41–45.

27. Morrison, *The New Leaders*, p. 1.

28. M. Haire, "Approach to an Integrated Personnel Policy," *Industrial Relations* (1968), 107–117.

29. J. Stuller, "Why Not 'Inplacement?' " *Training* 30:6 (1993), 37–44.

30. William J. Rothwell, H. C. Kazanas, and Darla Haines, "Issues and Practices in Management Job Rotation Programs as Perceived by HRD Professionals," *Performance Improvement Quarterly* 5:1 (1992), 49–69.

31. Matt Hennecke, "Toward the Change-Sensitive Organization," *Training* (May 1991), 58.

32. D. Ancona and D. Nadler, "Top Hats and Executive Tales: Designing the Senior Team," *Sloan Management Review* 3:1 (1989), 19–28.

Chapter 2

1. See William J. Rothwell, "Trends in Succession Management," *The Linkage, Inc. eNewsletter*, Issue 2/15/00 (2000). Presented on the Web at http://www.linkageinc.com/newsletter26/research.htm.

2. Michael Leibman, "Succession Management: The Next Generation of Succession Planning," *Human Resource Planning* 19:3 (1996), 16–29.

3. William J. Rothwell, Robert K. Prescott, and Maria Taylor, *Strategic*

Human Resource Leader: How to Help Your Organization Manage the 6 Trends Affecting the Workforce (Palo Alto, Calif.: Davies-Black Publishing, 1998).

4. Ibid.

5. P. Smith and D. Reinertsen, *Developing Products in Half the Time* (New York: Van Nostrand Reinhold, 1991).

6. See Jac Fitz-Enz, *How to Measure Human Resources Management* (New York: McGraw-Hill, 1984).

7. "The Aging Baby Boomers," *Workplace Visions* (Sept.–Oct. 1996). Found at http://www.shrm.org/issues/0996wv01.htm.

8. "Cross-Generational Approaches," *Workforce Strategies* 17:11 (1999), WS63–WS64.

9. Shari Caudron, "The Looming Leadership Crisis," *Workforce* (September 1999), 72–79.

10. "The Aging Baby Boomers," op. cit.

11. "Gap Between Rich and Poor Keeps Widening," *The CCPA Monitor* (1995). Presented at http://infoweb.magi.com/ccpa/articles/article 21t.html (Unfortunately this site is restricted.)

12. Peter Cappelli, "A Market-Driven Approach to Retaining Talent," *Harvard Business Review* (Jan.–Feb. 2000), 103–111; Joseph Dobrian, "Amenities Gain Ground as Recruiting/Retention Tools," *HRFocus* (November 1999), 11–12.

13. Charlene Marmer Solomon, "The Loyalty Factor," *Personnel Journal* (September 1992), 52–62.

14. David L. Stum, "Five Ingredients for an Employee Retention Formula," *HRFocus* (September 1998), S9–S10.

15. Lynn E. Densford, "Corporate Universities Add Value by Helping Recruit, Retain Talent," *Corporate University Review* 7:2 (1999), 8–12.

16. See, for instance, Thomas A. Stewart, "Have You Got What It Takes," *Fortune* 140:7 (1999), 318–322.

17. Richard McDermott, "Why Information Technology Inspired but Cannot Deliver Knowledge Management," *California Management Review* 41:4 (1999), 103–117.

18. Dawn Anfuso, "Core Values Shape W. L. Gore's Innovative Culture," *Workforce* 78:3 (1999), 48–53; Donald Tosti, "Global Fluency," *Performance Improvement* 38:2 (1999), 49–54.

19. William J. Rothwell and John Lindholm, "Competency Identification, Modelling and Assessment in the USA," *International Journal of Training and Development* 3:2 (1999), 90–105.

20. Rothwell, Prescott, and Taylor, *Strategic Human Resource Leader*, op. cit.

21. Bradley Agle, "Understanding Research on Values in Business," *Business and Society* 38:3 (1999), 326–387.

22. "PPG Industries Speeds, Refines Succession Preparation Process," *Workforce Strategies* 17:10 (1999), WS57–WS58.

Chapter 3

1. The source of this case study is Dennis C. Carey, "Where the Board Drives Succession Planning," *Directors and Boards*, 21:3 (1997), pp. 54–56. Used by permission of *Investment Dealers Digest 1997*.

2. The source of this case study is Jay L. Johnson, "How Kmart Plans for Executive Succession," *Discount Merchandiser*, 32:5 (1992), pp. 108–110. The article is reprinted here by permission of *Discount Merchandiser*.

3. The source of this case study is Joyce E. Johnson, "Succession Management: A Model for Developing Nursing Leaders," *Nursing Management*, 25:6 (1994), pp. 50–56. Used by permission of S-N Publications Inc.

4. U.S. Department of Labor, "Workforce 2000—Work and Workers for the 21st Century," Publication No. 0-250-433. U.S. Government Printing Office, 1989, pp. 79–82.

5. J. C. Robinson, "Hospital Competition and Hospital Nursing," *Nursing Economics* 6:3 (1988), 116–119.

6. Ibid.

7. R. Hansen and R. H. Wexier, "Effective Succession Planning," *Employee Relations Today* (Spring 1988), 19–24.

8. R. Nardoni, "Successful Succession Planning," *Personnel Journal* 5 (1985): 106–110; D. Dolan, "Management Succession: Know Your Management Talent," *Healthcare Executive* 2:6 (1987), 10–11.

9. D. Dolan, "Management Succession: Know Your Management Talent," *Healthcare Executive* 2:6 (1987), 10–11.

10. Ibid.; D. Burda, "CEO Turnover Tied to Hospital Straits," *Modern Hospitals,* November 28, 1988, 3.

11. R. S. Dunne, et al., "A Management Development Program for Middle Level Nurse Managers," *The Journal of Nursing Administration* 18:5 (1988), 11–16; M. F. Fralic, "Patterns of Preparation: The Nurse Executive," *The Journal of Nursing Administration* 17:7,8 (1978), 35–38; E. K. Singleton, "Nursing Leadership: The Effects of Organizational Structure," *The Journal of Nursing Administration* 18:10 (1988), 10–14; C. M. Freund, "CEO Succession and Its Relationship to CNO Tenure," *The Journal of Nursing Administration* 17:7,8 (1987), 27–30.

12. J. Johnson, et al., "Moving Your Nursing Department Forward: Win-

ning Strategies for Nursing Executives," *Nursing Economics* 7:6 (1989), 332–334.

13. This paragraph is based on information in C. Derr, C. Jones, and E. Toomey, "Managing High-Potential Employees: Current Practices in Thirty-three U.S. Corporations," *Human Resource Management* 27:3 (1988), 278. For more recent information, see also William J. Rothwell and H. C. Kazanas, *Building In-House Leadership and Management Development Programs* (Westport, Conn.: Quorum, 1999), and David D. Dubois and William J. Rothwell, *The Competency Toolkit*, 2 vols. (Amherst, Mass.: HRD Press, 2000).

14. See William J. Rothwell, *The Action Learning Guidebook: A Real-Time Strategy for Problem-Solving, Training Design, and Employee Development* (San Francisco: Jossey-Bass/Pfeiffer, 1999).

15. See S. Cunningham, "Coaching Today's Executive," *Public Utilities Fortnightly* 128:2 (1991), 22–25; Steven J. Stowell and Matt Starcevich, *The Coach: Creating Partnerships for a Competitive Edge* (Salt Lake City: The Center for Management and Organization Effectiveness, 1987).

16. Charles E. Watson, *Management Development Through Training* (Reading, Mass.: Addison-Wesley, 1979).

17. Manuel London and Stephen A. Stumpf, *Managing Careers* (Reading, Mass.: Addison-Wesley, 1982), p. 274.

18. James E. McElwain, "Succession Plans Designed to Manage Change," *HRMagazine* 36:2 (1991), 67.

19. James Fraze, "Succession Planning Should Be a Priority for HR Professionals," *Resource* (June 1988), 4.

20. Ibid.

21. Ibid.

22. Ibid.

23. Thomas North Gilmore, *Making a Leadership Change: How Organizations Can Handle Leadership Transitions Successfully* (San Francisco: Jossey-Bass, 1988), p. 10.

24. Fraze, "Succession Planning Should Be a Priority for HR Professionals," 4.

25. David W. Rhodes, "Succession Planning—Overweight and Underperforming," *The Journal of Business Strategy* 9:6 (1988), 62.

26. Ibid.

27. Ibid.

Chapter 4

1. See R. White, "Motivation Reconsidered: The Concept of Competence," *Psychological Review* 66 (1959), 279–333.

2. David C. McClelland, "Testing for Competence Rather Than for 'Intelligence,' " *American Psychologist* (January 1973), 1–14.

3. See J. C. Flanagan, "The Critical Incident Technique," *Psychological Bulletin* (April 1954), 327–358; J. Hayes, "A New Look at Managerial Competence: The AMA Model for Worthy Performance," *Management Review* (November 1979), 2–3; Patricia McLagan, "Competency Models," *Training and Development Journal* (December 1980), 23; L. Spencer & S. Spencer, *Competence at Work: Models for Superior Performance* (New York: John Wiley & Sons, Inc., 1993).

4. A. R. Boyatzis, *The Competent Manager: A Model for Effective Performance* (New York: John Wiley & Sons, Inc., 1982), pp. 20–21.

5. David D. Dubois and William J. Rothwell, *The Competency Toolkit*, 2 vols. (Amherst, Mass.: HRD Press, 2000).

6. Ibid.

7. Ibid.

8. See David D. Dubois, *The Executive's Guide to Competency-Based Performance Improvement* (Amherst, Mass.: HRD Press, 1996); D. D. Dubois, ed., *The Competency Case Book: Twelve Studies in Competency-Based Performance Improvement* (Amherst, Mass.: HRD Press and the International Society for Performance Improvement, 1998).

9. Bradley Agle, "Understanding Research on Values in Business," *Business & Society* (September 1999), 326–387.

10. W. G. Lee, "A Conversation with Herb Kelleher," *Organizational Dynamics* 23:2 (1994), 64–74.

11. A. Farnham, "State Your Values, Hold the Hot Air," *Fortune* (August 1993), 117–124.

12. See, for instance, William J. Pfeiffer, ed., *The Encyclopedia of Group Activities* (San Diego: University Associates, 1989); and Barbara Singer and Kathleen Von Buren, *Work Values: Facilitation Guide for Managers, Teams & Trainers* (Durango, Colo.: Self-Management Institute, 1995).

13. Michael Hickins, "A Day at the Races," *Management Review* 88:5 (1999), 56–61.

Chapter 5

1. Jac Fitz-Enz, *How to Measure Human Resources Management* (New York: McGraw-Hill, 1984), p. 48. See also Jac Fitz-Enz, *The ROI of Human Capital* (New York: AMACOM, 2000).

2. Fitz-Enz, *How to Measure Human Resources Management*, p. 48.

3. Particularly good articles on this topic include: Paul Brauchle, "Costing Out the Value of Training," *Technical and Skills Training* 3:4

(1992), 35–40; J. Hassett, "Simplifying ROI," *Training*, September 1992; J. Phillips, "Measuring the Return on HRD," *Employment Relations Today*, August 1991.

4. For example, see especially C. Derr, C. Jones, and E. Toomey, "Managing High-Potential Employees: Current Practices in Thirty-three U.S. Corporations," *Human Resource Management* 27:3 (1988), 273–290; O. Esman, "Succession Planning in Small and Medium-Sized Corporations," *HR Horizons* 91:103 (1991), 15–19; *The Identification and Development of High Potential Managers*, (Palatine, Ill.: Executive Knowledgeworks, 1987); Meg Kerr, *Succession Planning in America's Corporations* (Palatine, Ill.: Anthony J. Fresina and Associates and Executive Knowledgeworks, 1987); and E. Zajac, "CEO Selection, Succession, Compensation and Firm Performance: A Theoretical Integration and Empirical Analysis," *Strategic Management Journal* 11:3 (1990), 217–230.

5. P. Linkow, "HRD at the Roots of Corporate Strategy," *Training and Development Journal* 39:5 (1985), 85–87; William J. Rothwell, ed., *In Action: Linking HRD and Organizational Strategy* (Alexandria, Va.: The American Society for Training and Development, 1998).

6. Karen A. Golden and Vasudevan Ramanujam, "Between a Dream and a Nightmare: On the Integration of the Human Resource Management and Strategic Business Planning Processes," *Human Resource Management* 24:4 (1985), 429.

7. William J. Rothwell and H. C. Kazanas, *Human Resource Development: A Strategic Approach,* rev. ed. (Amherst, Mass.: HRD Press, 1994).

8. For research evidence, see William J. Rothwell and H. C. Kazanas, "Training: Key to Strategic Management," *Performance Improvement Quarterly* 3:1 (1990), 42–56.

9. Robert C. Camp, *Benchmarking: The Search for Industry Best Practices That Lead to Superior Performance* (Milwaukee, Wisconsin: Quality Press/American Society for Quality Control; White Plains, New York: Quality Resources, 1989), p. 3. See also Michael J. Spendolini, *The Benchmarking Book* (New York: AMACOM, 1992).

10. Ibid., p. 17.

11. Diane Dormant, "The ABCDs of Managing Change," in M. Smith, ed., *Introduction to Performance Technology* (Washington, D.C.: The National Society for Performance and Instruction, 1986), pp. 238–256.

12. Ibid., p. 239.

13. Ibid., p. 241.

Chapter 6

1. James L. Gibson, John M. Ivancevich, and James H. Donnelly, Jr., *Organizations: Behavior, Structure, Processes,* 5th ed. (Plano, Tex.: Business Publications, Inc., 1985), p. 280.

2. Walter R. Mahler and Stephen J. Drotter, *The Succession Planning Handbook for the Chief Executive* (Midland Park, N.J.: Mahler Publishing Co., 1986), p. 8.

3. "Choosing Your Successor," *Chief Executive Magazine* (May/June 1988), 48–63; Jeffrey Sonnenfeld, *The Hero's Farewell: What Happens When CEOs Retire* (New York: Oxford University Press, 1988); Richard F. Vancil, *Passing the Baton: Managing the Process of CEO Succession* (Boston: Harvard Business School Press, 1987); E. Zajac, "CEO Selection, Succession, Compensation and Firm Performance: A Theoretical Integration and Empirical Analysis," *Strategic Management Journal* 11:3 (1990), 217–230.

4. Joan C. Szabo, "Finding the Right Workers," *Nation's Business* 79:2 (1991), 16–22. See also "U.S. Chamber Calls for Congressional Action to Ease Worker Shortage," *News* (March 7, 2000). Presented at http://www.uschamber.org/media/releases/0003/030700.html.

5. Equal Employment Opportunity Commission, "Uniform Guidelines on Employee Selection Procedures," *Federal Register* 43 (1978), 38290-38315.

Chapter 7

1. Allen Kraut, Patricia Pedigo, Douglas McKenna, and Marvin Dunnette, "The Role of the Manager: What's Really Important in Different Management Jobs," *Academy of Management Executive* 3:4 (1989), 287.

2. See, for instance, R. Smither, "The Return of the Authoritarian Manager," *Training* 28:11 (1991), 40–44.

Chapter 8

1. M. Pastin, "The Fallacy of Long-Range Thinking," *Training* 23:5 (1986), 47–53.

2. B. Staw, "Knee-Deep in the Big Muddy," *Organizational Behavior and Human Performance* 16:1 (1976), 27–44.

3. Karen Stephenson and Valdis Krebs, "A More Accurate Way to Measure Diversity," *Personnel Journal* 72:10 (1993), 66–72, 74.

4. Rosabeth Moss Kanter, *The Men and Women of the Corporation* (New York: Basic Books, 1977), p. 48.

5. Ibid.

6. Glenn E. Baker, A. Grubbs, and Thomas Ahern, "Triangulation: Strengthening Your Best Guess," *Performance Improvement Quarterly* 3:3 (1990), 27–35.

7. Arthur W. Sherman, Jr., George W. Bohlander, and Herbert Chruden,

Managing Human Resources, 8th ed.(Cincinnati: South-Western Publishing Co., 1988), pp. 95–96.

8. For one excellent approach, see Roger J. Plachy and Sandra J. Plachy, *Results-Oriented Job Descriptions* (New York: AMACOM, 1993). See also *Model Job Descriptions for Business* (N.p.: Local Government Institute, 1997).

9. W. Barlow and E. Hane, "A Practical Guide to the Americans with Disabilities Act," *Personnel Journal* 71:6 (1992), 54.

10. Kenneth E. Carlisle, *Analyzing Jobs and Tasks* (Englewood Cliffs, N.J.: Educational Technology Publications, 1986), p. 5.

11. See Barlow and Hane, "A Practical Guide to the Americans with Disabilities Act," 53–60; M. Chalker, "Tooling Up for ADA," *HRMagazine* (December 1991), 61–63, 65; and J. Kohl and P. Greenlaw, "The Americans with Disabilities Act of 1990: Implications for Managers," *Sloan Management Review* 33:3 (1992), 87–90.

12. See, for instance, Max Wortman, Jr., and JoAnn Sperling, *Defining the Manager's Job*, 2d ed. (New York: AMACOM, 1975).

13. William J. Rothwell, "HRD and the Americans with Disabilities Act," *Training and Development* 45:8 (1991), 45–47.

14. Richard Boyatzis, *The Competent Manager: A Model for Effective Performance* (New York: John Wiley & Sons, Inc., 1982).

15. David Dubois, *Competency-Based Performance Improvement: A Strategy for Organizational Change* (Amherst, Mass.: HRD Press, 1993), p. 9.

16. Ibid.

17. R. Norton, *Dacum Handbook* (Columbus, Ohio: The National Center for Research in Vocational Education, The Ohio State University, 1985). See also D. Faber, E. Fangman, and J. Low, "DACUM: A Collaborative Tool for Workforce Development," *Journal of Studies in Technical Careers* 13:2 (1991), 145–159.

18. Ibid., pp. 1–2.

19. See A. Osborn, *Applied Imagination*, 3d ed. (New York: Scribner, 1963), and A. Van Gundy, *Techniques of Structured Problem Solving* (New York: Van Nostrand Reinhold, 1981).

20. A. Van Gundy, *Techniques of Structured Problem Solving*, op. cit.

21. G. Huet-Cox, T. M. Nielsen, and E. Sundstrom, "Get the Most From 360-Degree Feedback: Put It on the Internet," *HRMagazine* 44:5 (1999), 92–103; "Finding Leaders: How Ameritech Feeds Its Pipeline," *Training Directors' Forum Newsletter* 15:5 (1999), 4.

22. Leanne Atwater and David Waldman, "Accountability in 360-Degree Feedback," *HRMagazine* 43:6 (1998), 96–104. The article asserts that over 90 percent of Fortune 1000 companies use some form of multisource assessment. For more information on full-circle, multi-rater as-

sessment, David D. Dubois and William J. Rothwell, *The Competency Toolkit*, 2 vols. (Amherst, Mass.: HRD Press, 2000); see: Keith Morical, "A Product Review: 360 Assessments," *Training and Development* 53:4 (1999), 43–47; Kenneth Nowack, Jeanne Hartley, and William Bradley, "How to Evaluate Your 360-Feedback Efforts," *Training & Development* 53:4 (1999), 48–53; David Waldman and David E. Bowen, "The Acceptability of 360-Degree Appraisals: A Customer-Supplier Relationship Perspective," *Human Resource Management* 37:2 (1998), 117–129.

23. See, for instance, Paul J. Taylor and Jon L. Pierce, "Effects of Introducing a Performance Management System on Employees' Subsequent Attitudes and Effort," *Public Personnel Management* 28:3 (1999), 423–452.

24. See, for instance, *Performance Appraisals: The Ongoing Legal Nightmare*, Anonymous (Ramsey, N.J.: Alexander Hamilton Institute, 1993).

25. Mary Walton, *The Deming Management Method* (New York: Perigee Books, 1986), p. 91.

26. See, for instance, S. Cunningham, "Coaching Today's Executive," *Public Utilities Fortnightly* 128:2 (1991), 22–25; David L. Dotlich and Peter C. Cairo, *Action Coaching: How to Leverage Individual Performance for Company Success* (San Francisco: Jossey-Bass, 1999); Steven J. Stowell and Matt Starcevich, *The Coach: Creating Partnerships for a Competitive Edge* (Salt Lake City: The Center for Management and Organization Effectiveness, 1987).

27. *BLR Encyclopedia of Performance Appraisal* (Madison, Conn.: Business and Legal Reports, 1985). See also Richard C. Grote, *The Complete Guide to Performance Appraisal* (New York: AMACOM, 1996).

Chapter 9

1. See William J. Rothwell and H. C. Kazanas, *Planning and Managing Human Resources: Strategic Planning for Personnel Management* (Amherst, Mass.: HRD Press, 1994).

2. William J. Rothwell and H. C. Kazanas, "Developing Management Employees to Cope with the Moving Target Effect," *Performance and Instruction* 32:8 (1993), 1–5.

3. See, for instance, Newman S. Peery, Jr., and Mahmoud Salem, "Strategic Management of Emerging Human Resource Issues," *Human Resource Development Quarterly* 4:1 (1993), 81–95; Raynold A. Svenson and Monica J. Rinderer, *The Training and Development Strategic Plan Workbook* (Englewood Cliffs, N.J.: Prentice-Hall, 1992). For works specifically on environmental scanning, see F. Aguilar, *Scanning the*

Business Environment (New York: Macmillan, 1967); Patrick Callan, ed., *Environmental Scanning for Strategic Leadership* (San Francisco: Jossey-Bass, 1986); L. Fahey, W. King, and V. Narayanan, "Environmental Scanning and Forecasting in Strategic Planning—The State of the Art," *Long Range Planning*, 14:1 (1981), 32–39; R. Heath and Associates, *Strategic Issues Management: How Organizations Influence and Respond to Public Interests and Policies* (San Francisco: Jossey-Bass, 1988).

4. Harry Levinson, *Organizational Diagnosis* (Cambridge, Mass.: Harvard University Press, 1972); A. O. Manzini, *Organizational Diagnosis* (New York: AMACOM, 1988); and Marvin Weisbord, *Organizational Diagnosis: A Workbook of Theory and Practice* (Reading, Mass.: Addison-Wesley, 1978).

5. This is an issue of classic debate: Does structure affect strategy or does strategy affect structure? The first discussion appears in A. Chandler, *Strategy and Structure: Chapters in the History of American Industrial Enterprise* (Cambridge, Mass.: Massachusetts Institute of Technology, 1962). Other authors are not sure that strategy always affects structure. See, for instance, J. Galbraith and D. Nathanson, "The Role of Organizational Structure and Process in Strategy Implementation," in D. Schendel and C. Hofer, eds., *Strategic Management* (Boston: Little, Brown and Co., 1979).

6. See Kees Van Der Heijden, *Scenarios: The Art of Strategic Conversation* (New York: John Wiley & Sons, Inc., 1996); and William J. Rothwell and H. C. Kazanas, *Human Resource Development: A Strategic Approach,* rev. ed. (Amherst, Mass.: HRD Press, 1994).

7. See, for instance, J. Wissema, A. Brand, and H. Van Der Pol, "The Incorporation of Management Development in Strategic Management," *Strategic Management Journal* 2 (1981), 361–377.

8. See remarks in Larry Davis and E. McCallon, *Planning, Conducting, Evaluating Workshops* (Austin, Tex.: Learning Concepts, 1974).

9. Rothwell and Kazanas, "Developing Management Employees to Cope with the Moving Target Effect," 1–5.

10. See Rothwell and Kazanas, *Planning and Managing Human Resources,* op. cit.

11. Melvin Sorcher, *Predicting Executive Success: What It Takes to Make It Into Senior Management* (New York: John Wiley & Sons, Inc., 1985), p. 2.

12. William J. Rothwell and H. C. Kazanas, *Building In-House Leadership and Management Development Programs* (Westport, CT: Quorum Books, 1999).

13. Ibid.

14. E. Lindsey, V. Homes, and M. McCall, *Key Events in Executives' Lives* (Greensboro, N.C.: The Center for Creative Leadership, 1987).
15. This approach is described at length in George S. Odiorne, *Strategic Management of Human Resources: A Portfolio Approach* (San Francisco: Jossey-Bass, 1984).
16. Ibid.
17. Ibid.
18. Ibid.
19. Ibid.
20. Rose Mary Wentling, "Women in Middle Management: Their Career Development and Aspirations," *Business Horizons* (January–February 1992), 47–54.

Chapter 10

1. Walter R. Mahler and Stephen J. Drotter, *The Succession Planning Handbook for the Chief Executive* (Midland Park, N.J.: Mahler Publishing Co., 1986).
2. Peter F. Drucker, "How to Make People Decisions," *Harvard Business Review* 63:4 (1985), 22–26.
3. Lawrence S. Kleiman and Kimberly J. Clark, "User's Satisfaction with Job Posting," *Personnel Administrator* 29:9 (1984), 104–108.
4. Lawrence S. Kleiman and Kimberly J. Clark, "An Effective Job Posting System," *Personnel Journal* 63:2 (1984), 20–25.
5. Malcolm Knowles, *Using Learning Contracts: Practical Approaches to Individualizing and Structuring Learning* (San Francisco: Jossey-Bass, 1986), pp. 28–32.
6. R. Fritz, *Personal Performance Contracts: The Key to Job Success* (Los Altos, Calif.: Crisp, 1987).
7. Arthur X. Deegan II, *Succession Planning: Key to Corporate Excellence* (New York: Wiley-Interscience, 1986), p. 167.
8. Robert F. Mager, *Preparing Instructional Objectives*, 2d ed. (Belmont, Calif.: Lear-Siegler, 1975).
9. M. Lombardo and R. Eichinger, *Eighty-eight Assignments for Development in Place: Enhancing the Developmental Challenge of Existing Jobs* (Greensboro, N.C.: The Center for Creative Leadership, 1989).
10. A. Huczynski, *Encyclopedia of Management Development Methods* (London: Gower, 1983).

Chapter 11

1. James L. Adams, *Conceptual Blockbusting: A Guide to Better Ideas*, 3d ed. (Reading, Mass.: Addison-Wesley, 1986), p. 7.

2. Michael Hammer and James Champy, *Reengineering the Corporation: A Manifesto for Business Revolution* (New York: HarperBusiness, 1993), p. 32.
3. G. Rummler and A. Brache, "Managing the White Space," *Training* 28:1 (1991), 55–70.

Chapter 12

1. For assistance in conceptualizing a skill inventory and/or a record-keeping system for that purpose, see D. Gould, *Personnel Skills Inventory Skill Study* (Madison, Conn.: Business and Legal Reports, 1986).

Chapter 13

1. William J. Rothwell and Henry J. Sredl, *The American Society for Training and Development Reference Guide to Professional Human Resource Development Roles and Competencies*, 2nd ed. (Amherst, Mass.: HRD Press, 1992), II, p. 411 and William J. Rothwell and Henry J. Sredl, *The American Society for Training and Development Reference Guide to Workplace Learning and Performance*, 3rd ed. (Amherst, Mass.: HRD Press, 2000).
2. See Nancy Dixon, *Evaluation: A Tool for Improving HRD Quality* (Alexandria, Va.: The American Society for Training and Development, 1990); Jack Phillips, *Handbook of Training Evaluation and Measurement Methods*, 2d ed. (Houston: Gulf Publishing, 1991); Leslie Rae, *How to Measure Training Effectiveness* (Brookfield, Vt.: Gower Publishing, 1991); William J. Rothwell, ed., *Creating, Measuring and Documenting Service Impact: A Capacity Building Resource: Rationales, Models, Activities, Methods, Techniques, Instruments* (Columbus, Ohio: The EnterpriseOhio Network, 1998).
3. Paul Brauchle, "Costing Out the Value of Training," *Technical and Skills Training* 3:4 (1992), 35–40; W. Cascio, *Costing Human Resources: The Financial Impact of Behavior in Organizations*, 2d ed. (Boston: PWS-Kent Publishing, 1987); C. Fauber, "Use of Improvement (Learning) Curves to Predict Learning Costs," *Production and Inventory Management* 30:3 (1989), 57–60; T. Jackson, *Evaluation: Relating Training to Business Performance* (San Diego: Pfeiffer and Company, 1989); L. Spencer, *Calculating Human Resource Costs and Benefits* (Somerset, N.J.: John Wiley and Sons, Inc., 1986); Richard Swanson and Deane Gradous, *Forecasting Financial Benefits of Human Resource Development* (San Francisco: Jossey-Bass, 1988).

4. See Donald Kirkpatrick, "Techniques for Evaluating Training Programs," *Journal of the American Society for Training and Development* [now called *Training and Development*] 14:1 (1960), 13–18.

5. R. Brinkerhoff, "The Success Case: A Low-Cost High-Yield Evaluation," *Training and Development Journal* 37:8 (1983), 58–61. See also Rothwell, ed., *Creating, Measuring and Documenting Service Impact,* op. cit.

6. See William J. Rothwell and H. C. Kazanas, *Planning and Managing Human Resources: Strategic Planning for Personnel Management,* rev. ed. (Amherst, Mass.: HRD Press, 1994).

Chapter 14

1. See Thomas Hoffman, "Labor Gap May Drive Mergers," *Online News* (July 13, 1998), at http://www.idg.net/crd_it_9–65593.html.

2. Jennifer Reingold and Diane Brady, "Brain Drain," *Business Week* (September 20, 1999), 112–115, 118, 120, 124, 126.

3. Ibid.

4. Ibid.

Index

ABCD model for management commitment, 113
academic institutions, 300–302
action plan *see* program action plan
active role in succession planning, 120
Adams, James L., *Conceptual Block-busting*, 239
adopters of change, 113, 115
adoption stage of innovation acceptance, 116
Age Discrimination in Employment Act (1967), 141
American Management Association, 109
American Society for Training and Development, 109
Americans with Disabilities Act (1990), 145, 177
anecdotes
  collecting and using, 90–91
  in program evaluation, 275, 280
assessment
  competencies, 78, 199–200
  of current practices, 91, 94–96
  full-circle, multi-rater, 182–183
  full-circle, multi-rater, worksheet, 184
  internal development alternatives, 239–240, 247–249
  of performance, 69
  rapid results assessment, 181
  see also individual potential assessment
attitude surveys, 297
attitudes, quick-fix, 70

automated talent inventory system, 267–268
avoidable turnover, 216
awareness stage of innovation acceptance, 113, 116

balance in life, 303
behavioral event interviewing, 85
behaviorally anchored rating scales approach to performance appraisal, 189–190
bench strength
  testing, 215–217
  what it is, 216
  see also weak bench strength
benchmarking, 53, 108–109, 257
  interview guide, 110–113
"best-in-class" companies, 109
Black Lung Benefits Reform Act (1977), 143
bottom-line value, of succession planning, 99–102
bottom-up approach to succession planning, 22
Brache, A., 240
brainstorming, 181
  on use of online and high-tech methods, worksheet, 260–261
business needs, 53
business process reengineering, 240

Camp, Robert C., 108
career maps, 25, 67
career path meetings, 72
career planning
  as approach to integrating strategy and succession plans, 16

career planning (*continued*)
form, 211, 221
important characteristics, 304–305
by individuals, 18
meetings for, 72
succession planning integration, 302–303, 306–307
training tied to, 164
Carlisle, Kenneth, 178
Carrington, Edward, 41–44
Champy, James, 240
change champion, 95, 124
change, need for, 89
chart for replacement planning, 217
chief executive officer
and program rollout, 138
replacement planning, 57, 65
succession planning case study, 40–44
support for training, 162
China, age distribution of population (2025), 298
Civil Rights Act (1991), 145–146
Civil Rights Act, Title VII (1964), 140
Civil Service, 301
closed communication strategy, 151
closed program, 23
combination approach to succession planning, 22
Comins, Frederic M., 44–48
commitment, 73–75
from management, 113–116
communicating program action plan, 149–152
communication strategy, 146–147
consistency in applying, 151
Competence Expert, 265
competencies
approaches to identification, 81–83
assessment, 78, 199–200
conflict between present and future, 200
for high-tech and online methods of succession management, 269–270
identification studies, 79–80

identifying, 180
importance of, 37–38
using in succession planning and management, 78
what they are, 77–78
Competency Coach for Windows, 265
competency identification, 77
competency model, 77, 78, 180
future-oriented, 264
using, 80
Web sites, 264
competitive skill inventories, 28
computers
conference calls using, 258
see also high-tech methods of succession planning
conference calls, 258
Congressional Accountability Act (1995), 146
consultants, 29, 228, 291
for training, 157
Contract Work Hours Safety Standards Act (1962), 140
Cooper, Kenneth Carlton, *Effective Competency Modeling & Reporting*, 265
coordinator, for succession planning and management program, 153, 165
corporate politics, 69
cost/benefit analysis, 102
counseling for managers, 164–167
requirements for, 165
crisis
and change, 90
to demonstrate need, 96–99
key position vacancies as, 91
critical incident interviews, 209
critical questioning, 56
critical turnover, 216
crown prince phenomenon, 150, 302
current practices, assessment of, 91, 94–96
customer satisfaction, in evaluation of succession planning and management, 273

customized generic model method, 82

DACUM method, 180–182
data collection, for policy formulation, 257
Davis-Bacon Act (1931), 139
deadwood in performance/potential grid, 205
debate on succession planning mission, 127–128
decision making, network charting, 175
Deegan, Arthur, 222
delegation of work, 292
Deloitte, Senior Leaders Program, 292
Deming, W. Edwards, 186
demotion, 25, 26
derailment
    competency study, 79
    counseling to avoid, 166–167
development meetings, 72
developmental gap closure, 265–266
developmental programs, 55
The Dictionary of Occupational Titles, 178, 262
dimensions/activity rating to performance appraisal, 189
direct training, 163
directive role, 120
discrimination in employment, 9, 18–19
    and performance assessment, 69
dissemination of program processes, 23
diversity, promoting, 9
document distribution, 257
document imaging, 257
document storage and retrieval, 256–257
domino effect, 291
Dormant, Diane, 113
double loop learning, 7
downsizing, 20
    impact, 36
    and middle management reduction, 8–9

Drotter, Stephen J., 122
Drucker, Peter, xx
dual career ladders, 27
Dubois, David, *Competency-Based Performance Improvement*, 80

e-mail, for survey of management, 95
Economic Dislocation and Worker Adjustment Assistance Act (1988), 144
economic expansion, 35
Effective Competency Modeling & Reporting (Cooper), 265
employee hoarding, 220
employee loyalty, xvii
Employee Polygraph Protection Act (1988), 144–145
Employee Retirement Income Security Act (1974), 142
employees
    ability to respond to environmental change, 19
    evaluation process, 52
    morale, 19
employment discrimination, 9, 18–19
empowered individual potential assessment, 211–212
entitlement, 212
entry into job, 25
environmental change, employee ability to respond to, 19
environmental scanning, 194
    worksheet, 195
Equal Employment Opportunity Commission, 136
Equal Pay Act (1963), 140
essential job function, 177
ethics, 38
evaluation of succession planning and management program
    anecdotes, 275, 280
    checklist, 284–286
    guidelines, 276–277
    key questions, 272
    periodic evaluation, 280
    programmatic evaluation, 280–281

evaluation of succession planning and management program (*continued*)
  steps for completing, 282–283
  what it is, 271–272
  worksheet for identifying methods, 278
evidence to test bench strength, 217
Executive Order 11246 (1965), 141
executive retreat, 153–154
exemplary performers, vs. high-potentials, 203–205
exit interviews, 297
expansion of planning, 132, 134
expectations of superiors, 186
external talent pool, 67–68

Fair Labor Standards Act (1938), 139
Family and Medical Leave Act (1991), 146
family time, 303
Fayol, Henri, 5
Federal Coal Mine Health and Safety Act (1969), 141
Fitz-Enz, Jac, 99–101
flexible job competency model method, 82–83
flexible staffing, 248
focus on succession planning, 53
Formtool, 269
France, age distribution of population (2025), 299
full-circle, multi-rater assessment, 182–183
  software and Web-based instruments, 265
  worksheet, 184
future competency study, 79
future-oriented competency modeling, 264
future trends in succession planning, 287
  flexible strategies for organizational talent needs, 290–293
  global impact, 297–300
  government, academic institutions and nonprofits, 300–302

integrated retention policies, 293, 297
integration with career development, 302–303, 306–307
organizational openness, 302
realtime technological innovations, 300
work/family balance and spirituality, 303
worksheet to structure thinking about, 288–289
futuring approach to integrating strategy and succession plans, 16

gambler's fallacy, 171
generic model overlay method, 81
Gilmore, Thomas, 16
glass ceiling, 9
global assessment of individual potential, 205–206
Global Business Network, 264
global population trends, 297
global rating approach to performance appraisal, 188
Golden, Karen A., 107
government, succession planning trends and, 300–302
greenmail, 302
Gridley, John D., 17
group facilitators, 127
groupware, 257, 258–259, 264

Haire, M., 25
halo effect, 69, 206
Hammer, Michael, 240
hands-on stage of innovation acceptance, 115, 116
headcount reduction to essential workers, 27
healthcare organizations, human resource development, 48
Hercules, succession planning case study, 41–44
hierarchy
  of online and high-tech applications, 256–258

of succession planning and management evaluation, 274
of training evaluation, 272–273
high potential workers
counseling, 166
opportunities for, 10–11
response to knowledge of status by, 150–152
values clarification, 85
what it is, 203
high-tech methods of succession planning, 253–255
competencies for using, 269–270
hierarchy of applications, 255–258
hiring, 25
former employees, 292
from outside, 290
historical evidence to identify key positions, 174
holes, 216
homosocial reproduction, 9, 175
horizontal advancement, 187
horizontal job loading, 26–27
horn effect, 69, 206
HTML, 269
Hudson Institute, *Workforce 2000*, 48
human resource development, 17, 65
human resource planning, 17
Human Resource Planning Society, 109
human resource professionals, opinions about succession planning and management, 115
human resource strategy, 106–107
human resources audit, 280

idea champions, 69
IDP *see* individual development plans
Immigration Reform and Control Act (1986), 144
incident reports, 275
sample, 279
individual career planning programs, 22
individual development plans, 215, 221–229

implementation, 228
methods, 232–233
preparation, 222, 224–229
sample, 230–231
software and Web-based help, 266
what it is, 221–222
individual potential assessment, 187, 202–212
approaches to, 205–209
empowered, 211–212
form, 208
leader-driven, 209–210
participative, 210–211
information
maintaining about key positions, 176
problems in sharing, 149–152
inplacement, 26
insourcing, 291
institutional memory, 7
intellectual capital, 18, 37
interactive online or high-tech methods, 254
internal development, 215, 229, 231, 236
alternatives assessment, 239–240, 247–249
key strategies, 234–237
internal talent pool, 67
internalizing roles, 118–119
international assignments, 231
Internet, 253
see also Web sites
interview, for individual potential assessment, 210
inventory, by position, 218

JAVA, 269
job analysis
future-oriented, 197–198
of key positions, 177–178
job competence assessment model, 81
job competency, 77
job description, 177
Web sites for training in writing, 262
job forecasting, 264

job movement
    alternative approaches, 27–29
    types, 25–27
job posting, importance of, 220–221
job rotations, 26, 29, 237
    for assistant managers, 28
job sharing, 28
Job Training Partnership Act (1982),
    143
job vacancy, replacement decision,
    240

Kanter, Rosabeth Moss, 9, 175
Kelleher, Herb, 83
key position incumbent, 54
    decision on unnecessary, 241–246
    vacancy in, 173
key positions
    avoidable turnover, 216
    determining work requirements,
        176–182
    evaluating need for, 250–251
    future-oriented descriptions, 198
    identifying, 172–176
    identifying for future, 193–197
    maintaining information about, 176
    preparing individual for, 222,
        224–229
    problems filling, 90
    work requirements for future,
        197–202
    worksheet for descriptions, 179
kickoff meetings, 72, 154–155
Kirkpatrick, Donald, 272
Kmart, succession planning case
    study, 44–48
knowledge management, trends, 37
Korn/Ferry International, survey, 8

Labor Management Cooperation Act
    (1978), 143
Labor Management Reporting and
    Disclosure Act (1959), 140
Landrum-Griffin Act (1959), 140
lateral transfer, 25, 26
leader-driven individual potential as-
    sessment, 209–210

leadership
    bias of, 171
    continuity in organizations, 24–29
    matching to strategy, 106
    shortage, 35
leadership skills, 17
learning
    diagnosing needs, 222, 224
    organizational, 7
learning contract, 221
learning objectives, 224
    evidence of accomplishment, 226
    worksheet for preparing, 225
learning resources, 226
    worksheet for identifying, 227
learning strategies, 226, 229, 231
legal framework, 136–138
Leibman, Michael, 31
life cycle of succession planning,
    57–68
    CEO and executive team replace-
        ment plan, 65–66
    CEO replacement plan, 57, 65
    external talent pool, 67–68
    internal talent pool, 67
    middle management, 66–67
    requirements for fifth-generation
        approach, 73
    in rollout strategy, 138, 146
localization strategies, 299–300
loyalty of employees, xvii
    reduction, 36

Mager, Robert F., 224
Mahler, Walter R, 122
management
    commitment from, 113–116
    counseling about succession plan-
        ning, 164–167
    succession planning for all levels,
        54
    see also middle management; top
        managers
management career planning form,
    211
management career track, 27

management succession, importance of, xx

mandated succession planning and management, 24

manual talent inventory system, 266–267

Manzini, Andrew O., 17

market-driven approach to integrating strategy and succession plans, 16

Marshall, Thurgood, 18

McClelland, David, 77

McLagan's Flexible Approach, 180

meetings, 152–156
  executive retreat, 153–154
  for input, 152–154
  kickoff meetings, 72, 154–155
  number as problem, 72–73
  periodic reviews, 155–156
  proposal development, 154
  to verify need for succession planning, 152

memory, institutional, 7

mental tryout stage of innovation acceptance, 115, 116

mentors, 47, 56, 236

mergers and acquisitions to gain talent, 291–292

metasearch engines, 255

middle management
  downsizing and reduction of, 8–9
  replacement planning, 66–67

Migrant and Seasonal Agricultural Protection Act (1983), 144

mission statement, 122–128
  preparation, 124, 128
  sample, 130
  succession planning questions to be answered by, 123–124
  what it is, 122–123
  worksheet to formulate, 125–127

modified job competence assessment model, 81

moving target effect, 193

Multi-Employer Pension Plan Amendments Act (1980), 143

multiculturalism, 18
  promoting, 9

multimedia, distribution and delivery, 257

musical chairs effect, 291

National Labor Relations Act (1947), 139

need for succession planning assessment of current practices, 91, 94–96
  crisis to demonstrate, 96–99
  e-mail to focus on, 95
  informal discussions, 93–95
  survey to evaluate, 95–96, 97–99
  worksheet for demonstrating, 100

NetMeeting, 258–259

netphone, 258

network charting, to identify key positions, 175

nondirective role, 120

noninteractive online or high-tech methods, 254

nonprofit enterprises, succession planning trends and, 300–302

nursing departments, succession planning case study, 48–52

Occupational Safety and Health Act (1970), 142

Older Workers Benefit Protection Act (1990), 145

online methods of succession planning, 253–255
  competencies for using, 269–270

open communication strategy, 151

open program, 23–24

organization charts, to identify key positions, 173–174

organization, determining requirements, 102–103

organizational analysis, 194
  activity, 196

organizational change, 70–71, 290

organizational learning, 7

organizational meetings, 72

organizational needs, strategies to address, 290–293

organizational redesign, 27
organizational strategy, 103, 106
OrgPlus, 268
outsourcing, 27, 248, 290
overstaffing, xviii
overtime, 29

paperwork, 71–72
part-time employment, 29
participative individual potential assessment, 210–211
passive role in succession planning, 120
People Manager, 267
People Trak, 267
performance appraisal, 184–187
  approaches to, 188–190
  formal methods, 69
  and future potential, 54
  link to succession planning, 186–187
  meetings for, 72
  online and high-tech methods, 262–263
  vs. potential, 203
  worksheet, 191
performance contract, 221
performance management, 185
Performance Now!, 263
performance/potential grid, 204
performance standards, monitoring, 52
periodic evaluation, 280
periodic reviews, meetings for, 155–156
pigeonholing, 69, 206
placements, in evaluation of succession planning and management, 273
policy writing, 128–129
  high-tech methods, 258–259
  sample, 130
population, global trends, 297
position analysis, 178
position description, 177–178
  advantages and disadvantages, 178

potential assessment meetings, 72
Pregnancy Discrimination Act (1978), 143
present competency study, 79
priorities, 134–136, 303
  activity for establishing, 137–138
problem solving, 165–167, 239–240
problems, assessment of current, 90–91
procedures, 129
  sample, 130
process redesign, 27
professional positions, as initial target for planning, 132
program action plan, 148–149
  communicating, 149–152
  components, 148–149
  establishing, 149
  value of, 148
  worksheet for preparing, 150
program process, in evaluation of succession planning and management, 273
programmatic evaluation, 280–281
progress in place, 26
promotable workers, increasing number of, 13, 15
promotion, 25–26
  from within, 215
  avoiding impression of guarantee, 212
  internal policy formulation, 219–221
Pygmalion effect, 69, 186

question marks, in performance/potential grid, 205
quick-fix attitudes, 70

Ramanujam, Vasudevan, 107
rapid results assessment, 180–182
  future-oriented, 200, 202
  steps in conducting, 201–202
realistic future scenarios, 197
recency bias, 69, 206
recruitment, global or local, 292

Rehabilitation Act (1973), 142
replacement charting, 216–217
replacement needs identification, 11, 13
replacement planning, vs. succession planning and management, 7
researching secondary information, 255
responsibilities, 54
retention, 297
retirees, return to work, 29
retirement
knowledge of executive plans, 54
of senior executives, xvii
retreat, 153–154
rewards, delayed or immediate, 36
rifle approach to integrating strategy and succession plans, 16
risk management, replacement planning as, 7
role conflict, 119
role receivers, 119
role senders, 118–119
role theory, 118–120
applying to succession planning and management, 120–122
rollout of succession planning program
life cycle of succession planning in, 138, 146
strategies, 138, 146–147
Rummler, G., 240

scenario analysis, 197
scenario planning, 264
search engines, on World Wide Web, 255
secondary information, researching, 255
secrecy in individual potential assessment, 209
in succession planning, 23
self-assessment, individual responsibility for, 211
self-concern stage of innovation acceptance, 115, 116

self-fulfilling prophecy, 186
Service Contract Act (1965), 141
site visits, in benchmarking, 109
skills, seller's market, 35–36
Society for Human Resources Management, 109
survey, 9–20
speed, 32–35
of organizational change, 70–71
spirituality, 303
stars in performance/potential grid, 204
stereotyping, 69
strategic alliances, 292
strategic plan, succession planning and management as component, 15–16
strategies for program rollout, 138, 146–147
success factor analysis, 206–209
worksheet, 207
succession management, 6
succession planning, 6
succession planning and management
characteristics of effective, 53–57
characteristics of effective, questionnaire, 63–65
characteristics of effective, survey, 58–62
defining, 5–7
dramatizing need for, 66
importance of, 7–9, 93
life cycle of programs, 57–68
measuring results, 101–102
performance appraisal link to, 186–187
program difficulties, 68
replacement planning vs., 7
resistence to implementing, 92
values use in, 83–84
succession planning and management approaches, 21–24
amount of individual discretion, 24
bottom-up approach, 22
combination approach, 22
degree of dissemination, 23–24

succession planning and management
    approaches (*continued*)
    planning requirements, 22–23
    scope, 23
    timing, 22
    top-down approach, 21–22
succession planning and management
    model, 73–76
    assessment of work requirements,
        75
    commitment, 73–75
    developmental gap closure, 75–76
    performance appraisal, 75
    potential assessment, 75
succession planning and management
    problems, 68–73
    corporate politics, 69
    lack of support, 69
    low visibility, 70
    paperwork, 71–72
    quick-fix attitudes, 70
    speed of organizational change,
        70–71
    too many meetings, 72–73
succession planning and management
    survey, 9–20
    career plans of individuals, 18
    diverse group advancement, 18–19
    downsizing, 20
    employee ability to respond to envi-
        ronmental change, 19
    employee morale, 19
    headcount reduction to essential
        workers, 20
    intellectual capital, 18
    opportunities for high potential
        workers, 10–11
    replacement needs identification,
        11, 13
    respondent demographic informa-
        tion, 10–11
    respondent job function, 11
    retention strategies, 14–15
    statistics on reasons, 12–13
    strategic plan implementation,
        15–18

talent pool increase, 13, 15
termination decisions, 20
voluntary separation programs,
    19–20
workforce reductions, 21
successors, informal selection, 9
supervisory positions, as initial target
    for planning, 132
support, lack of, 69
survey
    formal for assessment, 95–96
    formal for assessment, example,
        97–99
    online methods, 257
    questionnaire to assess manage-
        ment of trend consequences,
        33–34
    using e-mail, 95

Taft-Hartley Act, 139
talent inventories, software and Web-
    based help, 266–268
talent pool, 13, 15, 28, 212
    creating, 187, 191–192
    external, 67–68
    internal, 67
target groups, 129–136
task analysis
    future-oriented, 197–198
    of key positions, 177–178
task inventory, 177
technical career track, 27
technical positions, as initial target for
    planning, 132
technology
    and paperwork overload, 71
    realtime innovations, 300
temping, 28
templates, 267
temporary workers, 291
termination, 25
    decisions about, 20
testing bench strength, 215–217
360-dgree assessment, 182–183
    software and Web-based instru-
        ments, 265
    worksheet, 184

time
  requirements for individual devel-
    opment plan, 222
  as strategic resource, 32–33
Tobias, Randall, 83
top-down approach to integrating
    strategy and succession plans, 16
top-down approach to succession
    planning, 21–22
top managers
  global assessment by, 205
  as initial target for planning, 132
  interest in succession planning and
    management, 8
  opinions about succession planning
    and management, 114
  participation and support, 53
  preparation of successors, 55
  questioning to learn key positions,
    174
  questioning to test bench strength,
    217
  replacement planning, 65–66
  requirements for succession plan-
    ning, 102–103
  requirements for succession plan-
    ning, interview guide, 104–105
  support for training, 162
  values clarification, 84
  see also chief executive officer
trading talent, 27–28, 292
training, 156–164
  ensuring attendance, 157, 162
  hierachy of evaluation, 272–273
  key strategies, 234–237
  matching to program planning,
    156–157
  methods, 163–164
  sample outlines, 158–161
  Web-based, 269
  Web sites for, 262
training meetings, 72–73
trait rating approach to performance
    appraisal, 188
trangulation, 175
transfers to fill vacancy, 291

trust, 211
turnover, 216
  tracking, 297
two-in-the-box approach, 28

unavoidable turnover, 216
*The Uniform Guidelines on Employee
    Selection Procedures*, 138
United Kingdom, age distribution of
    population (2025), 298
United States
  age distribution of population
    (2025), 297
  aging of population, 35
  employment law, 136, 139–146
  population age distribution, xviii
  population by age, xix
  retirement trends, 297
uproar method of identifying key po-
    sitions, 173
U.S. Department of Labor, 178

values, 80, 83
  importance of, 37–38
values clarification, 80
  studies, 84–85
  in succession planning and manage-
    ment, 85
verified succession planning and man-
    agement, 24
vertical advancement, 187
vertical job loading, 27
video cameras, 258
videoconferencing, 259
videotape for training, 163
Vietnam Era Veterans' Readjustment
    Assistance Act (1974), 142
Vine, David, 44–48
visibility, 70
voluntary separation programs, 19–20

Wagner Act, 139
Washington Hospital Center, 49–52
weak bench strength, 90, 95
  locating, 132–134

Web sites
  about competency modeling, 264
  about performance appraisal poli-
    cies, 263
  about 360-degree assessment, 265
  search engines, 255
Whistleblower Protection Statutes
  (1989), 145
word processing, for talent inventory,
  267
work processes, in organizational
  analysis, 194
work requirements
  awareness of, 171
  future, in key positions, 197–202
  meetings, 72
  present, high-tech assessment, 259,
    262
Worker Adjustment and Retraining
  Notification Act (1988), 145
Workforce 2000 (Hudson Institute),
  48
workhorses, in performance/potential
  grid, 204
workplace trends, 31–32
  importance of values and compe-
    tencies, 37–38
  intellectual capital and knowledge
    management, 37
  questionnaire to assess manage-
    ment of consequences, 33–34
  reduced loyalty, 36

seller's market for skills, 35–36
speed requirements, 32–35
worksheet
  for action plan preparation, 150
  for alternatives to traditional suc-
    cession planning, 250
  brainstorming on use of online and
    high-tech methods, 260–261
  for demonstrating need for succes-
    sion planning, 100
  environmental scanning, 195
  for establishing program priorities,
    137–138
  full-circle, multi-rater assessment,
    184
  for global assessment, 206
  for identifying evaluation methods,
    278
  for identifying learning resources,
    227
  integration of career planning with
    succession planning, 306–307
  for key position description, 179
  for learning objectives preparation,
    225
  for mission statement creation,
    125–127
  performance appraisal, 191
  to structure thinking about future
    trends, 288–289
  to structure thinking about meeting
    succession needs, 294–296
  success factor analysis, 207
World Wide Web *see* Web sites

About the Author

William J. Rothwell, Ph.D., SPHR is professor of human resource development in the Department of Adult Education, Instructional Systems and Workforce Education and Development at The Pennsylvania State University. He was previously assistant vice president and management development director for The Franklin Life Insurance Company in Springfield, IL and training director for the Illinois Office of Auditor General. He is also president of Rothwell and Associate, a private consulting firm, and has offered consulting services to many organizations. He has worked full-time in human resource management and employee training and development from 1979 to the present. He thus combines real-world experience with academic and consulting experience.

Dr. Rothwell received his Ph.D. from the University of Illinois at Urbana-Champaign, specializing in human resource development (employee training). He received his M.B.A. from the University of Illinois at Springfield and his B.A. from Illinois State University. He bears life accreditation as a senior professional in human resources (SPHR).

Dr. Rothwell's latest publications include Rothwell, W. (2000). *The Role of the Analyst*. Alexandria, Va.: The American Society for Training and Development; Rothwell, W. (2000). *The Role of the Evaluator*. Alexandria, Va.: The American Society for Training and Development; Rothwell, W., & Sredl, H. (2000). *The ASTD Reference Guide to Workplace Learning and Performance*, 3rd ed. 2 vols. Amherst, MA: Human Resource Development Press; Dubois, D., & Rothwell, W. (2000). *The Competency Toolkit*. 2 vols. Amherst, MA: Human Resource Development Press; Rothwell, W., Hohne, C., & King, S. (2000). *Human Performance Improvement: Building Practitioner Competence*. Houston: Tex.: Gulf Publishing; King, S., King, M., and Rothwell, W. (2000). *The Complete Guide to Training Delivery: A Competency-Based Approach* (New York: AMACOM Books); Rothwell, W., & Kazanas, H. (1999). *Building In-House Leadership and Management Development Programs* (Westport, Conn.: Quorum Books); Rothwell, W. (1999). *The Action Learning Guidebook: A Real-Time Strategy for Problem Solving, Training Design, and Employee Development* (San Francisco:

Jossey-Bass/Pfeiffer); Rothwell, W., Prescott, R., and Taylor, M. (1998). *Strategic Human Resource Leader: How to Help Your Organization Manage the 6 Trends Affecting the Workforce.* Palo Alto, Ca.: Davies-Black Publishing; Rothwell, W., & Kazanas, H. (1998). *Mastering the Instructional Design Process: A Systematic Approach* (2nd ed.). San Francisco: Jossey-Bass.